THE NINTH GEAR

The Valuepreneurship Method®

Sanjeev Loomba

WMP

The Ninth Gear

© Sanjeev Loomba

First published in April 2022
WM Publishing

ISBN 978-1-912774-87-6 ebk
ISBN 978-1-912774-89-0 Hbk
ISBN 978-1-912774-88-3 Pbk

Disclaimer: *The Ninth Gear* is intended for information and education purposes only. This book does not constitute specific legal, financial, health, clinical or commercial advice unique to your situation.

The views and opinions expressed in this book are those of the authors and do not reflect those of the Publisher and Resellers, who accept no responsibility for loss, damage or injury to persons or their belongings as a direct or indirect result of reading this book.

All people mentioned in case studies have been used with permission, and/or have had names, genders, industries and personal details altered to protect client confidentiality.

Note:
Registered titles of Sanjeev Loomba *Valuepreneurship*®
Copyright, Pending Trademarks: *Value Onion, Response Onion, VORO Model, S-VOC Model, Christmas Tree Model, Circles of Value (COVS), Circles of Response (CORS), EV/BV/PV Model, Valuepreneur, Trust Capital, Depth of Impact, Me SFEAR You SPHERE, Point Of Zero Conflict (POZC)*

Contents

Dedications And Gratitude

I Dedicate This Book

To You The Reader

Committed to engaging your *ninth-gear* through valuepreneurship, I wish you every success.

To Karuna

My soul mate, inspiration and inner voice. My wife.
You've brought me here, galvanised my ideas and resonate throughout this book.

With Loving Gratitude

To my parents, who shaped my values to see the world with integrity.

My father, Dr Satya Dev Loomba – a passionate doctor and the first valuepreneur I ever knew.

Upanishad, my son – for challenging and stress testing my methods and ideology, with fervour and immense love.

Anushka, my daughter-in-law – for immutable support and visualising the principles of valuepreneurship in work.

Aviral Johri a brilliant colleague, I consider as my son
and has contributed invaluably.

Kumkum, Rajeev, Manisha and Vivek, my adoring siblings
who nurtured and cultivated my values with love and care.

My parents-in-law for their infinite blessings and support.

Gurudev Swami Chinmayananda and the gurus of the
Chinmaya Mission, notably Swami Swaroopananda –
for showering grace and an ocean of knowledge.

I Warm-Heartedly Thank and Appreciate

The thousands of individuals and organisations I've had
the privilege to coach and accompany on their achievement
journeys such as Cognizant and Johnson & Johnson.

Martyn Dadds (author of the foreword), a true valuepreneur,
who as CEO of different corporations invited me to help
in their quest for value-impact and growth.

Karim Vissangy, an excellent coach and my other dear
colleagues who have admirably accompanied me on this
crusade, notably Ritu Iyer, Milan Samani and G George.

All family, friends, clients and colleagues
thanks to whom I continue to evolve.

The fabulous, scenic, serene locations and their staff
where I wrote the book. Notably: Stanrose Café, Mussoorie,
India; Krini Beach Resort, Crete; Bulls Head, Riverside, London.

Foreword: Martyn Dadds

"Life and work is truly meaningful when we use our skills, efforts, talents and interest to serve others' values."

Words that still resonate with me twenty years on since I first met Sanjeev during a break for lunch at a sales and marketing conference in an old monastery in north-eastern France.

Since then, I've worked with Sanjeev and implemented his unique, original and inspirational approach to life and business many times, in many companies, in many sectors, in many countries. Every time they have brought value and success to many customers, as well as to me, the teams I've worked with and the companies and organisations I've worked for.

Along the way they've helped transform the lives of many people and many firms by giving them the tools and means to unleash their real potential and successfully challenge and change the status quo within their organisations as well as in their wider markets, to their and their customers benefit and often to the benefit of society too.

Sanjeev brings an original and refreshing approach to business and life that positions caring and bringing value to the forefront of all that we do. He is a magical storyteller with a Mary Poppins-like bag of real-life examples that reveal his methods and models in an engaging and entertaining way.

Sanjeev is a game-changer his teachings dramatically re-shape how you not only see business but also how you see yourself and how you fit in the world around you. He lives and breathes Customer Value, how you determine it and how you respond to it. His methods are not theoretical but honed and precise, built on practical real-life situations and experiences.

Two particularly satisfying business transformations come to mind that I've led since learning Sanjeev's methods and focussing on bringing Value in all that we do. They were in very different market sectors, but both involved multi-site, multi-cultural, multi-country organisations and both resulted in a major change of narrative both within the firms themselves as well as in the wider marketplace they operated in.

The first was at a capital-intensive pan-European manufacturing business and the second a global software as a service organisation. In each case we started by actively listening to and really understanding our customers worlds and in particular the value they brought their customers and where our products and services fitted into this value chain. We then honed our responses perfectly to their needs.

We moved from a focus on telling our customers what we were doing to discussing with them their needs and the value we were bringing. Our customers, in turn, valued us much more and as we reassured them that we could respond to their values, so we gained their confidence and eventually their full trust and moved from being just another supplier to a true partner with a seat and voice at their senior team strategy discussions.

By discovering the outer layers of our customers' onions and responding perfectly to them we not only built great relationships with our customers, we also transformed our internal conversations from being predominantly price-based to how do we bring value that helped us improve the internal team's motivation, release their full potential, grow the business and increase our profitability.

As for me, I try to speak and teach Sanjeev's methods and models in all that I do. My experience over the last twenty years has shown that his methods work effectively in business and perhaps more importantly they work wonderfully in life generally.

You too can share in this. Please read on and enjoy.

Martyn Dadds

Founder & CEO

Giuoco Piano Advisory Limited

dream. dare. discover.

The Ninth Gear
And The Valuepreneurship Method®

Valuepreneurship

A new age transformational method and culture which has catapulted thousands of leaders, business people, professionals and organisations, reaching unimagined destinations.

- Valuepreneurs fly well beyond entrepreneurs.
- They create a legacy of impact.
- They are trusted, admired, valued and distinguished.

For leaders of today and the future, in enterprise, organisations or public service. For professionals in all fields – business, creative, sports, welfare, philanthropy, art and all other activities.

Not just a business book, it's a set of practical techniques and methods built on a culture and understanding of the essential human principal of bringing value and becoming valuable to achieve immense success and fulfilment.

Let's Reset – Wake Up Call

What will be your legacy? What impact on the world will you make? From where will your most profound satisfaction come? What wealth will you create?

You are an ocean of creativity and innovation and have the fire-power for attaining magnificent outcomes you haven't even imagined until now. If this sounds lofty, evangelical, and ordinarily motivational, then wake up. It's not a motivational lecture to help you achieve just a little bit better. It really is a wake-up call. It's the mirror we need to hold up. Currently, the image in the mirror is distorted and clouded by complications, constraints, fears, prejudices, the ego, the mind, and other emotional distractions. They distort our view of the world and of every initiative we pursue – be it work, business, or any other activity. We limit ourselves.

The answer is practical and much more straightforward than you think. Our thinking needs a one hundred and eighty degrees reversal to develop a strategic mind. We need workable methods with solutions, simple techniques, and formats that will become our reflexed modus operandi along with an illuminated, stilled, and available mind.

Whichever endeavour in life you are engaged with, whether professional, business, creative, music, sports, welfare and charity, public service, or any other pursuit – this strategic mind is epitomised by integrity and serving genuine value-impact. You will be shocked to discover just how close you are to it and how easily it has been missed, but most of all, how effortlessly it can be unfolded. If this book seems substantial and the explanations long and even repetitive, it's because the change needs to be drastic. The message is drummed hard and continuously – no apologies.

The essence, however, is shockingly straightforward.

It's time to set the record straight. The change we make will re-shape the environment around us and then the wider world, and goodness me, it needs to change. We really have lost our way. There is selfishness, dis-unity, loss of integrity, the destruction of society, and eventually our precious planet. In this age, there is no such thing as democracy. It has become a distant ideal. It's all about self-propulsion and preservation at the cost of everyone else. Business is principally about grabbing as much as possible with low regard for the value of those we serve. The irony is that the reverse will achieve what people are yearning for much faster, a lot better, and with total integrity.

There is nothing wrong with power, wealth, or capitalism. The problem is the arrogantly self-serving intention and motivation behind it. A transplant surgeon who is removing an organ to replace it to give life is using the same process of surgery as the surgeon who is removing the organ to sell it – don't blame surgery. Surgery is excellent; the intention and motivation behind it cause the entire problem.

Similarly, business, politics, capitalism, etc., are great things. They provide livelihoods, growth, protection, and the freedom to fully leverage the opportunities life offers. If we can shift the intention, we will make a formidable impact on the world. We will do that through the methods and thinking we are laying down here.

Nine Prime Questions
Stellar Leaders Of Tomorrow Must Ask

1. How do I discover the value-impact I can make on my world of business, society, family, and myself?

2. How do I determine my work purpose - define it, direct myself to it and build my personal legacy?

3. How do I design strategies for my goals to achieve extraordinary outcomes from my capabilities and potential. Growth, prosperity, and eminence for me personally and for my business or organisation.

4. Where do I find the inspiration to do maximum work and feel the minimum effort?

5. How do I inspire others, unite them, lead them to success, raise their performance, be respected, and build excellent relationships?

6. How do I win the confidence of others, persuade and influence them, gain their trust, converse and communicate well with them, and be seen as an engaging, comprehensive leader?

7. How do I handle challenging situations and people, bring solutions and win the trust of others?

8. How do I dynamise my mind and make it fully available to me, undistracted, undisturbed, fearless, unstressed, and calm to allow my talents to flow, handling obstacles with ease and strength?

9. How do I build my self-respect, be more confident, shift my ego from weakening me to becoming a net bringer of value-impact in the world?

Depth Of Impact

Our ultimate quest and trajectory to attain all nine dimensions is the *depth of impact* you can make on the value of people, organisations, and the world.

Notice I didn't mention the depth of impact to yourself.

I'm not saying that impact on your own life and achievement is unimportant. It is fundamentally important and why you are reading this book; however, it is a result, not the driver.

The driver is how much impact you can make on others' value. The more you do that, the more your own value and attainment will be assured. After all, who would you rather buy from – someone trying to sell you things and make as much as possible from you or someone oblivious to their own rewards but obsessed with *your* value and outcomes?

The answer is simple.

Who will you argue more on prices with and negotiate harder with? The first person, right? So, who will become richer in any case? There is no conflict whatsoever with becoming an obsessive server of true value and becoming wealthier, more satisfied, and successful yourself. It's the finest path to immense prosperity for you, yet this self-gain should not be your prime motivator.

Shift the motivation to bring a depth of impact, and then one of the delightful outcomes is your own lucrativeness.

Don't Chase Profit

I was doing a strategy program for a group of CEOs from different companies recently, and at one point I said, 'Don't chase profit.'

Very quickly, a hand went up, and a CEO said, 'I don't understand. Are you really telling us not to make a profit?'

I said, 'Stop. Who said don't *make* a profit, is that what I said?'

Another CEO interjected. 'I think he said don't *chase* profit.'

'Exactly, in fact, I am here to help you become wealthier, so don't chase profit, *make* it.'

Then he said, 'OK, so what should we chase?'

My answer?

'Obsessively understand the value of your market, people, and broader stakeholders and build perfect responses to impact it. You will be far more rewarded than you had ever imagined, be respected, wealthier, satisfied, work with absolute integrity, and build a valuable legacy.'

Release the valuepreneur within you.

The Four Objectives

This book has been written with these four objectives in mind:

- First – to set the record straight and re-shape the world to conduct all work and activity with the integrity of bringing sincere and profound value-impact. It's a mindset, a culture, a raison d'être, and the natural way forward.

- Second – to furnish you with a practicable method, frameworks, and techniques for triumph in your profession, business, work, and all endeavours. A step-by-step guide to constructing your strategies, directions, and actions to distinguish you and generate outstanding outcomes for you and whose value you serve. It's an invaluable tool kit for taking ideas and innovations through to fruition and then to ongoing growth and achievement.

- Third – to shape the extraordinary and inspirational leader in you in all respects – admired, adored, advocated, respected, valued, and followed. Igniting the talents and capabilities of people to raise their performance and attain incredible outcomes.

- Fourth – Provide you with a sledgehammer to smash the fears, prejudices, constraints, and barriers that are coming in the way of our own successes. It is about dynamising the mind, making it effective to discern, decide and act without apprehensions, stress, worries, and concerns. Activated yet serene, available yet balanced.

The What And The How
– Technique + The Mind

Technique without a fortified mind and vice versa will not suffice and often proves dangerous. We all have technique, expertise and know-how, i.e., the what. But our endeavours and actions become so much more potent when we structure technique through value-impact and then combine it with a strengthened mind, i.e., the how. The clarity, composure, confidence from an uninhibited, bolstered mind will propel us to exceptional destinations. Objectives one and two of the book give you the what of business, work, and leadership, objectives three and four give you the how.

There is a wide availability of literature on either the what or the how. However, the two co-exist and must be utilised in a total coalition; they are intertwined.

In all five sections of this book, we cover tangible techniques, and that too in a simple invincible way through valuepreneurship, but fuse them totally with the strength of mind, attitude and approach. These two phenomena, the what and the how are totally and completely interconnected. We cannot do the what without the how and vice versa.

I am associating the what with our intellect – the logic, know-how, and frameworks, and the how to our emotional or even spiritual dimensions.

When the two are combined, our capabilities in any sphere of activity are switched on to take pristine decisions, make changes with confidence and execute with phenomenal puissance and outcomes.

If this is what this is book is expected to deliver, then we can ask the question: *to whom does this matter?*

Who Is This Book For?

- Across the globe – every individual engaged in any professional, business, political, creative, public service, charitable, sporting, or artistic pursuit.

- CEOs and all business leaders + Managers/Directors working in organisations.

- Owners of businesses or people planning to start their own enterprise (valueprise).

- Anyone who wishes the world to work with integrity and wants to make a contributory impact and create a legacy of value.

I Devote This Book

- To every decision-maker responsible for delivering on business or project strategy, no matter how big or small. To every CEO and aspiring CEO. It will not only help you at the pinnacle of your strategic career but at all stages – from management trainee up to CEO.

- To every business owner, no matter the size of the operation, from a single small shop owner to the chairman of a multi-trillion-dollar conglomerate.

- To anyone who aspires to their own business or organisation – with the independence and freedom to design their life on their own terms.

- Finally, to anyone who wants to unveil their thought dimensions, regardless of working in an organisation or not. We are merely borrowing business as a comprehensive theme to explore the many methods in this book, but you can apply the tools in any part of your own life. You might be a philanthropist, a musician, an artist, a writer, sports person, etc. Your capabilities will be optimised and enhanced to accelerate you in your quest and outcomes.

- The bottom line is that the book is actually about YOU.

Why *The Ninth Gear?*

If the title evokes – engaging the best of your capabilities, amplifying your capacity, raising the game, reaching beyond; acceleration, winning, etc., the title is justified.

A Formula One (F1) racing driver has eight gears at their disposal. This technical capability is available to all racing drivers. The ninth-gear is the *you* factor that distinguishes you and sets you apart. It is technique refreshed and well beyond, into your mental resolve, your clarity, vision full utilisation of your capabilities. It's the valuepreneur within you – fearless, selfless, commanding, and confident bringer of value-impact.

I dedicate my work to that exceptional you and invite you to your supreme you.

The Five Sections

The Ninth Gear is comprised of five sections that follow a logical journey into shaping the ultimate, supereminent, new age trailblazer – the valuepreneur!

The book will deliver you the most if you read all sections in sequence. Sections 2 to 5, although fully interwoven, each stand on their own and can be read individually if you are particularly interested in one dimension. However, Section 1 is essential to grasp first as it ultimately contextualises the entire work.

Before a brief description of the Sections and titles, here are the five dimensions edifying each section.

The Valuepreneur's:

1. Spirit and Culture

2. Method and Strategy

3. Psyche and Mind

4. Character and Leadership

5. Magnetism and Relationships

Section 1 The Spirit And Culture Of A Valuepreneur Distinguished By A Culture Of Value – Valuepreneurship And Value-Impact

- Valuepreneurship – a new wave of thinking, which, although natural to the human psyche, we find ourselves far away from it.

- Exploring and redefining value and value-impact. It's not added value.

- Models to understand value and the integrity of responses and solutions to value.

- Why this ethos, quest, and direction is urgently needed in organisations, individuals, and the world.

Section 2 The Method And Strategy Of A Valuepreneur Strategic Thinking Planning And Execution Of Any Activity, Initiative, Program Or Organisation

- A Step-by-Step Practical Method and Toolkit for Valuepreneurs

- Having established the culture of value-impact in Section 1, we now turn it into a full-blown, comprehensive framework and methodology.

- Step-by-step, it will guide you with models, examples, and techniques to establish, re-engineer or vastly augment your work, business, or organisation – whatever its nature.

- You will be able to input the variables and information of your real initiatives into the models and structures easily and practically. Then develop strategies and actions for clarity, implementation, a unified team, and achievement of goals and results.

Section 3 The Psyche And Mind Of A Valuepreneur
A Mind Available And Energised To Accomplish Fearless, Composed, Unstressed And Potent

From Sections 1 and 2, we adopt a culture of value-impact and then deploy it to shape our work, programs, and organisation. But without the right psyche and mind positions, all of this understanding, culture, and method may go to waste or, at best, remain underutilised.

In this section, with the impactful dimension of valuepreneurship, we examine the workings of the mind. Where it falters, the constraints and barriers we impose on ourselves. We are derailed by harsh attitudes and challenging people and situations daily, which affects our progress. With shockingly simple techniques, we clear everything.

The many examples, techniques, and simple practices will lift the constraints and free the mind, bringing composure and availability, leaving it void of fears and stresses.

The freed mind will be potent and energised to perform at your natural best and amplify your capabilities and capacities to accomplish.

Far from a lecture on just what to do, this section will provide you with tangible ways and practical techniques to achieve it. It's the state and nature of a valuepreneur.

Section 4 The Character And Leadership Of A Valuepreneur
The New Age Trailblazer

Leadership is no longer about a simplistic, hierarchical command of people with naïve do's and don'ts. It's about the value-impact to their total people environment bringing immense growth and achievement above, below, and sideways in all relationships.

This section examines and redefines the new-age leader as a trailblazer. They are distinguished, admired, followed, and build a robust legacy of inspiration and exemplarity for others to grow and achieve.

With cases and methods, this section will provide the means to develop your natural capacities of value leadership.

Section 5 Magnetism And Relationships Of A Valuepreneur
Unity Collaborative Relationships And Trust Capital
The Way Of A Valuepreneur

Having shaped their culture, strategy, mind, and leadership, the valuepreneur is ready to impact their environment and the wider world.

Dis-unity is the current plague of the world, and in every walk of life, work, and running organisations, it fails us and our endeavours. The result is poor cooperation, collaboration, and relationships.

This section examines these aspects and equips you to win deep trust in all your professional relationships (Trust Capital). People will collaborate and cooperate with you and with each other and take on their responsibilities joyfully.

With the simple practice to eliminate conflict, we will achieve unification leaving everyone satisfied and productive.

Do I make it sound too easy?

Let's see after you have read Section 5. This is the compelling, magnetic nature of a valuepreneur.

My Eight-Point Promise To You

If you apply these principles you will gain:

1. 30% heightened outcomes and results as a minimum achieved from all your endeavours – be they projects, a job, a business, public or welfare service, creative or sports activity, etc. Why 30%? We calculate the progressions and results of people pre and post-adoption of these methods of valuepreneurship, and the amplified range is 40-60%.

2. A sharpened vision – seeing clearly and taking best opportunities in a rapidly changing world to bring incredible value-impact on anyone you serve and amplifying your own achievement far ahead of expectation.

3. Design goals and destinations with a higher purpose and make it happen smoothly with significantly removed obstructions and constraints.

4. Methods, techniques, tools, and thinking to apply immediately in your work with clarity, practicality, and ease. Strategic thinking and implementation centred on value-impact.

5. A mind available, dynamised, and energised to perform and accomplish. Fearless, composed, unstressed, confident, and brilliant in all areas of work and life.

6. A legacy and amplified profile as a value leader and bringer of huge value-impact to people, organisations, and the wider world who is respected, admired, advocated, and followed.

7. Distinguished, not just differentiated as an individual and organisation.

8. Attain Trust Capital and exceptional relationships. Inspire collaboration and cooperation from people – with you and with each other. Unify people at work and outside.

Section 1

The Spirit And Culture
Of A Valuepreneur

1.1

Making This Method Work For You

In Section 1, I am laying the foundation of valuepreneurship, the essential philosophy and thinking which turns into a practical step by step methodology in all five sections of the book.

In subsequent sections, we will explore them, give you more practical techniques, tools, models and frameworks to apply in your real work and life.

These practices are born out of decades of real application and outstanding results for individuals and organisations. I will enjoy sharing many of these with you as we go along.

The techniques generate incredible outcomes and impact our work, life, people, and ourselves. I invite you to transpose and input your own real situations into the examples and models. It will make the methods immediately and practically useable to achieve exceptional results.

1.2

The Valuepreneur
And Valuepreneurship

We've had the age of the entrepreneur. It worked, but it's done, dusted and over. Then came the intrapreneur, an employee of an organisation, who thinks and operates with an entrepreneurial mind within the organisation as a risk-comfortable visionary. This is a great ideal, but it had limited practical success.

The new age belongs to a new breed of person, a star, whether they own a business or are involved in any creative, professional, public service, charitable, sporting or artistic pursuit. I call this star the valuepreneur – the one who is obsessed with, sensitive to, driven by and responds to the true value of whom they serve.

Whom we serve through or work includes our customers, bosses, colleagues, team members, suppliers, etc. But in the broader sense, it includes everyone we have a relationship with or are concerned with or concerned for. It naturally includes our family and friends and the wider world of people we want to see grow and live better and happier lives.

The valuepreneur's constant quest is to discover the true value of whom they serve and deliver responses to bring significant value-impacts on them.

A valuepreneur's mind doesn't live in the me – what can I get. It lives in the you – what can I bring you? Your outcomes and value-impact.

This is the person we will respect, admire, listen to, follow and most of all, trust.

Naturally, they will be more prosperous, regarded, influential and distinguished, but this is not their aim and goal – it's a fortuitous and deserved by-product, an inevitable outcome.

1.3

What Is Value And Valuepreneurship?

Value is the most misunderstood word in business today.

When people speak of value, they are talking about ordinary, low level added value – which is not value at all. Frankly, it's a bribe to entice people to buy more. Added value means providing a little more product or service for no more money. For example, if you take your car for a service and they wash it as well, that is added value, added free of charge. It's good, it makes the customer happy, but true value is far more profound and valuable.

In today's day and age, we don't buy products and services per se. We buy the value-impact it represents to us.

Digital Banking App Developer

I was in Frankfurt coaching a group of high potential youngsters in their late twenties, all graduates of top universities in Europe. They were a mixture of Dutch, German, Swiss, French etc. and worked for one of the largest global IT corporations in the world. I was teaching them value leadership, and I asked one young lady, Klara, 'What are you working on now?'

She said, 'I'm on a project developing digital apps' and then gave me a brilliant technological description of the apps, the data, the platforms, the software etc.

I pushed further and asked her, 'So what? What does it bring?'

She answered that it is an easy method for making faster and more convenient payments. Now we are getting closer to value, but we are still far away from it.

I then asked, 'What impact does it have on whom?'

'I'm not sure what you mean, but, I suppose it helps our clients who are banks to help their customers.'

Not bad, but nowhere near enough to the ultimate value-impact. She couldn't go any further in trying to answer my question and maybe wasn't even sure what I was getting at.

We broke for lunch, and as it happened, I was having lunch with her senior director, and I asked him what Klara is working on, using the same questions – what, for who, why etc., and I got some fascinating answers.

Coming into the post-lunch session, I asked, 'Klara, do you know what you are working on? Your client is one of the largest retail banks in South Africa. They have launched a new strategy to increase their business by expanding services to a fast-growing market segment: poor farmers and small traders in the country's most rural areas. They don't have credit lines available to them and transact in cash. While travelling to the city to buy fertilisers, feed or stocks, they lose two days of farm yield or income in their shops. Your app helps them with protected credit to buy without leaving the business and manage their cash much better. So, what you are really bringing is helping the livelihoods of these poor farmers and traders.'

She gazed silently. I knew it had a profound impact on her, and she said, 'I had no idea.'

So what she was doing was developing digital apps for banks. This is essential yet ordinary. But why she was doing it and therefore what she was bringing: helping livelihoods of these poor farmers and traders. And this is value-impact.

Also let's be clear, by taking this story with a strong emotive impact I'm not saying that value is associated only with social or charitable impacts, although it does helps to illustrate the point, the direct impact to her client, the bank, is to grow commercially, gain market share, strengthen their brand and be more profitable. i.e. value is the net impact to whoever we are serving.

A week later, Klara wrote to me saying that nothing had changed about her work or what she was doing, but, everything had changed about how she was feeling.

She now feels she has a lot more energy, enjoying the work, going to work is not feeling like a chore, has brought a couple of great innovative ideas to the client, feeling more engaged and confident, her skills, talent and knowledge seems to have a greater meaning and application, nothing is mundane anymore as her mind is constantly on the end outcome, the impact of her digital apps and not just the technique.

This is one example. I see this change in people constantly as their *purpose* re-shapes through the value they bring to others.

So, our quest is to transition from and make the link between what we are *doing* and what we are *bringing*.

We are all knowledgeable about what we are doing, which may be intellectually stimulating and interesting, but we are rarely fully aware of what we are *bringing*, generating as *value*, and positively impacting who we are serving that is not just interesting but inspiring. It is in a state of inspiration that our creativity, innovation, work success and personal uplifting really flows.

I requested all seventeen young professionals to write down what they were *doing*, and before the next day's session, to research and focus on the end impact of their work – what they were *bringing*.

As one-by-one they spoke about the end impacts value to their clients and indeed their client's clients, I heard a different engagement and joy in their voices. Two of them actually had tears in their eyes as they spoke. They were genuinely inspired.

Since then they've connected with me and amongst the many comments, one common element for almost the whole group is that *we now go to work with a very different feeling – a feeling of satisfaction, sense of greater purpose, enjoyment, less fatigue, inspiration with a greater flow of ideas.*

One of them wrote I am able to handle small inconveniences and issues with others which trouble me less as my focus has changed and rather than *me and my concerns.* I have shifted to *you*, whose value I am serving and I feel stronger.

This is the pursuit of value and the ways of a true *valuepreneur.* The valuepreneur not only has greater impact on the world but also finds much greater success, satisfaction and personal elevation. This is the way of tomorrow.

The interesting thing is that we are all *bringing* this level of value but we just don't see it, realise it or enquire it. So we are just *doing.*

We now need to shift from *doing* to *bringing.* This would make valuepreneurs of us all. It is very important to understand that it's not our fault that we think the way we do. That young lady's intention was a good one but it is just our natural human tendency to think and speak in terms of what we *do* and less on what we *bring.*

Medical Devices – A Valuepreneurial Acquisition

I was facilitating a strategic transformation program, with the CEO and top management team, of a huge medical devices company in electro-cardiology. I was taking them through the process described in Section 2 of this book to construct a strategy for business growth and accomplishment.

One of the key initiatives was the potential acquisition of another medical device business in the domain. There was an urgency from the board as the previous acquisition made three years ago had failed. They had acquired that company because it was known in the market and it would bring instant market value growth, and for the first year, it did. Another reason was their efficient research capabilities and processes which would bring a significant cost saving. Despite this admirable logic, the project failed. They were now looking to sell that business, at a considerable loss, and acquire another.

In identifying the perfect acquisition target, they were still looking at criteria like market valuations and cost savings. But using a valuepreneurial approach we changed this and started from a completely different point.

We examined their customer and end customer markets, understood their changing priorities in the new healthcare environment and the depth of impacts to patients, hospitals, cardiologists etc. We calculated these values (see the method in Section 2), in other words, established the greater purpose and value to whom we serve, similar to Klara's case.

We then mapped the capabilities and ethos of each of the three short-listed target companies choosing the one with whom we could make the best response and value-impact to our new customer segments. Cost, process, market valuation, although still relevant, became secondary considerations. In other words, we drove it from a position of what we bring rather than what we do. Interestingly, the company acquired was on initial examination the least likely candidate.

That acquisition, despite generating incredible growth and return on investment, unified the two teams with ease. There was energetic innovation, creativity, collaboration and cooperation.

1.4

Why Is The Valuepreneur Needed?

Why is the valuepreneur needed and indeed called for by the world today? We are living through a dramatic re-shaping of the world, whether it is through a destructive pandemic, rapidly evolving technology, climate change, social modifications, widening market reach and opportunities, climate or acrimonious divisions on lines of religion, territory, politics and much more. There is massive concentration on self-preservation and protection and often, self-propulsion, but the keyword here is self.

We behave with the nature of wanting something, being someone and acquiring selfishly. Yet, the irony is that what we appreciate most in other people is the polar opposite – care, generosity and the bringing of value to others and the world.

Let's take the US President until January 2021. (I take this example observationally and not politically). Was he working with genuine value to whom he served, or was supposed to serve? Or with self-propulsion? Destructive policies like trade wars with Canada, China, Europe, unreasonable aggression with Mexico, NATO, reneging on the Iran nuclear agreement, the Paris Climate Accord, or the ratification of violent regimes across the globe or incitement of violence amongst his own people, are all the anti-thesis of bringing value. It was all about appearing strong and tough to a faction of the voting public in the US to be re-elected as President. It seemed a purely self-motivated agenda.

For someone who has a significant influence on seven billion people, can you imagine if they all had a vote? Would he ever be electable? And this is just one example.

I am not taking a political stance here but simply using an example of what is not valuepreneurship.

Most political leaders in the world are a perfect example of self-preservation and propulsion against the true value of whom they serve. Of course, there have been exceptions, and names like Nelson Mandela and Abraham Lincoln arise, and these we can call valuepreneurs, but they are few and far between.

In valuepreneurship, there is longevity and a respected legacy.

Dis-Unity – The Tragic Disease

Note: this is just a brief point on a fundamental issue solvable by valuepreneurship. Unification is explored in Section 5.

The biggest scourge to blight the world, countries, peoples and organisations is dis-unity. Propelled by self-motives, self-preservation and gains, it is divisive and destructive.

Within organisations, there are negative differences and conflicts between individuals, departments, teams – some overt but mostly subtle. Everyone is trying to get their way and for their own gain. The drastically reduced cohesion, collaboration and co-operation result in compromised productivity and underutilised potential. I see this every day, and there are real examples in Section 5.

For example, 75% of mergers and acquisitions fail within the first two years simply because self-protection and interest of the two merging parties collide and conflict. Or two departments or individuals in an organisation pushing their own methods, processes, or preferences in solving a problem disregarding the possibility that the other may be right. Each is motivated by self-interest and feels safer and more in control of their own knowledge, idea or perspective.

This is classic self-preservation. There is often no ill-intention but just our natural human tendency to look after number one. Sadly, in this quest, we often miss the bigger picture and the possibility that the other may be right, and adopting their idea or way will also benefit me. So, we are often the architects of our own misery through not listening, non-collaboration and dis-unity.

At What Point Are Dis-Unity And Conflict Actually Eliminated?

We need to find that missing joining point – the definitive point of alignment with each other. Does this definitive point of alignment really exist? I feel you asking. It is there, but our self-motivation prevent us from seeing it. So, again what is this point at which dis-unity and conflict are indeed eliminated and the only point at which we are unified? Yes, it is the value-impact of whom we are working together to serve. It's as simple as that.

We shall explore this point, which I call *The Point Of Zero Conflict* (see 5.4).

But for now, let's think about two individuals or departments pushing their own method – one says, let's automate the process, the other is arguing for a more manual approach. We are stuck in this non-collaborative argument. The answer is to forget both methods for a few minutes and understand the end outcome, the value-impact to the customers. For example, if flexibility and advice at every step are vital to the success of the customer's project, then we may find the manual approach as more appropriate. If speed and accuracy deliver more value, then automate.

So you see, *The Point Of Zero Conflict* is the value-impact to whom we are working together to serve. That value is factual and independent of the two parties and yet the only reason they are working together. Combining to serve it correctly will benefit both. It's with that end gain for each of the two individuals in disagreement that we will find unity, collaboration and co-operation. Job done. This argument holds from petty differences to major disunities in the world.

It's a delusion to think that people will collaborate just because you tell them to, or because it is morally desirable. Maybe idealistic, but it's not the way human psyche works. They will collaborate if they stand to gain themselves. The beauty of collaborating from to customer's value-impact is it breaks down the me and mine argument and each knows they will gain by co-operating.

The Future Looks Better

So let me ask you these three questions. On a scale of 1-100 (1 being low, 100 being perfect).

- What is the level of valuepreneurship in your organisation?
- What percentage of people in your organisation are valuepreneurs?
- And those who are higher up that scale, how valuepreneurial are they?

I ask these questions every day to business leaders and general employees, and the answers on all three questions range between 10% and 30%. And this is for well-intentioned people, so you can imagine.

1.5

Why Entrepreneurship Is Passé

An entrepreneur creates a business to sell products/services to generate as much money as possible through sales and profits. It's a valiant pursuit but is it a noble one? We will question the difference between the two words, *entrepreneurship* and *valuepreneurship* and ask whether it needs to be noble? Is being noble a just dream-like ideal or can it make you tangibly more prosperous? Can it exist in a business environment, or is it only relevant in public service or charitable environment?

The short answer to these questions is a resounding *yes*.

We will explore why and how.

But before that, let's understand the dynamics of this entrepreneurialism. It is driven by the *me*, the *I*, *what can I make, what will it do for me? How can I do it? How can I become rich?* It worked, and it did make a vast number of people wealthy.

So, who will be the new winners in the future? Those who don't live in the *me* and *I*, but live in the *you* and *why*. No longer asking the question *what* you want, but *why*. These are valuepreneurs. Klara in Frankfurt transitioned to becoming a valuepreneur.

Klara's Example From An Entrepreneurial Standpoint

The banking world is going more digital so let's develop new apps to increase our market share, sell more and generate profits. So, you go from bank to bank, show them the virtues of your products and try and win more and more contracts for them. It's valiant but motivated by self-gain.

Klara's Example From An Valuepreneurial Standpoint

'Small rural businesses and farmers in Africa find it difficult to operate as they don't have credit lines to buy supplies from the city. We help banks improve the work and lives of their customers, the farmers,with cards preloaded with cash. Then use easy-to-utilise apps to make these payments so they can have secure livelihoods. With this argument, small businesses and farmers are more confident, banks make more money and expand their brand. And we as an organisation will sell more, be wealthier, and bring this value to become more fulfilled.' Who doesn't win?

The entrepreneurial approach is still good, and frankly, why wouldn't it? There is a market out there with a hungry demand, and we can provide products and services to satisfy that demand. There is nothing wrong with this. It is bold and courageous, spotting and taking opportunities, taking risks, going for it, proactive, positive and determined, which are all classic traits of an entrepreneur. These traits are natural to human beings, but only some actually utilise them, and they are entrepreneurial or enterprising.

Sounds good, then why is it passé?

Because the market is becoming sensitised to it and valuepreneurship will take you further, faster. Who wants to be *sold to* anymore? Technology and information availability has shifted the power even more to the market. We have a massive array of suppliers at our fingertips and can choose from whom we want to buy. So, products and services, per se, offer little or no differentiation and then it will always descend to a discussion on price.

For example, in the retail environment: just stacking your shelves with products and displaying them well is no longer sufficient. It is the undifferentiated norm and people will just buy from the cheapest supplier. Worse, we cut corners to save cost and maximise profit, in the process compromising further with customer's true values which we haven't fully understood and don't realise we have short served them. Valuepreneurs go a different route, making life convenient for customers and addressing their values, examples of which maybe – an excellent online ordering experience;categorising food by vegan, health, gluten free etc; sourcing ethical products etc. They think of costs as investments in bringing value-impact and don't just trim for profit but make the right resources and processes available to serve the value. It also means that costs irrelevant to the serving of value are easily identified and removed. This is cost appropriation as opposed to cost minimisation. The returns are significantly higher than the outlays and profitability is greater in any case. This will take you well beyond *differentiation* – it will make you *distinguished*.

As businesspeople and even entrepreneurs you have up to eight gears at your disposal and the better you are the more you will deploy. However, all eight and then the ninth gear is open to valuepreneurs. It's the distinguishing factor.

Depth Of Impac (DOI)

I am simply a response to the value of whom I deliver to, i.e., the end-beneficiary of my work, knowledge, skills, talents, products and services. This could be our customers, team, colleagues, bosses, suppliers or even friends and family.

It literally is anyone whom I can benefit.

When we see ourselves as this response to value and making an impact on others, our skills, knowledge, and talents take on a whole new importance. We are giving ultimate respect to ourselves and recognition of our capabilities. We will be much more confident in knowing that someone has benefited from what I do and what I am. You can call this self-esteem. Yet, we are not doing it with the objective of self-recognition – it is one of the outcomes and a bi-product. The self-objective would defeat the entire argument, and we are back in the *Me Sphere* rather than the *You Sphere*, the latter being our endeavour. Think back to Klara's example, and there are many more to come. The more significant the impact on value you make, the more effective and magnificent you are.

Depth Of Impact (DOI) can be defined as the magnitude of the value you can affect. We will quantify this in the next section in the SVOC model (see 2.11 and 2.12).

I am introducing the notion of *Depth of Impact* here. It will be fully unveiled, discussed as we continue.

A Clarification On Terminology

- Value

- Value-Impact

- Depth of Impact

These there terms are interchangeable, but here are the subtle nuances between them.

Value is what the customer cherishes as the true benefit to them. I am using the word customer liberally as anyone or organisation whose value we serve. These could be people who buy from us, our team members, colleagues, bosses, suppliers or anyone in this definition.

Value-Impact, as the term suggests, is getting or achieving that value and outcome.

Depth Of Impact is the magnitude of value you can achieve for them. There are several values, and some are higher in priority than others. The more we can serve higher-value priorities, the greater the *DOI*.

For example, for the farmers in Africa. *Value* could be their livelihood, income and taking care of their family. *Value-Impact* may be the four days of yield gained. The DOI may be that you have solved several problems – ease of access to funds, getting fertilisers on time to maximise the crop, higher income etc.

I still emphasise that all three are the same thing, and I will use them interchangeably.

Note: The Simplicity And Practicality Of Examples Used

This is a comprehensive book and valuepreneurship with all its methods is as applicable to CEOs, heads of organisations and Presidents of countries as it is to early career professionals in any field and budding business men and women.

Although with this methodology I am advising and helping organisations daily to solve complex strategic questions as well coaching individuals at all levels of leadership – most of my examples are kept at a simple and comprehensive level. It's not the situation in these examples that's important but the principle and practical application.

You will easily be able to translate every example into your own or organisation's reality, irrespective of the level of the issue. I invite you to do so.

1.6

The Valuepreneur Will Be Wealthier And More Fulfilled Than The Entrepreneur

I emphasise that I am not arguing against being wealthy and only working for a noble cause. Think about this: who would you buy from – someone who is trying to sell to you, get a contract from you so that they can make their revenues? Or someone obsessed with your value, your success? Who will you negotiate harder with? Naturally the seller/entrepreneur. Who will you listen more to, trust, buy more from, recommend and be prepared to pay better rates? The valuepreneur, of course.

So who will become wealthier? It's a no-brainer.

Think about Klara's digital apps for banks. When the client bank sees that as a technology company you are not only interested in but obsessed with giving them access to a market of two million small businesses and farmers and expanding their brand, sales, and profits, they will choose you, the valuepreneur. An entrepreneurial tech company showing off its technology to impress you and sell you more may well lose out. Value-impact goes well beyond the product.

By giving the example of improving the lives of farmers and small business people, please understand that value is not just applicable in such socially beneficial situations, but even in hard commercial environments – like the banks who serve them. Value to these banks is more significant market share, brand expansion, profits, share value etc.

1.7

Now On The Issue Of Being Fulfilled

Thinking of Klara, in Frankfurt – which mindset will give her greater and deeper satisfaction – the entrepreneurial one of making and selling digital Apps or as a valuepreneur bringing that impact to farmers and small business people in Africa and indeed her direct customer the banks? The answer is clear.

Which of the two mindsets will inspire her more, find avenues to innovate, create, lead her team better, feel more engaged, become wealthier and therefore fulfilled. And interestingly, wealth is the least of the elements to chase. It makes us more desperate and we default to selling and being the entrepreneur. By pursuing the unmitigated understanding and delivery of value, one of the outcomes is much greater wealth. It's a result, not the driver. The driver is value and value-impact.

Shaping Your Legacy

Once we are done with this life, what can be claimed as ours and assigned to our name? Nothing tangible will go forward – Not our wealth, house, assets. Not even our relationships or our skills, knowledge and talents. There is only one thing we can claim authentically – *the value-impact we have had on others.*

This is indelible. It's an established reality for posterity, and no one can remove it or claim it. It isn't passed on to anyone – it will remain our true legacy. The more significant the impact and the larger the number of people we have impacted, the greater our legacy will be.

As dramatic as it sounds, I'm giving you the posthumous dimension for absolute understanding. However, this legacy is to be built, treasured, esteemed, highly regarded and respected during our lifetime.

Powerful Thinking About Ownership And Legacy

I own nothing. After all, so-called ownership can disappear in an instant. A sense of ownership weakens us as in the back of my mind, I know it is temporary and fragile. This triggers in us a more acquisitive nature of owning and holding on, which precipitates a sub-conscious intense fear of losing what we think we own. So, a sense of ownership leaves us vulnerable, weakened and less effective.

I'm at all not saying don't have. On the contrary, be stupendously wealthy, and valuepreneurship will give you that. Have wonderful friends and family, accumulate excellent knowledge and capabilities. Have all of this without a doubt, but change your relationship with it – appreciate it, be grateful for it but own something else – the value-impact you generated with it. It's not about what you have; it's what you do with it that matters.

Hundreds of millions of pounds are spent every summer buying footballers for a British Premier League team, but their results are appalling six months later. There are big egos – *I'm great, I'm famous* etc. But then there is a need to succeed and not fail; otherwise, I will lose that status. That fear of losing is greater than when I was unknown and didn't have a £100m price tag. I become vulnerable.

However, being lost and obsessed with the thought that with this skill, talent and opportunity, how can I best generate value for my team, my club, our fans etc? I now shift from ownership to applying it to generate value-impact. This is humbling, brings tremendous value as well as respect for me. It has a longevity of success and profound satisfaction. It's my legacy.

We are mere instruments of serving value, and the value-impact we generate will be our legacy. We will be known and recognised for it, and as a bi-product, it will undoubtedly make us more prosperous. Prosperity is a delightful, happy outcome, a result and not the prime motivation in our work, business and leadership.

1.8

I'm Not Asking You To Do A New Business, But To Do Your Business In A Completely New Way

This book gives you many practical tools to look at and apply in your business or organisation through the lens of value. But for the moment, please take a few minutes to think about your organisation and ask the questions I asked Klara and see the answers that emerge. (See 1.3 *What Is Value And Valuepreneurship?*)

Then ask how valuepreneurial are the people around you and what the shift to valuepreneurship will bring to the organisation.

- What are you working on at the moment?
- So what?
- So, what does it bring?

1.9

Realising Your Real Potential
By Becoming Valuepreneurial

Think about this.

If your unrestrained, absolute, professional potential for total success is 100, what number are you touching today?

You can think about this in the context of your whole organisation, a business unit or a function. I am giving you no framework or detailed analysis in reflecting on this point. I want a gut felt reaction. I repeat – if your absolute, unrestrained potential is 100, what are you touching today?

Do you have a number?

Interestingly, when I ask this question – and I have asked it to thousands of people – they all start at 60 or 70. As they reflect more, it soon comes down to 50. And then, thinking about it, even more, it tumbles to 20.

The exact number is not important: let's just say it's 30.

The real question is, *where is that difference of 70?* What's getting in the way?

Let's make a list.

Answering this question, everyone says the economic climate, a challenging market, tough competition, unclear strategic plans, uncertain objectives, market knowledge, processes, resource limitation, skill-base, politics, management, bureaucracy, etc.

I keep noting. Eventually, someone comes to the paramount issue and says, *It's me, myself; I come in the way of that 70.*

In other words:

- My confidence

- My reactions

- My reticence on taking risks

- My nervousness – What if I fail, what will they think of me, what will it mean for me, my future? etc.

It's that four-letter word beginning with F, which is propelling all of this, yes indeed FEAR! – the mother of all negative emotions – which derails us and limits our success.

So, we have two lists of what is blocking that 70.

1 External factors, and situations – Factors external to us as individuals and mostly out of our control.

2 Internal to us as individuals – from our emotions and notably fears.

   a. Hand on heart, which of these two lists really comes in the way? Yes, the internal one. The external list is not a problem. How can it be a problem? Something or the other is happening every day in our lives. If it's not an economic downturn, it could be a terrorist attack, a disaster, a new government, the market has changed or a competitor has come up with a similar product, priorities have changed and so on. How could this be a problem? Something new will happen every day.

b. So, the external is not a problem. It is a situation, neutral, mostly unavoidable and a historical fact – it's happened, and that fact can't be reversed. What turns every situation into a problem is not what it is but how we personally, i.e., internally react to that situation. If we react with fear and concern, will we ever remain objective and clear-headed enough to take strong decisions? No, we will be affected. This point will become abundantly clear in Anita's story below.

We come in the way of our own success. Business is much simpler. We complicate it by constantly misperceiving everything. So, where is the problem? The problem is that we are all held back by certain self-imposed barriers to which we are completely oblivious as they reside in our subconscious mind. This will be explored in Section 3 as our three constraining natures. I can already tell you that our misperceptions are the first and significant constraining nature.

We rarely look at reality in its raw, factual, neutral form. For example, Suppose you are told that your project is being cancelled. In that case, you may take this personally, thinking my project is not up to it. This unnatural falsehood, not factual or neutral created by you will affect your confidence and prevent you from seeking other opportunities. In contrast, the reality may have been that there is a cash crunch, or there is a better market timing for this project in six months, etc. We will explore the state of the mind, misperceptions and how to get over them in Section 3.

With this in mind, let's look at Anita's story.

1.10

The Whole Story:
When You Deliver Value
You Are Magnificent

Anita is an entrepreneur who came to my 5-Day MBA program. She had a business in London, doing interior fit-outs with state-of-the-art kitchens and a charming showroom. After the first two days of the program, having explored strategy, customers, understanding the values of the market..., she came to me: 'You know, Sanjeev, I am getting this, I am certainly getting this, it's making a lot of sense, but how do I get over my big problem?'

Here is what our dialogue looked like on that day:

Anita's Kitchens

Sanjeev (S): Well, that's precisely what we have been talking about, but let's hear about your big problem.

Anita (A): My big problem is that my market is disappearing.

S: Really? Why is that?

A: Sanjeev, where are you?! Don't you read the newspapers? There is a global economic crisis! Thanks to the financial crisis that has hit the world right now, my world is destroyed. No one is thinking about buying kitchens now. My market is disappearing.

S: Think about this, Anita. One year ago, before this economic crisis, what was your turnover?

A: I was making a million pounds.

S: And what was your aspiration, your point of success?

A: Well, if I had put in the ideas that I had (look at the language she is using, look at where her mind is: the ideas *I had*, in the past) in two years, I'd be making two million pounds.

S: Wow, doubling your business in two years! Well, that's ambitious. Very good. So, why not go for it? (I was teasing her.)

A: Sanjeev, I think you are not listening to me. The downturn has hit my business. My market is disappearing.

S: Well, let's work on that. You said you were making one million, and you want to make two million. Now, tell me about your market; you say it is disappearing. What's the size of your market in the UK? How much do people spend on kitchens, fit-outs and so on?

A: Well, I think it's two billion pounds.

S: You say your market is disappearing but by how much?

A: Well, if things continue this way, I think one-third of my market will have disappeared in six months.

S: Wow, that's rough. But let's be even more drastic. Let's say not just a third but half of your market disappears. Your sales were one million, and you wanted to grow it to two million. Your market size is two billion, going down to one billion. In other words, you now have to make two million from a one billion market. Please do me a favour, Anita, take a calculator, and divide two million by one billion.

Do you get the picture? It's such a small ratio! It doesn't even feature on the calculator.

A: Oh, well, Sanjeev, if you put it like that.

S: Absolutely, I put it like that. Why haven't you put it like that? The opportunities are immense! In fact, if you think about it, what happens in a downturn? Your competitors struggle, as does everyone else. That presents ample opportunity. Half of your market is still there. The supplier who brings differentiated value at that time, and keeps their cool and has the guts to do it, to bring value, and not just the desperation to sell their goods, who will absolutely cream it. It's a great opportunity!

I read somewhere at that time, and it stuck to my mind: Don't waste a crisis. Think about that.

I said to Anita, 'Now that we've put it like that, shall we start working?

She said, 'Yes, sure, let's do it.' And then she started thinking in a way that relates to everything else I am going to say.

Do you want the epilogue of this story?

I asked her, 'To whom do you sell?' A simple but critical question with which to start.

A: Well, I sell to many wealthy people in the more affluent areas of London, such as Chelsea and Kensington.

S: How do you sell to them?

A: Oh, through architects.

S: Great, so sell more through architects! (I was teasing her, of course).

A: But you don't understand, architects don't come to my showroom!

S: Why is it so important that architects come into your showroom?

A: It's fundamental. When architects don't come to my showroom, when I just send them proposals on jobs they specify, I get a one in twelve conversion rate because they request proposals from my competitors, too. But when they come to my showroom, I get a one in three conversion rate.

So, now comes the key question: *What are we really selling?*

Long before we think about kitchens or interiors or fit-outs, what we are actually trying to achieve is selling the idea of architects coming to my showroom. Yet, we are always desperate to sell our products and goods and get sucked into some system and some business process. You send a proposal showing the attributes of your products and services, you wait and hope for the sale, whereas the real issue here is different. So, know exactly what you are selling - those critical responses to value, and the know-how to serve that value.

> Then I said to Anita, 'Get architects to come to your showroom!'
>
> She said, 'But how? It's easy for you to say. These are busy people, every hour of theirs is money, I can't get them to just come to my showroom!'

Here is what we did. Anita has state-of-the-art kitchens in her showroom, which are all operational. Every Thursday evening, she started a *cuisine evening*. One evening, she invited a Sushi chef from an excellent Japanese restaurant. The next week a Tandoori chef from a top Indian restaurant. Each chef does cooking demonstrations, which promotes their restaurant. She sends out a lovely, personalised invitation. There's a jazz guitarist playing in the corner, and guess who's flocking into the showroom?

The architects come in, and she says, 'I appreciate that your clients are eager to see their kitchen designs once they've had an idea to change it. We understand for you the architect, that's a challenge, but achieving it will generate excellent business results for you.'

'So, come, let me show you our design cell where we do the design. If you give us information on the job to be done in a certain way and if we put our software on your computers as well, forget 24 hours, we can do a design turnover in ten hours.'

This delights the architects. Not only did she come up with innovative ideas to help the architects to build their own business, but she has even strengthened the relationship as true business partner in serving the value of the end customers. Now who will these architects go to? To Anita, of course, because she is solving their problems. In this way, Anita helped architects to succeed, and guess whose business boomed even through those tough times?

She absolutely bucked the trend. Her business grew, her margins grew, and she was strongly differentiated. Her revenue increased by thinking about the two billion turning into a one billion market size. She focused her mind on the one billion remaining, and not the one billion lost, being a massive pot of business that she could capitalise on if she served the right values.

The power of Anita's story is an understanding of how fears and anxieties can obscure the opportunities that the economic crisis presented. When all her competitors would be panicking into desperation to sell their services, Anita could differentiate by understanding true value to wealthy people in Chelsea and helping the architects sell to these customers and make them more money.

She allowed her creativity to flow, not be blocked by her fears and concerns and grow in a very tough climate. In this way, she became a true bringer of value which made her more confident and joyful in her work. What a shift from being a fearful victim to a hugely successful valuepreneur.

She sold her business two years later for a figure she had never imagined.

So, briefly, which lessons can we take from all this?

When You Approach A Situation From Fear Or Worry, The Real Opportunities In Every Changing Scenario Will Escape You

In Anita's case, she came to this program in a panic, saying to herself, *My business is finished, I am ruined.* Frankly, she came to the program because she wanted to close her business. Yet, it was this same situation which provided the most incredible opportunity. What an opportunity to miss! Her fears and worries obscured and prevented the simple understanding of what the architects and their customers genuinely valued.

The only thing to fear is fear itself. We really do get in the way of our own success.

By understanding and therefore managing our emotions – and the mother of all emotions is fear - then taking a logical strategic approach, nothing can prevent us from our own individual goals.

We will explore the mind, emotions and fear later. I will share practical tools to manage it all.

Shift From A Wanting Mode To A Delivering Mode Of Value

Please question whether you are in a *wanting* or a *receiving* mode, typically thinking, *I hope it goes well, I wish my business grows, I hope it doesn't sink* and so on. This thinking will make you weaker.

Moving from *wanting* to *delivering* mode, where you become an impactor of value, will definitely make you stronger. The pure joy of bringing that value will make you more confident and fearless, as it did for Anita. More on this point under the heading *Delivering The Gift* (see 1.13).

I am stressing the importance of *value-impact*, and I've used this word several times. Here we understand the importance of value and the that we rarely drive from it.

We will structurally examine value, what it is, a framework for understanding it, how to discover it and how to serve it. All will become clear as a practical, immediately applicable technique and tool.

Not Taking Risks Is A Precarious Place In Which To Be. Can You Afford It?

The fear of potentially losing it all made Anita weak and risk-averse to continue with the business or even open a new one.

It's All About Customer Value (Explored Later In Section 1)

Proper understanding of the values and their order of priority for your customers or whomever you are serving is the starting point, the be-all and end-all of every business or professional situation.

For Anita, understanding that helping architects provide a design for their customers within 24 hours will increase their business and became the source of success of her own business.

Only when you fully know these values should you even attempt to build responses. These responses will take on much more meaning, and you will be appreciated for it. For Anita, without understanding this 24-hour requirement, her proposals were mere ordinary undifferentiated technical responses, the same as those of her competitors.

To know the values of your customer or market, you must know who is your market and who are your customers. The genuine value of wealthy people in Chelsea would be vastly different to another set of customers.

Transitioning to a valuepreneur. Not only had Anita found the eight technical gears, but the *ninth* one – the mind-set of valuepreneurship.

There is a logical, sequential process not only in planning your business or work but also in the way you think about it. We will explore this step by step in Section 2. This process and thinking are strategic. As we shall see, strategy is simple to understand and practical to use to generate solid results beyond the textbooks.

1.11

The Skyscraper Model
To Get You Distinguished

This book is systematically and step-by-step, working on shifting your thinking, understanding, mindset and giving you practical and concrete tools to manage and become distinguished. This process is somewhat like building a skyscraper. There are four significant steps in building a skyscraper.

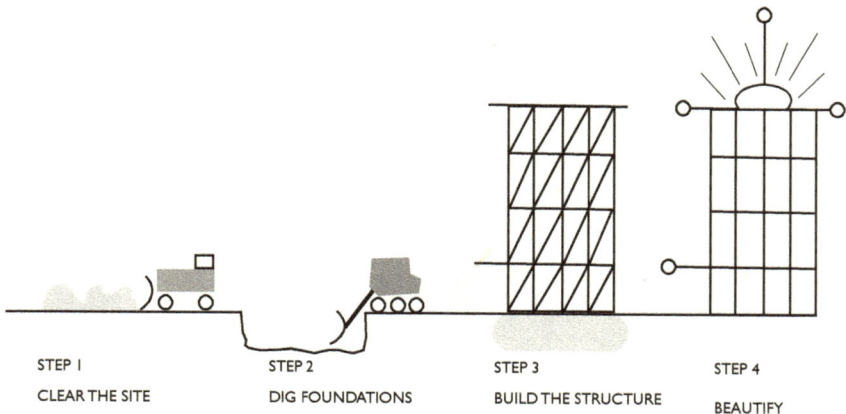

| STEP 1 | STEP 2 | STEP 3 | STEP 4 |
| CLEAR THE SITE | DIG FOUNDATIONS | BUILD THE STRUCTURE | BEAUTIFY |

How does this model translate into you becoming the best of you, being distinguished, achieving outcomes better than you had ever imagined, being deeply satisfied and creating a true legacy?

Step 1 – De-Clutter

The starting point of building a skyscraper is to pull down the old buildings, clear the rubbish and make the ground neat, flat and pristine. Similarly, we carry baggage, old ideas, irrelevant facts and complexities, academic but useless models, history and bad experiences.

Let's put up a mirror to ourselves, de-clutter and uncomplicate, remove the limitations and constraints we have put on ourselves, look forward and replace these with simpler and more robust thinking. We have built up prejudices and misconceptions and view the world through our fears, worries, distortions, expectations and other complex emotions, fuelling our egos. And all of this is done without bad intentions. In fact, the road to hell was built on good intentions.

How can we hope to build new fresh, powerful thinking, just like a shiny new skyscraper on this messy surface? I am not even talking about questioning what is already there. We don't have the time, and we need to move faster. When you are clearing your house, if you procrastinate on every object and ponder its usefulness, you'll waste time, energy and your progress will be hampered. De-clutter means a fresh, powerful, clean, simple look at business, work, people, ourselves and life itself. It needs to be stark and surgical. We will do this together!

Step 2 – Dig Deep To Lay Strong Foundations

The taller the skyscraper, the deeper you need to dig. To hold up the new structure, you need to lay stronger foundations so that the building will be secure, sustainable and whether all storms for longevity.

Similarly, look at our mind and emotions, self-imposed barriers, fears, concerns, regrets. Yes, we need to dig deep and lay strong foundations with mindfulness, clarity, and objectivity. Turn fears into passion, turn expectations into care.

Step 3 – Build The Structure

Using concrete, bricks, steel and metal structure and building blocks to get a tall and firm skyscraper, solid, long-lasting and fit for purpose.

Similarly, our own success through strategic thinking and valuepreneurship will need practical tools, techniques supported by frameworks, even models, which you will be able to apply immediately in your business, function, projects, transactions and personal life. While this is covered in all five sections, it will be even stronger in Section 2, where we talk about Strategy (see 2.6). It will make you fit-for-purpose. This discussion is not a philosophical lecture but a practical implementation of techniques in our actual work and indeed all life situations. They are practical and transformational.

Step 4 – Beautify

In the final step of building the skyscraper, now that the structure has been created, we need to put the finishing touches and beautify it with the right décor, glass, and aesthetics inside and outside to make it appealing and a joy work in and live.

What good is an excellent building if people don't see it like that? They must believe in it, trust it, and get the value from it and perceive its value.

How does this translate to developing yourself for complete business and personal success? From Step 1 to 3, we have gained clarity, a stronger mind and all the tools and thinking.

Now, let's get others around you to perceive the value you have. So they engage with you, are convinced by you and your ideas, have confidence in you and trust you. It's about how you wand your newly acquired thinking and technique comes across and make a personal impact.

We will work on your interactions with others and your communication to make this happen in Section 4 – Collaborative communication and building relationships underpinned by *Trust Capital*.

In summary, keep this skyscraper analogy in developing yourself by using this book. While each of the four steps is inter-twined, there is a logical flow from Step 1 to Step 4.

The book will also be most helpful if it is read in sequence. The skyscraper will be built; you will stand tall and distinguished.

1.12

Differentiation is Dead
Be Distinguished

Differentiation is ordinary and insufficient in this day and age. At best, mediocre. And yet, everyone seems to talk about it.

For example, laptops like Toshiba, Dell, IBM, Lenovo, Acer, HP, Sony... are all trying to differentiate against each other and therefore in head-on competition. But, if I said a MacBook Air, can you genuinely name me a competitor? Whether you're a fan or not, you have to agree that paying USD $1,500 for a machine that does the same job as a USD $500 Acer means they are extraordinary, stand out, and re distinguished.

What makes them distinguished?

To understand this difference between being *differentiated* and *distinguished*, I'd like you to think about something fascinating. If in the late 1990s, I said to you: In twelve years there will be a company which:

1. Actively chooses not to play in the biggest market available to it.

2. Sells its products at three times the price of its competitors – not double but treble the price; and

3. It will be the highest market capitalised company, the first trillion-dollar company in the world.

Would you have believed me? No way! You would have recommended I see a psychiatrist.

Of course, I am talking about Apple.

Look again at those three parameters above. What is the biggest volume market for laptops? Yes, its corporations. Almost all employees in all companies, are equipped with a laptop, yet Apple chose actively not to sell into that market. Yet it has the guts to sell at three times the price of an Acer or HP, and yes, it was the wealthiest company in the world in 2012 and twice the value of Microsoft. Of course, this was thanks to all its products, including the iPhone – but the reason was the same.

So, what is that reason, and how is this possible?

It's because Steve Jobs had an absolute obsession with understanding the customers' real values in the market segments they have chosen to serve and then set about serving and responding to those values. I would argue that he didn't make products. I hear you saying, really? Then what was the iMac, the iPod, the iPad and the iPhone? These weren't merely products; they were brilliant responses to the perfectly discovered value of his chosen customers. He set about understanding value and then and only then building these perfect innovative responses to that value.

There is a captivating video footage of the time they were designing the mouse in the 1980s. On one side of a room are Steve Wozniak and the tech team deeply engrossed in writing algorithms on a whiteboard with brains fuming. On the other side of the room is the main man himself, Mr Jobs, rocking in his chair, and he is lost to the world and deep in thought. He is playing with an imaginary mouse.

He wasn't even in that room and was lost in the thought, *which problem of which customer am I solving here?*

Such obsession for understanding, engaging with, and serving values makes organisations and indeed people such as Apple, Steve Jobs, Google, Toyota, and Elon Musk/Tesla *distinguished*.

This is not an advert for Steve Jobs, but an example of how a mind obsessed with bringing value creates, innovates and generates with relative ease. In subsequent sections, we will leave no doubt on how this is within reach of every individual and what you must do to achieve it.

These are all valuepreneurs.

The future of Apple is less certain as it moves from total value leadership under Steve Jobs into a mere competing corporate.

Can you imagine, had he been alive, the iPhone and all subsequent models would have been radically different. Frankly, what is the difference between these and Samsung phones? Everything before at Apple was revolutionary, and now that fan base and brand value is continuing on a legacy. They are keeping up, but they are not radical in innovation. They used to keep ahead of rapidly changing value and creatively dedicated to serving it. They are now having to compete and try to differentiate with their products.

So, differentiation is dead. Becoming *distinguished*, you will stand well above the rest.

What do I mean? Let's look at the three levels.

- Level 1 – Undifferentiated
- Level 2 – Differentiated
- Level 3 – Distinguished

- Companies at the lowest Level 1 are *undifferentiated*. This is where you do what everyone else can do – but everyone else can do what you do. It's a rat race, and you are lost in the noise.

- Companies that are at Level 2 are *differentiated*. In some respects, you are better than your competitors, but they might be better than you in other elements. You're merely competing, as in the example of the laptop above.

- At Level 3, you're *distinguished*. At this level, it's not about competition anymore. It's about the market and the values of the customers in it. It's when you stand alone and stand out. You're not even concerned about competitors.

Shift From Competitor To Customer Value Focus

I am not saying competitors should not be considered. But they are much less important than we think or make them. Most organisations and people in it are over-engaged with thinking about what their competitors are doing and then subtly or overtly try to match them or beat them. I request you to resist this temptation. Squarely set your focus on the market, customers value and how you can make value-impacts. This is much more powerful than looking at competitors in which case you will at best be as good as them and not distinguished – your energies, efforts, talent and capabilities are underutilised, even wasted. What competition do Google, Toyota, Tesla worry about? They don't need to and frankly have the time to – they are engaged with their customers value. Apple used to but sadly have had to turn the other way. Tesla need to take care as well – having been distinguished for years they are not innovating faster than competitors and are turning from being distinguished to differentiated.

Sure, look at competitors but only as a secondary cross check. Direct your energies, resources, know-how and talent towards your customers and their value. Be distinguished.

1.13

Delivering The Gift –
Shifting From What I 'Do'
To What I 'Bring'
Shifting From The 'Receiving' Mode
To The 'Giving' Mode

What gives you greater satisfaction: giving a gift or receiving one? And for the cynical amongst you who said receive, ha-ha! I said *satisfaction*, not pleasure.

Whenever I ask this question, most people respond that *giving a gift gives me more satisfaction*. And by gift, I don't mean chocolates or taking your customer out for lunch. I mean something far more valuable—their outcomes, impacts, value and success.

Think about Klara (see 1.3). What she was *doing* was developing digital applications, but what she was *bringing* was livelihoods to poor farmers and small tradespeople in the villages of South Africa. Which was more purposeful and, therefore, more powerful?

For Anita, the gift was not the kitchens, designs and fit-outs, but a service that gives architects the ability to provide their discerning clients 24-hour design turnarounds and win more business. And for the end customer – inviting friends home and having great dinner parties.

Let's say you need a new tire for your car. Providing the right tire with the correct specifications is *not the gift*. It is essential, but it's not the gift. Suppose that tire prevents your car from skidding and causing an accident - that's a gift. If delivering the tyre, replacing it without you having to leave your home or office saves you the hassle and unnecessary usage of your valuable time, that's a gift.

A piece of machinery or an engineering tool you sell to your customer, a car manufacturer, is not a gift. It's a gift if, thanks to your product, his costly production line stoppages are prevented, the plant manager's performance is raised, and his subsequent promotion to a director etc.

It's not just about what you *do*; it's what you *bring* that really matters.

Then why, time and time again, and perpetually, are we pre-occupied with our product, service, quality, price, and competition? Our mind is in the wrong place.

I am not saying that these variables are unimportant. On the contrary, your product, specifications, and quality are critical, but those things are not the gift. The gift is the value-impact and outcomes it brings to the customer. This is value.

As a result of our preoccupation with these core essentials, we can miss understanding and serving the real high priority need. That is the gift.

Sitting in front of a customer, if my mind thinks: *I hope I can get the contract; I hope they like my product; I hope they don't argue on price; I hope competitors aren't good as me; I wonder how much I can sell; my targets; my sales etc.*

In this case, I'm in *receiving* mode. I want something; frankly, I am begging. This will undoubtedly make me weaker and less confident. And the fear of *not getting* will certainly make me less successful.

Although the example I've used is in sales, exactly the same principle applies to all of us in every situation. For instance, you're a project manager, you want more resources, and you justify to your bosses logically, saying, *I need those resources to make this project work, please sign off on it etc.* You are *wanting*, not *giving*.

Suppose you are trying to sell an idea to your management, colleagues, or team. It's the same thing. You're asking for something. You're asking for them to agree, to listen to you, to give you something. In all these situations, you're in *receiving* mode.

Now let's resolve it.

- If you get more satisfaction from giving gifts than receiving.
- If you have many gifts for your customers, your management or to whoever you bring value.

Then daily and several times a day, why do we find ourselves with our hands spread out, *asking* for something? *Please sign off on my contract* and so on.

When we have so much to give and so much more value to bring, why do we make ourselves simply beggars? We're in *receiving* mode. It's soul-destroying. And whenever we are asking for something, we are in expectation. Expectation is the killer of man.

Expecting and wanting generates the fear of not getting. Fear is destructive. When we want, we are in fear; when we give, we are confident.

So shifting from the *receiving* mode to the *giving* mode is the answer to uplifting ourselves and being confident. Never again do you need to ask for anything from anyone.

In everything you do, the gift exists, but if you don't see it, like Klara, then it's soul-destroying. Deliver the gift, be a valuepreneur.

Andy's Story – From *Receiving* Mode To *Giving* Mode

Andy, a senior marketing director, was eager to get his boss, George, to agree to a project to take the entire export sales force and distributor team for a sales conference in Marrakesh.

Andy: I have an excellent idea. Let's arrange a sales convention in Marrakesh.

George: Really? Sounds like an expensive social gathering, a holiday. What does it involve?

Andy: No, it's not a holiday, it's a serious project. I think it will be very worthwhile, getting everyone together for three days, discussing important business issues, so that everyone gets on the same page.

George: How much will *all* of this cost?

Andy: $90,000

George: *How much?!* In these tough times? *Are you crazy?*

Andy: Honestly, it's a good project, and I'll be really grateful if you could consider it.

Is Andy in a *receiving* or *giving* mode? He is *wanting*, and it's nothing short of begging. What's going through Andy's mind? *I hope he doesn't think it's just a fun trip, a holiday, and I hope he's not too resistant...* Andy is in *receiving* mode. In this *receiving* mode, how confident does he feel?

Let's shift Andy's conversation into *delivery* mode.

Andy: Hi George, I've been reflecting on our forecasts for next year, and I have a proposal, which will generate sales of 12% over and above our current targets.

George: Really? 12%? Are you sure? How?

Andy: Three very lucrative markets, specifically A, B and C, are growing at an incredible rate. To tap into them and take the full opportunity, we need the buy-in and action from our entire sales force and distributors, as it will bring them excellent sales and therefore personal gains.

George: Hmm, sounds interesting. Tell me more.

Andy: We can do this in one hit, explore the opportunities, share experiences of what works and what doesn't, which would happen by getting them under one roof, so let's do a sales convention. I propose Marrakesh as a great location.

George: Sounds good. What will it generate, and how much will it cost?

Andy: 12% of sales growth equates to $25m for an investment of only $90,000.

George: What are we waiting for? *How quickly can you do it?*

In this second conversation, where is Andy? In *giving* mode or *receiving* mode?

Beating next year's forecast by 12% is in itself gift enough for George, let alone the fact that he is looking to be promoted to CEO when the current CEO retires in two years. That's a gift. This is not a trick or a game we are playing with the boss. Frankly, would you ask for projects to be signed off without having a tangible outcome like this? But we forget that part because we have a *wanting* mind, not a *giving* one.

In every situation, there is a gift, but you need to recognise it and use it. I am not asking you to manipulate anyone with this gift delivery mentality. It is a superior way of understanding genuine value and articulating and serving it.

Manipulation uses these as a tool for self-gain, irrespective of whether it benefits or harms the other person. However, applying this approach to genuinely serve value is a high integrity position, which is our quest. When you are giving, you will be much stronger, confident, and frankly, in value leadership.

Shifting From Receiving To Delivery Mode –

The IRC Stages – Intention – Realisation – Communication

Like Andy, most of the time, our intention is excellent in most situations. He genuinely brings a superb idea to help the company, George and his own work. But the problem is he doesn't realise the true end-value he can bring. This is because the state of the human mind is most often in expectation or wanting something which pushes us into the receiving mode, such as, I hope my boss signs off on the project, I hope he gets it etc. Inadvertently, despite the good intention behind it, we miss the value we have to bring and find ourselves nothing short of begging for a positive answer. It's a negative and self-deprecating mindset. However, we need to live in a constructive attitude which is even higher than a positive one. Positive would be: my boss will say yes to the project. That's good. But the superior, more constructive thought is he will gain $25m. Our mind needs to reside in the constructive, the end-impact, the gift.

There are three stages in our bringing of value.

- Stage 1 – Intention to bring
- Stage 2 – Realisation that I have value to bring
- Stage 3 – Communication so they clearly perceive the value

Let's understand each of these.

- **Intention.** Mostly, people genuinely have the right intention of bringing success and value to their customers, their company, their bosses and their own work. This is not where the problem lies. The problem lies in realisation.

- **Realisation.** It's the realisation that my skills, ability, knowledge can genuinely deliver huge value-impact. Andy was only subconsciously aware of the value this project would provide. It became all about his project and getting it signed off and the expectation, desire and even desperation of getting it approved. It became about himself and what he wanted. In that expectation, the realisation of value gets suppressed or even lost somewhere. So, controlling our state of mind and shifting from the receiving into the giving mode lights up that realisation of value. But then the next step is to make sure that the other person clearly perceives the value, i.e. have we properly communicated it to them?

- **Communication.** What good is having solutions to value if the beneficiary of that value doesn't see it and perceive the value? To build this perception and get the job done, hold back the project, the product, the idea. Make their end value your starting point in the communication and contextualise your solution to that point of gain, of value – as Andy did in the second conversation. He held back the sales convention, the location, the cost, i.e., the project features, and led with the value-impact, which was 12% of sales above the forecast and even George's promotion to CEO. Why would a project not get signed off?
So, don't go in to get the project approved; you will be in receiving mode if you do. Go in to genuinely serve the value, bring the gift. You don't need to worry about the project being approved.

Keep your mind focused on the fact that I am bringing George and the company 12% of sales growth. Now your approach is: *Would you like 12% sales growth above the forecast? I'm here to make it happen for you.*

1.14

Business And Management Is Not An Academic Subject, It's A Practical And Emotional One

I am explaining and over-explaining the simple notion of how a true valuepreneur operates, and we haven't yet described value in a structured way, but it's coming. The crucial word here is simple.

This is why I say business, management, strategy, leadership – none of these are academic subjects. They are practical and emotional subjects. After all, how many MBAs did Steve Jobs or JRD Tata, Richard Branson, Bill Gates, Ingvar Kamprad (IKEA), Walt Disney have? None. They had something else. They had a relentless passion for serving genuine customer values; and one other key factor – fearlessness. It's emotional. They didn't go through an academic process.

Now you might say, yes, but they were exceptional business-people. Well, I think there is an exceptional business-person inside every individual, whether they be an entrepreneur, intrapreneur or, more significantly, a valuepreneur.

Let's think about this.

Let's say you're proposing a project to top management which will require considerable investment. The moment they quiz you to justify the returns or pick holes in your idea or object on some point, what goes through your mind? *What do they think of me? Maybe they don't like my project; what if it's not signed off; what will it do to my promotion prospect; how will I be viewed in the future, etc.* And despite all the complex, fancy strategic logic, models, techniques you have used, these thoughts dominate the process and actions.

I am not speaking against models and frameworks.

The models I explore in later sections are efficient and incorporate the emotional reactions of human beings. These have been distilled from 30 years of application and generation of real results then transformed into practical tools which are simple, easily applicable and uncomplicated.

Business is much simpler than we make it.

Complex models, frameworks, and techniques have often been over-used by so-called professionals and academics, creating corporate confusion and lost opportunities. Having ejected Steve Jobs from his own company, replacing him with all the suits and excessive so-called professional management, they had to go back and beg for his return to save the company. The rest, as they say, is history.

I've got tremendous respect, there's no doubt, for great strategists, writers, thinkers who have brought a lot of theory and rigour to the business world. In no way am I putting their work down or discounting the immense amount of work done in strategy, models, processes, strategic thinking. The essence, however, is simple, easily applied, practical and emotional.

Let's put it this way.

Structured business education teaches you all about the what of business, which are the models, frameworks, definitions, analyses. It needs to evolve to the *how – how to do business?* That is the crucial ingredient.

Very often, a head full of extremely complex models, structures, concepts, theories put up more and more walls between you and your markets, your customers, your key people and your teams. We have over-processed business and management.

Take planning. How many strategic business plans have you ever seen genuinely adhered to that result in growth and success? On the contrary, everything appears disjointed. Someone somewhere is writing missions and visions, and someone else is doing the budgets; others are developing projects and programs; another is setting performance measures; someone else is doing an organisation chart, and others are working on critical success factors. It's all brilliant and clever stuff, but disjointed, over-complicated, and it's hardly surprising that it is not sustainable.

What we need is a single, simple point of alignment and reference from which everything is aligned linearly, every process, every project, every action of every individual, and every dollar expended becomes relevant and aligned to that one ultimate point of reference. It's simple, and in Section 2, we will expand on this, give you the tools and plenty of examples of how it generates success.

So, emotion has a massive influence and impact on business. Emotion is the driver of business, not the heavy models.

One of the largest mergers ever, Glaxo Smith Kline (GSK), involving hundreds of thousands of jobs, was held up for two years because the two CEOs could not work out who would be at the head.

Frankly, it is entirely emotional. Look at how the relationship between Steve Jobs and Bill Gates completely changed the shape of business. Look at how starting with an essential human emotion - college guys wanting to have relationships with college girls – shaped how we communicate in the world. Facebook was born out of pure emotion.

I am often asked the question, *When you say that business is not an academic subject, would that not shock many scholars?*

My response is: I think it needs to. It's about time we did, and it's time to wake up. You've tried to make a precise science of something which isn't. We have over-processed business and management. We are making the process an end in itself, rather than allowing processes to help us to make solid business decisions.

I am not speaking against processes. They are critical in shaping ideas and being well implemented to deliver growth and success. But the most successful businesses adopt only those processes which are fit and relevant for purpose. Section 2 will abundantly clarify how to plan processes and how every single process must exist and only exist with a single clearly visible purpose of serving customer value. This also makes it easy to change and adapt processes, in line with the changing nature of market values.

Clever academic techniques, theories and approaches could give you up to eight gears. But all eight gears and the *ninth gear* opens for you as the valuepreneur.

1.15

The Flow Of Creativity

Going back to Anita's story, someone recently said to me, OK, I get the story, but effectively what happened was she started seeing things and driving value more creatively. She was able to attract the architects to her showroom much more creatively.

So, is it about creativity and innovation?

It's very much about creativity.

Every one of us is endowed with an abundance of creativity. Geneticists are inconclusive about how much and whether our DNA determines our creativity. Having had the wonderful opportunity to develop thousands of people in different organisations, walks of life, countries and cultures, whether it was running corporations or in my last twenty years of coaching and growing people - I can definitively conclude that a lot more creativity exists in all of us. Still, the issue is that it is constrained, blocked to different degrees. We have all the equipment. We have all the creativity and innovation, and we only use a tiny proportion of it.

The real questions here are: *What gets in the way of it? What's blocking it?*

Creativity is something to unblock rather than force on someone. This blockage emanates from the mind. The state of mind is shaped by our egos interacting with every experience we encounter. The result is emotions such as fears, worries, concerns, hope, and even regrets. It's an emotional reaction of the mind which holds us captive and bound. How can we be free? How can ideas flow? Ideas exist, and creativity exists, but the state of our minds just traps it. For example, let's say the last time you proposed a similar idea, it was rejected. This experience will interact with your ego and raise a fear that this idea won't be accepted either. As a result, your behaviour may alter, you might speak with lower confidence, nervousness and worry. This may cause the rejection and not the idea itself, which is brilliant. So, we come in the way of our creativity.

The aggregate of our behaviours, formed by our minds in this way, can loosely be called our personality. And like the situations that we experience, it's transient. A situation is simply a situation and raw reality. We think it is the problem, but it's not; it's neutral. However, the way we engage with it through the state of our mind and emotion distorts it into a problem. For example, the situation in this example is the project and its benefits – that's the raw reality. Our mind distorts it as we see it through the previous rejection and mess it up. Our creativity is thwarted.

So, if the architect of my diminished creativity is me – I have the answer to unblock it. Having had the privilege to coach and observe thousands of people at close quarters, I see time and time again that with understanding, quietening, and balancing our minds, we liberate our creativity. We can change things, bring better solutions to problems and our flow of imagination and innovation gears up significantly.

We always were creative, but now, we have been released from some or a lot of that blockage. How much can be unblocked depends on the degree of the blockage, the gravity and volume of our experiences and even more importantly, the resolve and commitment of the individual to see clearly, understand reality and bring the mind into equilibrium. It's a dramatic release of our capacities, our potential and therefore our creativity.

What frees our creativity? The *giving* mind is uncluttered. Everything opens up when you shift your emphasis from being a *net taker* into being a *net giver.*

What do I mean by the *net taker* and *net giver?*

Let's go back to Anita.

Before the program, she was in a *receiving* rather than *giving* mode. The mind was emotionally distracted, locked in either regretting the past, e.g. *I wish the economic crisis hadn't happened...* or worrying about the future, *My business is finished, and how will I survive?* She had trapped her creativity.

When she moved to the *giving* mode, she asked, *What do those wealthy people in Chelsea and Belgravia value? What is value to the architects? What would help architects? What would encourage them to come into my showroom?* She moved from fear to clarity and the visibility of opportunities. Creativity suddenly flowed in the shape of the cuisine evenings. Her business boomed. So, the idea of the cuisine evenings was highly creative. That idea was always in her, but it was unliberated or even realised because her fears and emotions blocked it. She was unable to see it.

Again, I ask the question: *Is creativity something to be taught or released?* Of course, it's the latter.

A mind in the *receiving* mode is cluttered because it is overly concerned with *me and what I want,* my own expectations. These expectations are the killer of man. Wherever there are expectations, fear is guaranteed because the worry of *not getting* makes us vulnerable, subjective and obscured from reality. We are bound and not free.

Shifting to the *giving* mode releases us. The focus is on others and delivering value to whom I am serving. The mind is released from expectations and therefore fears.

Becoming objective we see reality. Our creativity will be unblocked and flow. In *wanting*, we are bound, fearful, constrained and held back. In *giving*, we are caring, confident, unbound, creative and productive.

It's our ninth gear. Making that transition takes conscious practice.

1.16

Understanding The Meaning
Of The Gift

So, have we understood the meaning of *the gift*?

Returning to Anita, the gift to architects was a fast, impeccable design service that delivered the ability to win more business from wealthy clients in Chelsea. To make the architects' lives easier and make them richer in a harsh economic environment. The kitchens themselves were not the gift; they were the means to deliver the gift. The gift to the customers in Chelsea was seeing remarkable designs *within 24 hours*, becoming distinguished in their social circle, if not ahead of their friends.

Again, the kitchen was just the means.

Deliver the gift. Be distinguished. Be deeply satisfied and, as a by-product, win the game, become wealthier.

1.17

What Is Value?

Value is one of the most misunderstood words in business. When we say *value*, we are normally just speaking about *added value*. It's not added value. Look at any discussion of added value, and you will find it essentially boils down to providing a little more product or service for no more money. It's mundane and ordinary.

It is nothing short of a bribe, trying to hook the customer with the desperation of winning the sale. This is not value or an attempt to serve it. The next supplier who offers another value-added bribe will move the customer to them and then the next. It is selling at its worst, yet people naively hail *added value* as something wonderful. For example, added value is when you take your car for a service and wash it for you. It's good and pleasing, but it is not real value. This so-called value is nothing but ordinary add-on services or products, not differentiated at all, but just a bit of self-satisfaction that we are doing just a little bit more for our customers to entice them, for our own gain.

Then there is that tired, ordinary and weak statement – *Going the extra mile*. Most of the time, it feels nothing more than an undifferentiated bribe to our customers to get them to buy more from us.

In Anita's story, the added value might have been a free colour consultation, a leather-bound proposal, let's yawn. This is not what we mean by absolute value, and it is just a pretext for selling more. Why go the extra mile when you can go all the way and sell much more?

It's Time To Understand What Value Really Is

Real value is about solving the problem by delivering the net gain, the outcome, and a value-impact that meaningfully fosters the customer's well-being. In Klara's story, value is the improved livelihoods of farmers in remote villages, not having to worry about how they will buy their fertilisers for the next season. In Andy's story, it's the 12% growth in sales for the company; and George getting promoted to the CEO position. In Anita's story, the value to wealthy Chelsea clients is the excitement of seeing the design within a few hours of deciding on a new kitchen. That brings a bigger wow factor. It's the joy of cooking in a convenient and fabulous kitchen, especially for people who find cooking a chore. The value to architects of offering this wow factor to their customers makes them see dollar signs. Why wouldn't they listen to you, engage with you, even trust you and, of course, buy from you and negotiate less with you if this immense value was served?

Don't you have a preferred airline, where you'd be happy to pay 10% more because your child could be entertained on an 11-hour flight? Or that restaurant who could adjust the food to your taste and allergies; that shop who can give you the right advice depending your usage and outcomes etc.

We are going to structure value and give it a practical shape but before that, let's clarify what we mean by the *customer*.

1.18

The Meaning Of Customer

I'd like to clarify I'm talking about value and its delivery from a customer's viewpoint. It is the easiest way to see it. This book includes customers not only in the traditional sense. But, well beyond that.

Let's define a customer as *anyone whose value is served and satisfied through your capability, including expertise, knowledge, products, services, etc.*

In this case, customers in this book include all the people you serve, including those you sell to and your bosses, colleagues, team members, suppliers, family members, friends, and the wider world you interact with. If you are a doctor, it is your patient; a Prime Minister – the country's residents; a charity – the people you are helping; the police – the people you are protecting.

So every principle, idea, or technique I illustrate with the example of a traditional customer, please ensure that it applies just as much to your *total* people environment.

1.19

It's Not About Your Value

Another misconception I want to clarify straight away is that we are not speaking about our own value. People often say to me, *You are telling us to understand people's value and serve it. What about my value, growth, outcomes, and success?* My answer may sound harsh. Forget about your value and yourself. The more you leave your own value out of it, the stronger you will be.

Let's be careful here. I'm not saying that your success and value are unimportant. Not at all; it is crucial; that's why you are reading this book. So, why do I say forget about your value? Because it is a result, not the driver. The more you forget your own value and obsessively engage with your customers' value; whom your talents, products and services are serving - the wealthier, more satisfied and successful in all its definitions you will be.

If you focus on serving *others value*, you never need to worry about the result *for you*. It will be much bigger than you can identify or imagine.

As we have said, from whom will you buy more readily, the seller who was trying to sell you things to win your business and make money, or the one who is obsessed with your value and outcomes?

With whom will you negotiate harder and argue more on prices, the entrepreneur or the valuepreneur? The valuepreneur will be more prosperous than the entrepreneur. You really don't need to worry about your own value.

Steve Jobs never had an objective to be mega-wealthy. He was obsessed with the value to his customers. Apple became the wealthiest, highest market capitalised, first trillion-dollar business. The same is true for other Valuepreneurs like Elon Musk, Kamprad or Branson, or valuepreneurial companies like Toyota, Tesla, Cipla etc.

Let's then give value a useable structure, a model, a shape.

1.20

The VORO Model
Value Onions And Response Onions

To understand value, think about the customers' value as rather as an onion.

Let's call this the *Value Onion* (see diagram below).

At the core is the actual product or service itself. The further away we go from the core, and as the layers become bigger and bigger, they represent more and more value to the customers. The bigger the layer, the greater the value to the customer.

In the diagram below, look at the Value Onion on the left. If this is the Value Onion for Virgin Atlantic's customers, then the analysis is a follows:

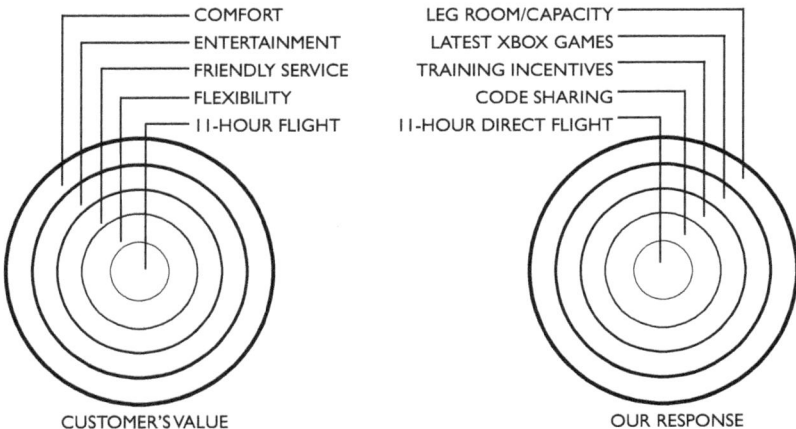

COMFORT	LEG ROOM/CAPACITY
ENTERTAINMENT	LATEST XBOX GAMES
FRIENDLY SERVICE	TRAINING INCENTIVES
FLEXIBILITY	CODE SHARING
11-HOUR FLIGHT	11-HOUR DIRECT FLIGHT

CUSTOMER'S VALUE   OUR RESPONSE

I am not saying that the core is unimportant. Let me be clear on this. By making the core (which is the product or service) the smallest part of the onion, it is far from unimportant. It's fundamentally important. After all, if the core is rotten, the whole onion will be rotten.

There can be no compromise with the excellence of the core. It's not even up for discussion. If there is a problem with core, you need to first address that and improve it to be second-to-none. Quality is no longer a differentiator. It's not even a point of discussion: it's a must, a given, the starting point. If you can't get the core to be perfect, give up and do something else.

Then why am I making the core, i.e., the product or service, the smallest part of the onion? Because to the customer it represents the smallest value.

When was the last time you said in excitement that my car has four wheels or that I had a meal in the restaurant, or that I had a room to myself in a hotel? This is the core product or service: it's not exciting in itself. Yes, there can be no compromise with the quality because if it were a bad room, you would undoubtedly comment on it. However, if it were a good room, you wouldn't comment - it's a minimum expectation of the customer.

It's the core.

So, what would you get excited about?

Suppose it had an adjoining door to your children's room for security and care. The decor and the pictures were so inspirational they would help you be more productive. A massage chair after a long travel to be refreshed for the meeting in the evening. Are you getting this point? It's not what it is, but what it delivers as the end-gain to the customer. The massage chair is not the layer of value. The layer of value is attending the meeting fresh after a long journey. The massage chair will be the response to value.

Let's take another example.

You can fly from London to Los Angeles in 11-hours direct. How many airlines can do that? They all can. Let's personalise this.

Air Travel Value Onion

When I travel with my family, with my young teenage son, one of the outer layers of my Value Onion is entertainment for him. Because you can imagine eleven hours on a plane can be tedious and uncomfortable.

Now, the airline, in this case Virgin Atlantic (VA), needs to grasp this value to me. Exactly where on the Value Onion does it sit? Let's say it's layer 2, and therefore a priority.

Only after understanding my Value Onion, does VA need to develop matching responses, layer by layer, to serve every layer of the Value Onion. And this we will call the *Response Onion*.

In our example, the matching layer 2 response to layer 2 of the Value Onion of entertainment could be the latest Xbox games in every seat, pre-released, expected to hit the market after three months.

When my son gets off the plane in LA does he pick up the phone and excitedly say back to his friends back in London, 'Hey, guess what? I just flew eleven hours direct.'

No, this is not exciting. He picks up the phone and says, 'Guess what? I just played the latest FIFA game, the one you're going to play in three months! Wow man, you should see the graphics! Clarity is crazy, and they have all the latest players in there.'

This is exciting. It's thrilling for him and enjoyable for my wife and me. Not only to see the joy in his face but also that for eleven hours we can get on with our own thing, a movie, champagne. The next time, which airline will I choose? And, for that end-grain, for that value, would I be happy to pay a little extra to fly to LA? $50 $80?

I don't assign a price to this value.

I wouldn't reason my decision by saying, *This game is worth $80*. It's not as logical and reasoned as that. It's far more subtle and emotional. I just feel cared for, looked after, and the VA brand in my subconscious occupies a very favourable position.

How is this difficult?

1. There are two onions in business, indeed in life; the Value Onion and the Response Onion.

2. The core of the Value Onion is the actual product or service itself, and the value is in the layers, increasing the further out you go.

3. The Value Onion must precede the Response Onion.
   However, the problem is that we are always putting Response before the Value Onion. When you go to buy that laptop, and they simply show you all the different models available, that is responding without understanding that you make movies and want a bigger screen, higher capacity, faster processing etc.

4. Layer by layer, invest in developing responses to value. And naturally, you will invest more in serving the outer layers than the inner layers. Let's face it, resources are limited, and this is what we mean by doing the right things.

5. The emotional factor for the customer increases as you go further and further out in the onion. People buy on emotions. They'll justify it on the core (we'll discuss this more in Price - see 2.25).

1.21

Product And Service
Are They Different?

Wouldn't you agree the definition of a product or service is: *something you create to serve customer value?*

Therefore, don't just think of your product as the core product or service. That is too limited. At best, you will be back to an ordinary added-value approach. Think of your product or service as a total *value response* to your customers, i.e., redefine your product as the entire Response Onion to the customer's Value Onion.

For Virgin Atlantic, doesn't the pre-released Xbox game serve value? Sure it does. So, it must be part of the product.

I'm using the words product and service interchangeably. Where is the difference between the two? I don't see it. Too much is made of the distinction between product and services. There is no difference. Yes, one is made in a factory, and the other is made live through people. That's where the difference ends. After all, just like a product, don't you research a service, innovate in it, develop it, doesn't it have a unit cost, a unit price, a life cycle, doesn't it deliver value, doesn't it serve value to your customer, so where's the difference?

Let's cancel the myth. From here on, product and service are interchangeable.

So, let's think of our product as the *total service offering* in delivering the whole Value Onion. Therefore, the complete Response Onion is the solution massively favoured by customers.

1.22

The Why That Deludes Us
Value Must Precede Response

In business and life in general, we invariably respond *before* understanding true value. The computer salesman selling you product features before understanding your usage – and therefore, your value-impact frustrates you.

Excel V SQL Example

I was coaching a director of a top IT company. Let's call him Rakesh. His client, Gerald, the head of a trading team for a major bank, called him into his office, and the conversation goes something like this:

Gerald: Rakesh, I don't know what your guys have installed on our computers, but I want Excel restored, and I want it done by 5pm tomorrow.

Rakesh: But Gerald, we are giving you something much better, its SQL Server technology and works on a better database access process.

Gerald: Thanks for your advice, but if you want to play with your toys, please do it at home. I have a business to run, and I like Excel.

Rakesh: But please understand Gerald, Excel is old-hat, school kids stuff. Trust me, I'm an expert in SQL, and it's much more professional.

Gerald: Listen, if you want your contract renewed, you'd better restore Excel by tomorrow evening.

Rakesh: Sure, we'll have it done by 5pm tomorrow.

Look what has happened. The moment Rakesh starts fearing the loss of the contract, he concedes. This fear distracts us and prevents us from truly engaging with the client and value. Knowing that SQL was the perfect answer for the client, who won and who lost? Actually, everyone lost.

The question is: *What was Rakesh putting first: value or response? What is SQL: value or response?*

It is a response. Not only did he put response first, but he also didn't address Gerald's value at all.

We *think* it is value (SQL) because, in our mind, we are clear it will help the client and be beneficial for them. It's looking at it from our perspective. Whereas value, if you remember, is subjective and needs to be seen from the perspective of the customer or organisation we are serving.

What was missing from this conversation? That simple three-letter word – WHY.

You might say, *Well, it's obvious he should have asked 'why' Excel.* This answer is easy to give as external observers as you are right now. You are not involved in that situation - you are objective. However, in that real situation, everyone is subjective, and the *why* is rarely asked or half-baked at best; we don't properly engage with the *why*.

The next day, after we had the coaching session, Rakesh went back to the client, Gerald, and this is how the conversation went.

Are you prepared to be surprised at just how simple the answer is? Here goes.

> Rakesh (says with confidence): Gerald, I just want to check something with you. Restoring Excel by tomorrow is no problem, and we can do that smoothly for you, but first, it would really help me to understand, *why Excel?*
>
> That simple three-letter word *why* is the one that certainly deludes us and prevents us from understanding true value.
>
> Gerald (angrily responded): What do you mean, *why Excel?* My team knows Excel. We write our macros and manage our data in Excel. Not having accurate data on currency movements can mean a loss of millions... in a matter of seconds. We lost $3 million on a deal a month ago when the Yen had suddenly moved against the dollar. Also, I travel a lot and I want to manage the data and reorganise it remotely, receive it on my laptop to guide my team on currency positions more effectively. I have a business to build, and you ask me why Excel?

With this onslaught, we only hear and engage with his anger and miss the gems of his points of value. Gerald's whole Value Onion is coming out. For this, we need a present mind. Rakesh was able to cut through the anger, not take it as an attack on him and therefore was able to listen to the fundamental three points of value to Gerald and responded like this:

> Rakesh: OK, sure, Gerald. As I said, restoring Excel is not a problem. But if in 45 minutes I could show you how your team *never* misses a deal, like that $3m lost because the data will be so real-time. And that you can re-arrange the data to support your team with greater ease, not just from your PC... but from your mobile... how would that be for you and the business?

With this, Rakesh is leading with value before response. There is no way that Gerald can say *I'm not interested.* His highest values are being impacted head-on.

Gerald will ask, *'Can you really do that? How?'*

And Rakesh says, 'SQL Server technology.'

The same SQL, which in the earlier conversation sounded like a justification and pushing product desperately into the customer, has suddenly turned into the highly desirable response to value and success. Wow, what value have we missed? And we thought this was about Excel versus SQL – No. It doesn't matter how good SQL is; it is a response. If we put it before or even without value, it will be a source of annoyance for the client and desperation for me. By reversing it, daring to care and listening for the real value to the customer - and then proposing it as a response, makes the client feel satisfied and trusts you with confidence.

Never Put Response Before Value

It's a simple arithmetical equation:

Responding – Understanding Value = Justification

As we will see, justification is a self-defence reaction that makes us lose credibility and hurts the relationship.

This missing magical little word *why* really deludes us in life, especially when we want something. We don't have the courage or simply the consciousness to understand why to discover actual value. We give answers before asking questions.

You more or less have an idea of *why* your customer wants this or that. Even if you do, by confirming your confidence in delivering that value and your customer's reassurance that you care about their value will be significantly heightened.

It's not enough to be brilliant at *what* you are doing.

When you understand *why* you are doing it, your skill, knowledge, and expertise become far more powerful and valuable. Not only does it bring you more contracts, easier negotiation, but the deep satisfaction, confidence, and motivation when you know what value you have delivered, what problem you have solved.

The value in this example is how many millions you can save him and how easy you can make his life when travelling and help him meet his business growth targets. Put value before response – understand their Value Onion then and only then set about developing the Response Onion, layer by layer.

It's worth it!

This is how a true valuepreneur operates.

1.23

What Precedes Value Onions?

We've established that the Value Onion must precede the Response Onion. And we've touched on the dangers of putting responses *before* value, like the computer salesman. But now think about this: something else comes, even before the Value Onion.

What do you think that might be?

The answer is: *Who's Value Onion?*

1.24

Whose Value Onions?

The who must come before the Value Onion. And Value comes before the Response Onion. It's because value is entirely subjective and therefore, different for each individual. At the end of the day, a customer is an individual, a human being (even in the B2B environment) who has their own Value Onion.

So, let's understand the importance of starting with the who.

Let's take an example of this flow:

Who > Why > Value Onion > Response Onion

Luggage To And From India

My wife and I travelled to Bali from London to attend a dear friend's daughter's wedding. A whole group of us travelled on Qatar Airways with a baggage allowance in Economy Class of 23kg. But folks, this is an Indian wedding! There will be at least ten saris, which by the way is six yards of material, shoes to match, the jewellery, the accessories, the gifts, etc., not to mention my clothes!

So, how will a 23kg allowance suffice? We were concerned.

Then I had an idea.

On the way back, my wife was coming straight back to London, and I was coming on Jet Airways as I had work in Mumbai. Jet Airways allows 46kg in Economy, so on the way out, we could pool in the luggage in a group but, I could bring a whole suitcase back myself on the way back. Problem solved? Oh no. Because when I booked my flight for the return, from Mumbai, on Jet Airways, my ticket showed an allowance of 23kg. I was most upset and called the airline complaining that they had suddenly changed the rules and now I am stuck with 23kg of extra luggage.

They asked me, 'Which route are you flying?'

And I said, 'Mumbai to London.'

'Sorry Sir, that's the problem.'

But, look at this.

If you fly London-Mumbai-London, you are allowed 46kg, but if you fly Mumbai-London-Mumbai, same class, same seat, it's 23kg!

Let's take this and understand the flow:

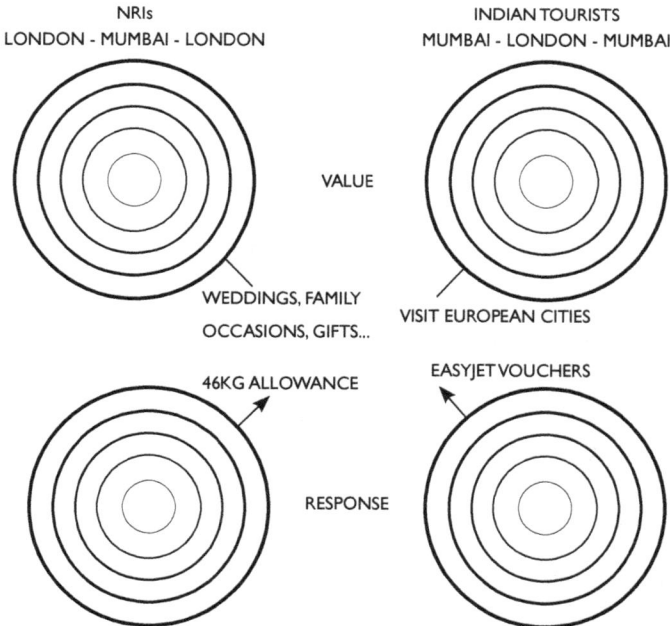

NRIs
LONDON - MUMBAI - LONDON

INDIAN TOURISTS
MUMBAI - LONDON - MUMBAI

VALUE

WEDDINGS, FAMILY OCCASIONS, GIFTS...

VISIT EUROPEAN CITIES

46KG ALLOWANCE

EASYJET VOUCHERS

RESPONSE

For Non-Resident Indians (NRIs) travelling London-Mumbai-London (look to the left of the diagram above):

- Who flies London-Mumbai-London? NRIs.

- Why? Family occasions, weddings etc.

- Value Onion – Carrying gifts and clothes – extra weight is required.

- Response Onion – 46kg.

Notice the core on all onions is the same – an eight-hour direct flight between London and Mumbai. But as the who changes, everything changes as follows (look to the right of the diagram above):

- Who flies Mumbai-London-Mumbai? Indian tourists.

- Why? To visit Europe.

- Value Onion – Easily enjoy multiple European cities from London like Paris, Rome, Madrid.

- Response Onion – Discounted EasyJet and hotel vouchers across Europe.

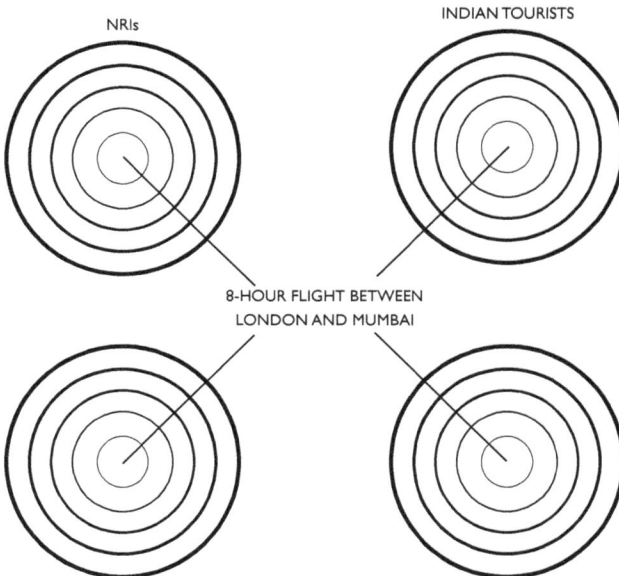

NRIs

INDIAN TOURISTS

8-HOUR FLIGHT BETWEEN
LONDON AND MUMBAI

The core on all four onions is the same:

Interestingly, on all four onions, the two Value Onions and the two Response Onions the core, i.e. the actual product or service, *are the same.*

NRIs, *as well as Indian Tourists*, will want an eight-hour direct flight between London and Mumbai and the response from Jet Airways will be an eight-hour direct flight between London and Mumbai. However, the real value is in the layers, and this is where the values will be different depending on whose Value Onion we are dealing with.

Suppose Jet wants to serve both segments' Value Onions. In that case, they will have to be honest and dedicated to investing in and developing different Response Onions to the two Value Onions.

So, in summary, if we are saying that business, leadership or indeed life itself is all about developing genuine responses to genuine discovered value, then we must always begin by understanding the *ultimate recipient* of that value.

This is why we must always start with the *who*.

Value really is subjective, and it belongs to individuals. We are merely the responses to that value, but that is what makes us very powerful, and it is also a position of absolute integrity, i.e., genuinely serving genuine value.

Ultimately, nothing is as enduring and attractive as impacting real value.

1.25

Multiple Stakeholders
And Their Value Onions

Each customer (unless it is just one person) is made up of multiple customers or stakeholders who each have their own sets of value. Value being subjective they each have different Value Onions. We must first discover who these stakeholders are they are and then their different Value Onions. The more we can do this the stronger we will be at serving the total Response Onions and winning that customer's business.

So, where there are multiple stakeholders there will be a collective Value Onion for the customer as a whole. Then individuals within the customer will all have their own individual Value Onions. For best results, you need to respond to both. In the example below, the family has a collective Value Onion, and then each family member has their own.

You will see how the responses are conceived.

Here is another example of *who* we are serving and why.

 Here the *who* is the customer or end beneficiary of our product or service, the *why* is their Value Onion and the *what* is our Response Onion.

Car Seat Manufacturers

I was invited to run a three-day strategy workshop for the executive management team of one of Asia's largest car seat manufacturers. To disguise their identity, let's call them Rolling Thrones.

I arrived a day earlier to understand the business and visit their main plant.

The next morning at the start of the session with the twelve executive and senior director team of Rolling Thrones, I opened with a simple question. 'Tell me, what business are you in?'

Simple and straightforward, the question was met with silence. I wasn't surprised. Their minds were thinking, We showed you around the plant and told you about our products, didn't we, Sanjeev?

I asked the question again. Eventually, one kind person decided to answer, thinking, *We had better just humour Sanjeev. He has come a long way from London to be with us.*

He said, 'We are in the business of making and selling complete car seat systems, including the frame, upholstery, electrics etc.'

'Oh really? Is that what you make and sell? So, has anyone bought a new car recently?'

A few hands went up, and I asked one gentleman, 'Please describe the step-by-step process of buying the vehicle.'

Exec: I went to the showroom.

Me: Then what did you do?

Exec: I saw all the cars there and went up to the model I liked.

Me: And then?

Exec: I opened the door.

Me: Then what happened?

Exec: I put my hand on the seat, and then I sat in it.

Me: Describe the feeling

Exec: Hmm... it felt comfortable, and the smell of the new leather was superb.

Me: Now we are getting closer to what you what you sell, but you've limited yourself to thinking you sell car seats. Why did you change your car?

Exec: As a family, we enjoy going out on weekends and especially with the children to visit historic cities.

Me: Great. Describe the journey. What is nice about it? And: what's a problem.

Exec: Well, it's nice being together, and we talk about what we have seen; but the problem is the children end up fighting over the iPad. My son wants to see action movies, and my daughter likes nature documentaries.

Me: I see. And what about your wife and you? What do you find inconvenient?

Exec: Well, she complains of backache on the long journeys, and I like the air conditioning to be quite high, but she likes it low...

Do you see where this conversation has led us?

It has identified the customer's Value Onions. Further, not only do we have the Value Onions of the buyer, who in this case is the Exec, but the other stakeholders, i.e., the son, daughter, and wife, each of whom have a completely different Value Onion.

Me: Think about your journeys and imagine if in the headrests of each of the rear passenger seats you could have built-in headsets which come down... and your son and daughter can watch different movies on the screens fitted in the seats in front of them. Also, imagine if, in the front passenger seat, there was a massager fitted to massage the back. And then the driver's seat was chilled – the opposite of heated seats – for you. How would your journey go?

Exec: That would be absolutely amazing!

I actually saw them *all* taking notes. I'm not joking.

'Seriously, folks, you've got to be kidding me. Do you mean you've never thought of this or discussed it as a strategy?'

'We have... kind of... but to a limited degree - more a nice idea rather than a serious strategic response to the customer's true values.'

Well, you'll be happy to know that two of their major automotive customers have already adopted these attributes in their seats generating significant business growth for Rolling Thrones.

So let's examine the *who, why,* i.e. Value Onion and *what,* the Response Onion.

Who?	Son/Daughter	Wife	Exec
Why? Collective value	Happy family weekends visiting fun places comfortable		
Why? Individual Value Onion	Enjoying own preferred programs/games	Keeping the back comfortable and massaged	Keeping cool and comfortable without distrubing others
What? Matching Response Onion	Personal built-in headsets and screens	Rolling massager, multi-program in seat back	Chilled driver's seat
How? Actions/Tactics	It's only when we have created the best responses to value that we will develop and action all design, production, processes, people, publicity, financial projections...		

1.26

Collective Value And Individual Value Of All Customers

My focus in this example has been on consumer values, but I must emphasise, precisely the same principle applies to a business's values with its multiple stakeholders. For example, Rolling Thrones sells to car manufacturers like Toyota, Hyundai, Jaguar etc. So as a customer, Hyundai will have a collective value of growing the company, acquiring new markets, becoming more profitable, etc. Then there will be many stakeholders involved, and each will have different values from Rolling Thrones.

Here are some examples of stakeholders at Hyundai and their central values:

- Procurement manager – Cost savings and delivery capability.

- Marketing manager – help me to brand the idea and make it appealing to my market.

- Sales manager – give me lots of options on the feature combinations for my different customers.

- Production manager – easy fit; productivity of my sales force.

- HR manager – train my workforce to fit it easily.

And it goes on:

- Quality manager.
- Finance manager.

If we seriously want to be exceptional suppliers. Then we must engage with and understand our customers and their true values—both collective and individual.

Then and only then build responses and then the detailed tactics to deliver that value.

1.27

What Makes You Distinguished?

A reminder. As we had said earlier, differentiation is not enough. Certainly not in today's day and age when suppliers can be easily researched, compared and chosen – thank you, Google.

So, how do you become distinguished?

Let's go back to the Value Onion.

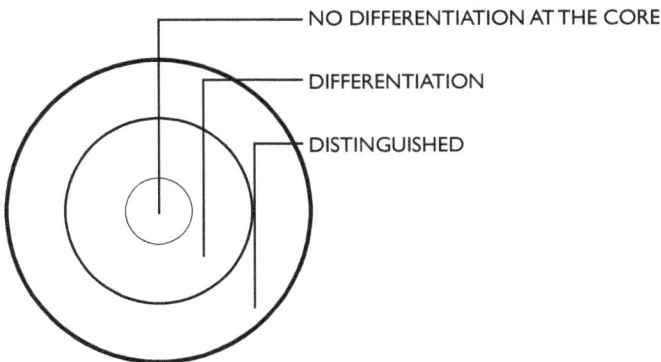

At the core, i.e. the product, service, process and nuts and bolts of what we do, there is no real differentiation. Everyone can do the same as the others. If you are a Holiday Inn or Ibis or Crowne Plaza etc., it's more or less the same as each other.

I'm not saying the core is unimportant. On the contrary, nothing short of excellence will do. If it isn't excellent, don't even dream of differentiating yourself, let alone distinguishing. After all, if the onion's core is rotten, the whole onion will be rotten. I'm not even going to speak about quality. Quality is not a differentiator. It is the starting point, an expectation, a minimum in today's world.

So first, fix the core.

Many restaurants have focused on the décor, ambience, service, decoration, menus, but the food has been poor, and they go out of business.

It is essential to make the core perfect, but it will only be a point of reassurance for the customer. Remember the examples of laptops like Dell, Toshiba, Acer? If you operate at the core, the only real differentiator becomes price – a demoralising and damaging downward spiral.

As you move onto the layers beyond the core, i.e., understand the middle layers of the customer's Value Onion and build Response Onion layers to serve them, you become *differentiated*. But these are still in the middle of the onion, and it's not too difficult for competitors to catch up. Microsoft laptops may be a good example. They are differentiated as they are thin, convenient to use as they are touch screen etc.

You start to leave the rest behind as you move to the outermost layers of the Value Onions and build genuine and innovative responses to serve those values. You are impacting the most potent values of your customers. You will be respected, trusted, admired, advocated and even advertised by your customers – yes, you are *distinguished*.

Businesses like Apple, Toyota, Tesla, Amazon are in that zone. They stand out and are respected by their customers as they deliver value at the outermost layers of the Value Onions of their customers.

They are courageous because they know they are holding the highest values of their customers in their hands.

Apple can courageously afford to price their MacBook Air at 300% above their competitors. Toyota understand the outer layers of the Value Onions of their customers as cost per mile of motoring and spending their time more productively rather than looking after or maintaining the car. As a result, when other car manufacturers build their vehicles to last seven years so that customers replace them and buy new ones, Toyota goes the other way and make their cars last much longer. They invest in building their cars for longevity and to not break down.

Conversely other manufacturers lead by product, cost and profit rather than value mentality. Their approach is to make more money from selling expensive replacement parts on breakdowns. Of course, this is a good revenue stream, but Toyota has the highest revenues and profits and doesn't need to look for desperate or even devious ways to make more money when serving value makes you richer in any case.

Another example of Toyota becoming distinguished is the hybrid car.

The outermost layer of the Value Onion of environmentally conscious people was a personal satisfaction from owning a car but causing less damage to the world. If I said the word *hybrid car*, the first word to enter mostly people's mind is Prius.

The Prius was the first hybrid car. It was distinguished, and it is why seventeen years after it was launched, there were dozens of hybrids, but the Prius is the first in mind. They were also ahead of the competition and distinguished in developing the first 4x4 SUV as a hybrid – the Lexus 400h, a hybrid brand.

I was in that segment and felt great pride and personal satisfaction driving it. It was my outer layer of the Value Onion, and Toyota had distinguished themselves, and they sold huge volumes.

It took another ten years for other 4x4 manufacturers to catch up.

It's not about competition. Think less about them. It is about the market, engage with customers' Value Onions.

Operate on the outermost layers of the Value Onions of your customers by building genuine Response Onions, and you will be distinguished.

The same arguments apply to Tesla. Despite hundreds of competing products, they remain the most respected brand in EVs.

1.28

Think Of Every Customer
As A Consumer – Valupreneurially

Business To Business (B2B) V Business To Consumer (B2C)

Too much is made about this distinction. Many books have been written and massive theories propounded on the distinction between B2B and B2C. Let's be clear; there is no difference.

Think about this; you are in senior management of a B2B company. Let's say it's a manufacturing company and you buy raw materials, for example, steel. You can choose from many different suppliers. The core is the same, i.e., grade XYZ steel - and ten suppliers can give this to you.

The price is more or less the same, so who do you select? Won't you choose the supplier who appears more interested in you, your production, your values? And they seem to be more flexible, will sort you out if there is a problem, are more communicative with your team, as opposed to another who is working to strict processes of their own? You will feel you can trust this supplier, have confidence in them and therefore sleep easy knowing that thanks to them your production will not have costly production stoppages. In choosing this supplier you are behaving like a consumer with a Value Onion and looking beyond the core, even into your personal values.

In the end, value is subjective. It belongs to human beings; it's personal, so where is the distinction between B2B and B2C?

Yes, there may be one slight distinction -In the B2C environment - the Value Onions of customers are much more evident and in your face. Especially with social media reviews etc. However, in the B2B environment you have to work a little harder and ask more questions of the right people to discover the value. The approach and method of understanding that value by engaging with the customer are exactly the same in both cases. In fact, the day that B2B companies start to think like B2C, they will achieve much greater success.

Think about the two examples earlier, the family buying a car for happy weekends; and Hyundai. The former is a B2C example, and the latter a so-called B2Bone. Looking at the multiple stakeholders in both; where is the difference? It was only the Value Onions of each stakeholder that were different.

The beauty of thinking in VORO (Value Onion, Response Onion) as a valuepreneur is that these naïve differences and complications are eliminated. Business and, indeed, life are much simpler, and the implementation of plans and actions are more transparent, decisive, and bring far more remarkable outcomes.

1.29

Dare To Care – A Spirit Of Enquiry

I hear you saying, *Ah yes, but what about where the supplier is being sought by a competitive bid like a Request For Proposal (RFP) process? Does this approach still hold?*

My answer is: *Absolutely it does.*

RFPs were made by humans, not God. To be a human is to have a Value Onion – it's personal.

Don't get stuck. If you dare to care, you will get to the outer layers, RFP or not. RFPs mainly focus on the core; they specify what the buyer is looking for - the steel quality, quantity, and supply logistics.

You need to engage the customer beyond this, and how you ask the question will determine how engaged with you they become. Who wouldn't if their real and most considerable value was being looked at and served?

Let me give you a real example. This is not just about an RFP process. You may not be involved in them. It is really about a *Dare To Care* attitude and a *Spirit Of Enquiry* to engage with the customer's Value Onions.

London Construction Bid Presentation

A vast construction consultancy in London, had a presentation of an RFP bid in four days on the proposed construction of a huge shopping mall. The COO asked me to help the team build a winning strategy. It was full of self-justifications and a detailed response merely at the core from start to finish.

Value was missing.

It began with, *We are ABC company, the best in the world...* and laboriously rolled out all impressive credentials. Then came the full details of their solutions, which were all about the service and responses at the core. It was Death-by-PowerPoint with fifty slides – all about themselves and their service.

It's impressive, but is it distinguished? Frankly, is it even differentiated? I asked, 'Won't your ten other competitors be saying, promising and able to deliver the same?'

Pensively they answered, 'Yes, they will.'

'So, it's the luck of the draw literally, and if one of the competitors happens to get lucky and hit a high value beyond the RFP, they will win it. Can you afford that?'

'No...'

'OK, so what should you do?'

'Call the client, the senior-most stakeholder involved and tell them you need an hour to understand a few more things around the project. I guarantee you the response will be *no*.'

So say, 'Whether we win the contract or not, our concern is with getting your construction to happen on time, within budget, meeting all your business priorities and getting all the shop units rented from day one.'

This will capture the buyer's interest.'

And then say, 'And to respond perfectly, we need to know a few more points.'

They will respond with, 'I'd like to, but I am unable. It's a competitive bid. Sorry, my hands are tied.'

Your response?

'Let me understand your main concern. You can't give any suppliers an unfair advantage by speaking to them. Am I right?'

'Precisely.'

'OK, I have a proposal for you. During that one-hour conversation, I will have a member of my team write down every question and the answers you give, word-for-word. We will send it to you immediately, and please feel free to share it with all our competitors. Would that solve the problem of not giving us a competitive edge?'

The answer was, 'Yes, that would resolve it.'

They had the conversation, fully understood the Value Onion, built perfect responses, and won the contract. Their competitors received the note, and because it was not driven by them, they became upset that the customer was looking for more information. Further, because my clients had dared to care and were genuinely interested in the customer's Value Onions, they were more liked and trusted.

Don't get stuck in the issue and the process - your creativity will be stunted. The issue here was an RFP bid without an unfair competitive advantage to any bidder.

The *issue behind the issue* was much more significant – a booming mall built with 100% occupancy from day one. Think like and be a valuepreneur, then you will see opportunities more clearly unrestricted by the process but built on value.

1.30

Unperceived Value

Value May Be Perceived Or Unperceived By The Customer

Value often exists without being known by or perceived by its owner. The best way to understand customers' value is to ask them. We will discuss how to do this in Section 4 under the *Spirit Of Enquiry and Questions for a Value Conversation.*

Customers will only tell you the values they are aware of or perceived by them. However, there are some values of which even the customer is unaware. We call these unperceived values. We will not discover these by asking unintelligent questions like, *Which of my products would you like?* But more intelligent ones.

Let's take an example.

Samsung Camera

I go into a phone store. A Samsung salesperson asks me, 'Would you like a camera in your phone?'

Whatever for? I wonder.

They are trying to propose me a product, in which I haven't seen the value (yet). They have made life more difficult for themselves. It's the wrong question.

My response may be, 'Is it free?'

When we don't see the value, the discussion will always descend to price. So Samsung responds, 'Yes, it's free.'

Well, I'm no fool! 'OK, put it in.'

What an ordinary, boring, transactional conversation. To get to value, a much better question is, 'What do you do for a living?'

So, the conversation goes:

Samsung: What do you do for a living?

Me: I speak on strategy and leadership.

Samsung: Oh really? What does that involve?

Me: Well, it's a lot of travelling – sometimes I'm out of the country seventeen nights a month.

Samsung: Wow, that's a lot! And how do you keep in touch with your son?

Me: When I finish I go to my hotel room and call him.

Samsung: And what's your son doing these days?

Me: He is in his final year at university.

Samsung: Imagine he is going to his final strategy exam and feeling a little nervous, and you are three thousand miles away in Dubai. How would it be if, on his way to the exam, he got a picture of the Burj Khalifa (the tallest building in the world) and an encouraging, loving video message from you on his phone?

Now you are selling me something completely different. You are no longer selling me a camera in the phone that is mere product, but you are addressing the love for my son and more transactionally that he will get a great result in his final exams – that is value, real value, not added value. Now I won't ask, *Is it free?* anymore. I'll ask, *How much?* Because now, it is valuable... *to me.*

It's not about what we *do* – that's just dull product-speak. It's about what we *bring* – that's of value.

But this is a shift in our mindset. I'm not saying it's something new or that we don't think about it, but it is intuitive, weak and not systematic. If we take it for granted and don't address it – we lose out.

May be the customer or owner of the value doesn't even know their value, i.e., it is unperceived value. In fact, as we see from the above example, it is rarely fully known or perceived.

Remember the Excel/SQL example? (See 1.22) The client was unaware that he could find a solution to prevent the loss of millions; or support his team's decisions remotely etc.

In Anita's example, (see 1.10), she was unaware that the real issue was to get architects to come to her showroom.

This begs the question, who's responsibility is it to discover this value? The customer or us? How can it be the customer's responsibility? They don't even perceive the value! The duty to discover the actual value, perceived or unperceived, by the customer rests squarely with us.

How?

- Asking sensible questions, not product-driven ones – Do you want a camera in your phone?

- Using the Circles of Value Model (see 1.39) –
  Conversing to discover the higher levels of value beyond the core.

- Look at the Issue Behind The Issue (see 1.29 and 3.25), and by navigating the conversation through their value.

- Use the BAF model (see 1.36) to open up the customer, engage in dialogue and give us their priorities.

1.31

Application Exercise:
Make It Real – Make It Yours

Make A Quick List Of Key Stakeholders
Whose Value Needs You Are Serving

Just two or three of the key stakeholders will do. It could be your customer, different stakeholders within a customer, or your boss, team members, or people you are helping through a charity.

Next, select one and do the following:

Draw a line across the middle of a blank page.

At the top of the page, write, I am that stakeholder – name them, be specific.

In the upper section write: *I want.*

In the bottom section, write: *I don't want.*

Then fill out your page.

The key here is that you are not writing I want, I don't want as if it's you. You have to forget yourself and imagine being the stakeholder you listed. Otherwise, you will probably write a boring list about your products and services you want to sell; or solutions you want to *bring*. You have the *who*. This list is *not* about Response Onions at all but their Value Onions. Now repeat this activity for the other stakeholders.

Sit back and examine where you have got to with this list. You will be pleasantly surprised. By all means, please go and check it out with the actual stakeholders. You will be surprised how much of their value you do really know.

Excel/SQL

Let's take the example of Rakesh and Gerald – the Excel SQL case. Rakesh needs to do this exercise. I am Gerald.

I Want

- To use excel.
- To support my team in currency placement decisions remotely when I am travelling.
- Real-time information on currency movements.
- To meet my business targets.
- To beat my targets.
- Clarity of information and data.
- To be the best division in the company.
- A promotion to a board position.
- A stronger relationship with my boss.
- My team to respect me even more.

I Don't Want

- To lose millions when currencies fluctuate.

- To waste time in administrative processes.

- Unclear, manual reporting.

- My team to be distracted by complicated technology and methods.

Can you see how simple and enlightening this is?

Interestingly, the first item is, *I want to use Excel...* in other words, the product, solution, response, but then, the list becomes extremely much richer in values. With this knowledge and insight, imagine the creative, innovative and valuable solutions Rakesh can provide, winning the confidence and trust of the client and more business at better prices.

He is now a valuepreneur.

I.32

The 'WHY' – The Purpose – The Value

Never do anything in life ever again, i.e., the what – without knowing the *why*. The *why* is the Value Onion; the *what* is the Response Onion. Value Onions must precede Response Onions.

Think about Klara. The *what* was developing digital applications for banks. The *why* was improving the livelihoods of poor farmers and traders in the villages of South Africa.

What will give her greater motivation, satisfaction and joy? What will make her more creative, innovative and productive?

Think of the Rakesh's list of Gerald's *I want* – only the first item, Excel, is a *what*, but everything else is the *why*. It is richer and will get you to the answer much faster and better. Not merely differentiated, you will be *distinguished*.

When our purpose in everything we do, regardless of how small or big the issue, is established with clarity, what we do takes on a different and more potent meaning. We do tasks with greater joy, brilliance and success.

And it's not about what I *do* but what I *bring* that ultimately matters. Sadly, this is why, the purpose evades us. We miss it. We always jump to doing things and rarely look at the ultimate reason, outcome, value, and why of what we are doing.

Working closely with people daily you see people just doing things because they have to, are told to, or to earn a living. It is soul-destroying. But in the very same so-called mundane work is hidden value, purpose, i.e. the *why*. They just don't see it. Or look for it. The routine saps energy, and frankly, today, I rarely meet someone who is enamoured by and joyous of their work. Who goes to work with a spring in their step? Klara does now –but not before. Our mind is missing the impact of what we do and is over-engaged with the process.

Making Our Apparently Mundane Work Energising

Someone asked me recently, How much do you travel?

I am away around fifteen to seventeen days a month. I take six to eight flights a month. She looked tired just hearing this and asked, 'Don't you get tired of all that travelling, airports, queues, delays?'

'Do you brush your teeth every day?' I asked her.

'Of course.'

'Don't you get tired and bored of it?'

'I don't even think about it; it's automatic.'

Why?'

'Well, I'd feel uncomfortable, and besides, people around me who meet me will not be impressed.'

So, her focus is not on what she is doing but intuitively on why; and the impact. Hence it's not mundane, boring or tiresome to brush her teeth.

'It's the same when I travel. I don't get tired because my mind is squarely fixed on the success of the people or organisation I am helping to grow and succeed. That energises me and travelling itself is a happy task for me.'

'Yes, I make sure I take early flights, so I will still make it if there is a delay. But delays don't trouble me. I use the time productively; I work and listen to music.'

When the outcome, purpose, and value are abundantly clear in the mind, the process becomes automatic, easy and energising.

So when the why is clear, you will be energised; and the what is purposeful and enjoyable.

In a later section of *Finding your purpose, building your legacy,* we will explore this further, and I will give you a simple framework to find your purpose, respond to it and achieve deep satisfaction.

There is a wonderful, famous old story of the President of the USA in the late 1960s who walks into the NASA building and sees a janitor sweeping the floor in the main reception area.

He goes up to the janitor, puts his hand on his shoulder, and asks, *'Gee bud, what are you doing' today?'*

The janitor continued sweeping. Despite the leader of the free world having his hand on his shoulder, he didn't stop his work. He looked up at the President, and, with deep pride and satisfaction, said, *'Putting a man on the moon, Sir.'*

Regardless of what it is and what he does, his work contributes to the greater impact. Now with which motivation will he sweep the floor? And sadly, people look down on a sweeper.

Similarly, suppose the mind of a person cleaning public toilets is focused on the fact that he is keeping the place sanitised, so people don't get sick. In that case, he will do his job with pride and satisfaction as opposed to the cleaner who is thinking, another horrible day doing a horrible job. I am pushing the example. It's tough, I know, but it's only as tough as you make it in your mind.

Free yourself. Nothing can ever disturb you again. You will do your work with a clearer purpose and never look down on anyone again.

In the same way, think about everything you do and work out what it brings, as I did with those seventeen bright youngsters in Frankfurt. Then that *why* will energise you, make you more innovative, creative ideas will flow.

The cleaner whose mind, instead of saying, *I'm a menial public toilets cleaner,* says, *I protect people's health,* is a great human being. They will always be satisfied and irreproachable.

I am not saying don't progress; resign to where you are; and simply accept your lot. On the contrary, go search for better *whys,* in other words, value to serve. Only when you are satisfied with where you have arrived can you more successfully move on to different *whats.*

So self-betterment, growth, and constantly aspiring to do better things and improve your life is intrinsic and absolute in what I am saying.

The question is *why.*

People want to move to better things because they are dissatisfied with what they are doing, and all I am saying is instead, look for better value to serve. Then whatever you do will become profoundly satisfying and a source of tremendous success and outcomes—more than you had ever imagined.

Similarly, in the Jet Airways example, the moment we ask the question, *Why do NRIs travel between London and Mumbai?* The outer layers of their Value Onion reveal themselves. We are now far more creative with the Response Onion and indeed accurate in our responses, which will undoubtedly generate favourable responses from customers to us, i.e. they will simply buy.

As a reminder, we are discussing everything from an external customer's perspective.

However, the same principle applies to anyone whose value can be served by our capabilities, knowledge, resources, etc. This could be our seniors, team members, colleagues, even family and friends. Ask the *why*. Focus on it. Discover it – not from yours, but the other's perspective.

This overarching mammoth question of *why* – to which everything and everyone is aligned – will recur throughout our book and be the guiding light in answering every question.

1.33

Value And Price
The Powerful Connection

People often say to me, *In the end, doesn't it all just boil down to price?*

Really? Then why is a MacBook Air - at $1,500 - more than 300% the price of a product which can do more or less the same thing? You can buy an ACER or an HP for $500. The engineering director of a plastics manufacturer who supplies raw materials and casings for laptops told me that Apple is quality crazy compared with other laptop companies and prepared to pay 30% to 40% more. Now look at this, Apple's costs are 30% more than competitors, but they have the guts to charge 300% more in price. It's all about that obsession for serving value.

Let's understand this. Price is much more of an *emotional* than a *technical* issue. (We'll talk about price from a technical perspective in 2.25).

Technically and financially, people come up with a unit cost. Let's say it's $75. Then you put a mark-up, a margin of 25% and therefore let's sell it for $100. How narrow is this? Why not $150 or $200? Or conversely, it may need to be lower - can the market handle a price of $100?

In all this discussion, we're just playing with numbers. And I'm being a little harsh, and of course, these numbers would be supported with some market analysis of what the market will tolerate. But it's still a tedious comparative study of what people are prepared to pay for laptops. Short-sightedly, it looks at the status quo of what happens currently and worse, historically. But all business parameters are changing rapidly - notably, Value Onions. Then history is unlikely to be a good indicator of the future. They're focused on the core and not the outer layers of the Value Onion. If Apple had done that, would the MacBook ever have been sold at 300% of competing products?

With this in mind, let's get to the crux and the real pricing issue.

I am saying that cost is only a tiny and low-level element to pricing. Let's not price to cost. By all means, cover cost, but let's price to value. Pricing, therefore, is much more of an emotional than technical issue built around cost and mark-up.

Think about the Value Onion.

When people ask, *Doesn't it all boil down to price?* in a way they are not wrong because price will always start at the outermost layer of the Value Onion.

It's the first port of call. To be human is to want to buy cheaper. However, genuinely understand the other outer layers of the Value Onion for that customer, and genuinely build super-responses on the Response Onion to serve that value. Price will start to move inward, and where it ends up on the Value Onion depends on your brilliance of understanding the Value Onion and developing the Response Onion.

When you are super-brilliant at responding to value in this way, as Apple has been then, price may simply merge into the core, become a hygiene factor, and become least important. Notice I use the words has been as I believe Apple's story of continued success is directly related to Steve Job's value obsession.

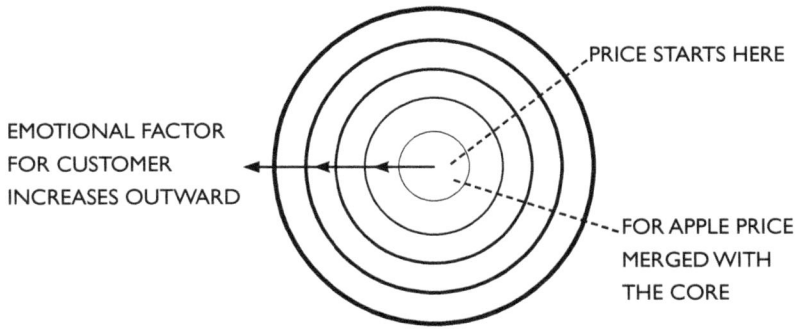

EMOTIONAL FACTOR
FOR CUSTOMER
INCREASES OUTWARD

PRICE STARTS HERE

FOR APPLE PRICE
MERGED WITH
THE CORE

So much so, that the brand value of his legacy has long survived him. The future for Apple may be less bright as they have fast become another laptop and mobile phone supplier.

There has been no real innovation in several years.

1.34

Emotional Value

Thinking about the Value Onion of any customer, is the emotional factor increasing as you go outwards - for the customer; or decreasing? It's increasing. As the value layers become bigger and bigger, it's representing more and more emotional value to the customer, which is why, again, the core generates the least emotion in the customer (see 1.33).

Now, back to pricing:

If a supplier was genuinely serving the outer layers of your own Value Onion, wouldn't your negotiation become softer? For the same product, wouldn't you pay that 10% or even 20% more to buy from the supplier or people you really like? Of course, you would. And in some cases, even 300%.

These are real examples. So, don't sell yourself short.

If you remain focused on the core, in other words, your essential product or service, can you genuinely be differentiated? No.

Let's face it, your competitors can do pretty much what you do. So, you are ultimately forced to differentiate only on price. Focus on the core, and you'll be non-differentiated and, in your desperation to sell, more malleable when your customers negotiate hard on price.

So, what is the answer? Move beyond the core. Genuinely understand the value of onion in its full glory and genuinely build excellent Response Onions. You will be distinguished, differentiation will become an ordinary word, and at that stage, you can hold your price at the deservedly higher and proper levels. If you are serving the outer layers of the Value Onion, the worst that can happen is that the customer says, *I wish we could afford them.* This is an excellent position in which to find yourself.

Alright, so you could lose three out of ten pitches as customers perceive you as expensive. But the seven you get will be customers who are prepared to pay at the right level for the value they are getting. And even the three you've lost will have respect for you and aspire to use you when they can afford it.

With this in mind, here are the three definitive and only statements you need in pricing perfectly:

1. Everyone wants to buy cheaper.

Yes, let's state the obvious. To be human is to want to buy cheaper. Don't you think if you offer a 10% discount on a Maybach (a $500,000 saloon car) to a multi-billionaire, they wouldn't appreciate it? What's $400,000 to them? Or indeed, when you get a $10 restaurant voucher, what's $10 to you? But it makes you *feel* good. It's not about what you can afford; it's simply that human beings like to buy cheaper. It's actually a value on the Value Onion! This is why I said earlier that price will always start at the outer layer of the Value Onion. It's simple.

2. It is our professional, business, ethical, moral, integrity filled duty to serve the best value at the lowest prices.

Look at the simple consistency of this statement. If integrity and our business duty are to serve the outer layers of Value Onions with matching layers on the Response Onions, and if price starts at the outer layer as we said in Statement 1, then, of course, it is our duty to serve that value at the lowest prices. End of story.

So, putting Statements 1 and 2 together, it seems like I am saying discount prices and sell cheaper i.e., if everyone wants to buy cheaper and it's our duty to serve the best value at the lowest prices, it seems as though I am saying just drop your prices, sell cheaper, right? - Wrong!

Because here comes Statement 3.

3. Don't give value away.

This puts the proper perspective and actually says hold price at the right level.

So, putting all three statements together, what I am saying is:

Price will start at the outermost layers of the Value Onion - but to not give value away, you need first to know what value really is, and I rarely ever see this being done. In other words, leaving price aside, look to the outer layers of the VO and build genuine responses to it, and you will see price moving inwards, and with brilliance, as in Apple's case, it can even merge into the core.

For example: returning to the Virgin Atlantic example.

If you were serving the value of *entertainment* with pre-released Xbox games as a response to the value of entertainment for families travelling with teenagers, the next time, you would happily pay $50 or even $80 more to travel on Virgin compared to another airline. But interestingly, you wouldn't reason with it and intellectualise it by saying, Oh look, Virgin gives my son or daughter pre-released Xbox games, which is worth $50 to me on a flight. No, this is too logical. Customers don't behave like this. They would simply feel looked after, cared for. And feeling and care is pure emotion, not logic. As a result, I wouldn't consider $50 or $80 expensive.

These customers would probably say, *I know Virgin are $80 more expensive than British Airways, but aren't they lovely people — they look after my family.*

This is value and the perception of that value being served: and customers are comfortable to pay it. When you genuinely offer perfect Response Onions in this way, then you can stand tall and hold your prices at the right and higher level. Emotionally, that in itself becomes a differentiator, as the higher price represents a level of comfort and is aspirational.

The customer thinks of it as *reassuringly expensive.*

This is an example, where value is more evident, and an obvious Value Onion exists. But what about highly commoditised products and services? Where it seems to be all about the core?

Does the same principle of holding your price to value apply? The answer is a resounding *yes.*

It's not lower prices, as much as discounts, that customers seek. When customers push us to lower the price, what's the reference point? *Lower compared to what?* For that matter, *expensive compared to what?*

They might be comparing it to the norm of the market, but actually, their real value here is a *discount.*

If you want to sell for $100, then price it at $115 and then discount it to $100. They'll enjoy getting a 15% discount, and you will enjoy giving it; and you'll be serving their value of the discount.

Putting this into the three pricing statements above:

- Statement 1 One of their values is to buy cheaper.

- Statement 2 It is your duty to serve the best value at the lowest price.

- Statement 3 Proudly hold the $100 because below $100, you would be giving value away.

Understand this fundamental distinction. We get messed up by thinking our customers are asking for a low price. But put yourself in the shoes of your customer. What really excites them is coming away with a discount. So, there is a fundamental difference between price and discount. It's frankly the latter that customers are seeking.

I was chatting to a senior-leader audience from across the Middle East, where the negotiations on pricing are hard. For most, it was a light bulb moment and realisation for them.

One of them, Dr Reza said:

We've been obsessively minded to lower prices, but realise, customers are willing to pay for value even in the Middle East. I now see that we ask for a lower price, but we are actually looking for a discount. When the other outer layers of the Value Onion are being responded to, even discount becomes less important and quickly dropped.

He nailed it!

1.35

Sell Nothing; Win Everything
Building Trust Capital
Why Listening Sells

From whom would you rather buy? Someone who was trying to grab you as a customer, make money from you, interested in himself, his products, his revenue, or someone obsessed with your success, value, and gain? It's a no-brainer. And with whom would you negotiate harder?

So, if you would buy more from the second person, negotiate less with them, then, in any case, the second one will be richer and more successful. How wrong do we get it! Obsess with the other person's value, their entire Value Onion, and success is yours - Guaranteed.

New Home Refurbishments

A few years ago, we bought a house in West London. We doubled it in size and added a new floor: a big project. Of the six contractors we interviewed, I distinctly remember two. One guy turned up in his Mercedes S-class with a project manager and company brochures. Their attitude was: *Right, we can sort it all out for you. You would need a two-tonne steel from that wall to this wall. And you see that arch? If you want to take that out, we will have to replace the lintel with a low bearing RSJ* - and so on. It was technical, even impressive.

And then, he asked us to look at page five in his brochure, which had their payment and commercial terms.

The second guy came in a chug-chug old van, and for the next three hours, he did just one thing and one thing alone. *He listened.*

His approach was: *Hmm, nice place. So, what was your last home like? And why the move?* This is a great question—what a place to start.

He did not start with his product or service, but our values and gain.

I answered, 'It was nice... but a little small.'

'Small? So, do you mean you entertain a lot or have many guests staying?'

'True, but also we are musicians, and we like to have classical music concerts at home.'

'Really?'

'Oh, yes. We invite excellent musicians, forty or fifty friends and have a great evening of music.'

'Imagine,' he said, 'Just imagine, your favourite musicians are playing in this room, and all your friends are here, where would the musicians be placed?'

I pointed to one end of the room.

'Ah, you see that arch over there? Ten people sitting behind it will not get a clear view. If you like, we can remove it. He continued with excellent responses, having understood our true value.

Look at this: both builders speak about two tonnes of steel lintels, RSJs, etc., except one is pushing his product, service, and contract, and the other is obsessed with my gain, value, great music evenings, and happiness. So, who gets the contract?

But here is the rub. My chug-chug man was 15% more expensive than the Mercedes man. And all weekend, my wife and I thought long and hard about who should we choose. Our logic was saying the Mercedes man as he was cheapest, but our heart said something else.

Come Monday morning, and we decided to go with the Mercedes guy. *After all, he is 15% cheaper...* and as we've said before, *price always starts in the outer layer of the Value Onion.*

But as we were dialling the Mercedes man, we both had the same reflex. *Hold on, let's just think about this!* And after a nice cup of tea and an hour later, we called the chug-chug man. Yes, the heart had won.

However, logic had not failed. It's just that the chug-chug man had reached the outer layers of our Value Onion and the Mercedes man remained stuck in the core. On the core of our Value Onion, both were strong and undifferentiated.

Logic resides at the core of the onion and the heart increasingly towards the outer layers. So, which one of these two sellers would we have negotiated harder on price? Right, the Mercedes guy. And what were we buying for that extra 15%? Absolutely – it was peace of mind, reassurance.

By listening to us, the chug-chug man had won our trust, and the feeling in our heart was if something goes wrong and all building projects go wrong, who is the guy who will listen to us, work it out, solve it and who is the one who will see it as an opportunity to earn more?

I call this Trust Capital. Build Trust Capital in your market with your customers. More on this in Sections 4 and 5 when we discuss *Spirit of Enquiry*. So, you see, listening sells.

When you are deeply immersed in – and I'd even say obsessed with the customer's value – you need sell nothing, and yet you win everything. In other words, not just the contract and at better margins, but also the trust and confidence of your customers – you have built Trust Capital.

What Is A Customer? What Is Selling?

I want to re-emphasise is that, in this story, we are talking about a customer/seller business relationship. But this principle of delivering value applies in all our transactions and interactions, be it with our business customers, colleagues, team members, senior leaders or even our family and friends. Because what is a customer? Wouldn't you agree that it is someone whose value we serve through our skills, capabilities, expertise?

Indeed, in that sense, what is selling? It is about serving someone's value through our skills and expertise? So, we are always selling. You don't have to be a salesman. We always have customers.

In all your dealings, personal, professional, business, become an obsessive bringer of value, even at the cost of not winning the deal. The reality is that your rate of deal wins will significantly increase in any case.

So, sell nothing. And win everything.

1.36

Convincing Convincingly – Win People's Agreement: Live In BAF, Not FAB

In work, in life, at every step, we need to convince people about something in business, professional and personal life. Let's just blatantly say that we are selling - whether it is a product, an idea, a project, a required action, an agreement, and so on.

When we try to convince anyone of anything, we do what I call The FAB Talk. My product is FAB, my project or my idea is FAB, which is short for Fabulous.

But in sales and marketing, what does FAB stand for? *Features, Advantages, Benefits.*

We first talk about *Features*. Sometimes, the *Advantages*. But rarely the *Benefits*. It usually goes in that sequential order:

- F = Features
- A = Advantages
- B = Benefits

Actually, I am being quite generous with FAB. Underperforming salespeople never really go beyond features at all. Remember the Mercedes guy?

Whether you are selling, presenting, conducting a meeting or in any interaction or dealing, change your approach from FAB to BAF.

Let's relate this to our chug-chug van builder, and the BAF looks something like this.

- B – happy, inspiring evenings of music with friends and family

- A – a pleasant, open space, everyone can see the musicians

- F – two tonnes steel, RSG, lintel, payment terms and price

So, you see, if you dare to care, you will start from benefits and then position your features to serve and only serve the benefits, i.e., values on the outer layers of the Value Onion.

However, if you start from features, you are less likely to win the customer's confidence and, therefore, the contract. You're in a hard-sell mode, desperate, desiring, and definitely in a weaker position.

After all, who likes desperate sellers?

1.37

Application of BAF
Make It Real – Make It Yours

How do you use the BAF Model?

At each step we will use the example of Andy and his boss George earlier, Andy was trying to get his boss to agree to a sales convention in Marrakesh. Please input your own situation using this example as a guide.

Take any situation where you are presenting or bringing an idea, wanting a decision to be made from someone, or simply selling.

Take a blank piece of paper, draw two lines, to divide it into three sections: upper, middle and bottom. (See p160).

Now talk to yourself and write as follows:

Putting yourself in Andy's shoes, we start writing on this template. Naturally, you will write on the bottom section first, which is *Features.* This is absolutely fine, i.e., when you are preparing, it is perfectly natural and makes sense to write *Features* first.

In the bottom section, *Features* would be the sales convention, the location, the price, etc.

Now, to move to the *Advantages,* you need to ask a simple question: *So, what will that bring?*

And then to move from *Advantages* to Benefits, again ask the question, *And, what will that bring?* This question, *And, what will that bring?* is a technical and critical one and within three times of asking this question, but a maximum of five, you will not be able to answer the question anymore. That's when you know you are at the endpoint, the real *Benefit*, the end gain, the big value.

The structure below defines the example.

What's going through your mind? And why is that important to you?

3. BENEFITS

- Growing sales to 12% above current forecast

- Greater margins and profits

- Differentiating the business, winning customer confidence and strengthening our brand

- Market share growth

- Increasing our market share

So what will that bring?

2. ADVANTAGES

- Sharing of ideas

- Getting a common understanding of the market and opportunities

- Uniting the sales force and distributors in serving the market

- Creativity and innovation

And what will that bring?

1. FEATURES

- Sales convention

- Location Marrakesh

- Cost $90,000

- 120 delegates

- 3-days duration

- Structure, agenda, speakers, workshops, hotels, dinners

1.38

The Sequence To Plan
Vs The Sequence To Communicate

It is essential to know that when you plan your idea and the meeting using the BAF Model, it will always start with *Features:*

- 1.Ask yourself what your project is about – write the *Features*.

- 2.Ask, So what will that bring? You will automatically write the *Advantages*.

- 3.Again, ask, *And... what will <u>that</u> bring?* You will instinctively write the *Benefits*.

Notice for *planning*, go F>A>B. This makes great sense as your starting point. By the way, I am speaking here about the mechanics of FAB>BAF as a process to communicate and convince others. Please don't confuse this with the overall thinking, and working, which in all situations will start with first understanding Value Onions (benefits) then building Response Onions (features).

Now having *planned* your communication as FAB… when you are having the conversation, *presenting, communicating* or *writing,* you first need to reverse the content. Start with the *Benefits,* then the *Advantages*, and then you could even go silent. You will have captured interest so much through the *Benefits* and *Advantages* that they typically ask, Wow, great, how?

And then, with joy and confidence, give the *Features*. So the *preparation* sequence is F>A>B, but the *communication* sequence is B>A>F. Please reread that.

It will bring you tremendous success, easily convince people and get great satisfaction in getting your ideas accepted.

Everything we do and our capabilities are far too important. We must leverage these to capitalise on the opportunities and make things happen. We are dependent on others, their decisions and inputs. Don't miss these opportunities.

Don't underutilise your capabilities. Go BAF.

BAF is not just about doing it in *Benefits >Advantages > Features* format, but it should become your innate psyche. It's a thinking. It's a way to be and exist. It is a modus operandi and an entire mentality in everything you do in your work; your social world, and life as a whole. It is fulfilling as it brings value and, of course, rewarding – personally, materially, and emotionally.

1.39

Valuable Conversations
Through Value Onions/Response Onions
Circles Of Value (COVs)/
Circles Of Response (CORs)

This is another way to look at the Value Onion/Response Onion

It extends the VORO Model to valuable conversations and daily practical application.

Circles Of Value (COVs)

This alternative look at the Value Onion will help us understand value even better. It is another practical tool in discovering the true value of who we are serving.

Let's divide the onion into three circles. We will call these EV, BV and PV.

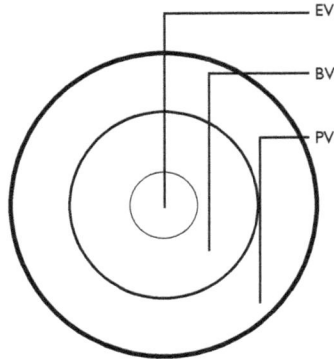

These stand for:

- Essential Value (EV)

- Business Value (BV)

- Private Value (PV)

- **Essential Value.** This is the core, as we had described in the Value Onion – the actual product, service, project etc. It's the smallest circle, and although essential, it represents the least value to the customer. See the example below.

- **Business Value.** This is bigger than Essential Value for the customer, i.e., it's what the customer gains in their business or organisation. It represents the end gain, the true value-impact for the customer from your service or product. It's the real reason they buy from you. If this value wasn't there, your product or service would be irrelevant, yet we miss most of this value. We know some of it but don't engage with the customer to discover it fully. It could be solving a business problem, getting more sales, more profit, growth, compliance, cost-saving, safety etc. See the example below.

- **Personal Value.** Ah! This is the ultimate value. It's the individual's personal gain, even beyond the organisation. For example - a job promotion, bonus, accolade for a successful project, respect from colleagues, recognition from senior management, esteemed by friends and family etc.

Let's not be deluded but accept simple human reality, this is the ultimate and most potent decision factor in any purchase. You may well say that this shouldn't be the case and people are paid by their organisation and should remain professional. Nice idealistic thinking and good moral stance – really? Think about any buying decision you've made at work; didn't you wish or even push for choosing the supplier who would bring you success. There is nothing wrong with personal success; in fact, it is a beautiful reality to embrace and build on. After all, everything every individual does is related to personal success. This is natural and reassuring. However, it is vital to align this personal value to business value, and in no way conflict with business value, i.e. it should not be at the cost of business value. So long as this personal value does not conflict with business value, it is perfectly legitimate, and far from ignoring it, we should embrace and welcome it.

Aligning personal values to business values is a powerful act of leadership.

Circles Of Response (CORs)

Having discovered the COVs, we would now and only now develop the CORs. This is the same point as building Response Onions, layer by layer corresponding to each layer of the Value Onions. Let's call these Essential Response (ER), Business Response (BR) and Personal Response (PR).

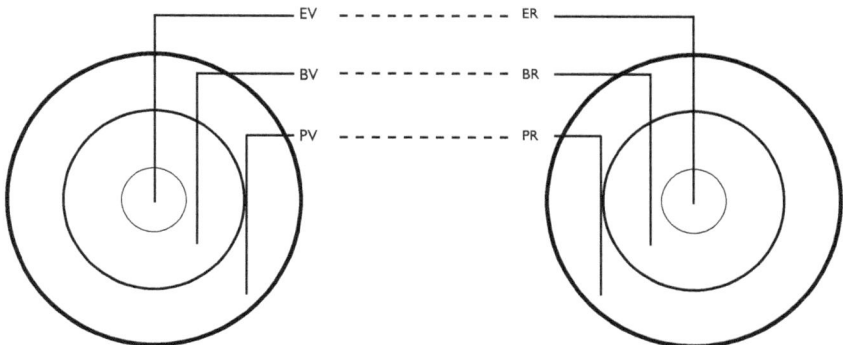

1.40

An Example Of COVs And CORs

Think back to the EXCEL SQL story (See 1.22) of the banking client – Gerald, asking for Excel; and the director in the IT company, Rakesh, trying to persuade him to take SQL. The COVs are:

Gerald's COVs	Rakesh's CORs
EV (Essential Value) • Excel • 12 users • Macros **Training** • Time lines • User interface **BV (Business Value)** • Not lose $3m in seconds! • Support my teams in currency • Decisions remotely • Meet targets **PV (Personal Value)** • Beat targets • Be best performing team in bank • Promotion • Solve problems with my boss	**ER (Essential Response)** • SQL server • Databases – wide and complete • App based interface for mobile • Time frames **BR (Business Response)** • Direct feed into all computers from Bloomberg • Real time data from multiple sources • Personalised information and parameters for each team member **PR (Personal Response)** • Automated daily reports to see business generated Vs targets • Provide information to make it easy for my boss to take to Board

The Impact of EV, BV and PV

By understanding EV, BV, and PV of who's value we are serving and then delivering that value with perfect ER BR and PR, we will earn their respect and build exceptional relationships. These will be lasting and powerful in generating superb outcomes for both.

These three words describe the progression of that relationship at each level of value:

- EV = REASSURANCE achieved

- BV = CONFIDENCE won

- PV = TRUST gained

When we address the customer's EV, the best we can achieve is to REASSURE them - This is what you are looking for, and yes, we can supply it to you.

When we understand their BV and serve it, we will win their CONFIDENCE. They will feel comfortable with us knowing we care for the outcomes they are seeking instead of your competitors who are only interested in selling their products and services. They will feel confident that you are the one who will sort out their problem or bring them the business value they need.

When you move into their PV, and they open up to you with personal requirements, issues, constraints, you know you have won their TRUST.

1.41

The Sequence Of EV BV PV

In a conversation, what sequence should you follow?

When I ask this question, I get varied responses. Some people say, *I would get all the EV… then BV… then PV.* The problem here is that you will get stuck on the EV and then respond with product/service and most likely miss the BV and PV.

You may not move beyond reassurance.

Others say, *I'll start with PV as its biggest value.* But PV is a private zone, and imagine beginning the conversation with, *Tell me, what's giving you a personal problem in this project?*

Not only will they not answer, but it could offend or make them closed to you. Understand, most people find it hard to open a sales conversation by admitting a problem even though the very fact that you are having a conversation infers one!

Earn The Right For PV

To get to PV, you must earn the right to go there. But go there you must, as decisions are ultimately made there.

The answer is to navigate the conversation in this sequence:

- **SMALL EV – no details.** This will contextualise the conversation.
  *May I understand the issue? I see, so you are looking to retain Excel.
  How do you use Excel? What do you like about it?*

- **BIG BV.** This is where the conversation really starts and pivots.
  You are risk-free in speaking about their business outcomes.
  *What happened in that incident when the Yen moved against the dollar?
  How can that be prevented? What would real-time knowledge of currency
  fluctuations do for your business? Which market segments do you serve today?
  How are they changing? Where are the best opportunities for you? What is
  needed to seize them?* And so on.

- **BIG EV.** Now go into details of what they need and even give high-level
  examples of what you propose. SQL and how it will serve the BV.
  The process. The time lines, and so on.

- **PV.** Having reassured on EV and won their confidence on BV,
  you have now earned the right to go into their PV. Summarise the
  EV and BV you have understood, confirm your understanding, and thank
  them, this will seal their confidence. Then with depth and care, ask,
  *May I ask you something? Personally speaking, what are your priorities?
  What would you personally call a success in this project? What are the
  barriers in your way? How can I help?…*

I want to remind you and emphasise that none of these approaches are tricks or manipulation of people. We're not using them just for our gain even if the other is at a loss – this would be against the fundamental principle of valuepreneurship. Instead, this method will help them open up and disclose their genuine value giving you a strong chance to respond to that value.

So once again, this is a method of utmost integrity and, therefore, the route to sustained mutual success.

1.42

Innovation –
The Constant Pursuit Of A Valuepreneur Distinction Between Innovation, Invention And Inconvenience

What is innovation? How is it different to invention?

If I asked you to name me the most significant innovation in commercial aircraft in the last century – after the jet engine - you would probably say the Concorde, as it was the first and only supersonic airliner. But I don't call this an *innovation*; I call it an *invention*.

Inventions start from a capability, knowledge, and product, and they may be innovative if they serve value. The Concorde was an invention – *We'd like to make a supersonic airliner because we can...* but the question is: *what value did it serve?*

Conversely, innovations begin with the value of whom we are serving and then develop responses to serve them.

This is why the total Response Onion, made to serve the outer layers of the Value Onions, is the ultimate innovation.

So going back to the Concorde, it was an amazing invention. Had it been an innovation, it would have been updated, and newer models would be flying around today.

Boeing came out and said, *We could make one.* They actually had a supersonic airliner in design which they never produced because there was no viable market to carry one hundred passengers, royally, but uncomfortably, between London or Paris and New York – even though it shaved three hours off the journey, compared to the price which had to be paid.

Also, it was a costly plane to operate.

They said show me a supersonic airliner carrying four hundred passengers between London and Sydney, and you've got yourself a market whose values can be genuinely served.

When the A380 super Jumbo came out – which can carry over five hundred passengers for 15,000 km non-stop – the first airlines to buy them were Singapore Airlines, Emirates, Qantas, Thai, and others followed.

The question is: why didn't these airlines ever order a Concorde?

Only two airlines ever did, which were Air France and British Airways, which were the national airlines of the countries who developed it, i.e., Aerospatiale of France and British Aerospace.

Don't get me wrong, I was a total fan and loved it as a remarkable feat of engineering, and if in the advancement of science and humankind you have the resources to put into it, then fabulous, it's a great invention. But it was intended as a commercial project, financially viable and expected to grow in sales globally – in this respect, it was a failure.

Valuepreneurial Innovation

What is the first product that comes to your mind if I say the word *hybrid car?* Toyota Prius.

It was the first mass-produced hybrid car long back in 1997. This means it was in design in 1995 and conceptualisation in 1993. Who, in 1993, was seriously speaking about the environment? It was thirteen years before Al Gore's movie about the environment, *An Inconvenient Truth,* came out.

The discussion of the impact of pollution on the environment was just bubbling at that time. Toyota anticipated this as outer layers on the Value Onions of huge markets in the west, starting with the UK and USA. The Prius was developed as the perfect matching Response Onion to it and over two decades later is going extremely strong as one of the best selling cars in the Western world.

This is powerful valuepreneurial innovation.

The best of innovation begins with understanding market segments, i.e., groups of customers with similar values and unravelling their Value Onions. Then as you set about devising the Response Onions to serve that value, it's bound to be innovative and much more creative. Starting from product design or improvement without fully understanding the Value Onion will rarely be innovative. Innovation is actioned on the Response Onion.

Its value may be on the core of the Value Onion, or one or more layers or the whole onion. In the case of the Prius, it was the core, i.e., a car, as well as the layers. In other cases, the core or product may remain unchanged, and the innovation may be on the layers. For example, Virgin Atlantic. The core, which is an eleven-hour flight between London and LA, may remain unchanged. Still, by understanding customers' value, the main innovation may be on the outer layers of the Response Onion, such as pre-released Xbox games or internet connectivity mid-flight etc.

1.43

Inconvenience

Innovation surpasses invention. The worst of all is inconvenience, the antithesis of innovation. This is where the business is only interested in itself and doesn't care for whom it's serving.

Apple, under Steve Jobs, was innovative and obsessed with solving customers' problems and values. It's fast turning into just another electronics supplier concerned with grabbing as much as possible for itself. Products are static with nothing revolutionary as the iMac, iPhone, iPod, iPad were in their time.

The MacBook Air is as it was over a decade ago. The iPhone, at best, follows Samsung's changes. When the iPhone 8 came out, their greatest claim to innovation was to get rid of the headphone socket to sell wireless earpieces called AirPods for an exorbitant £159. This is inconvenience. They missed the point that people use high-end listening headsets to get almost all their music and entertainment on the go. So the customer is left inconvenienced.

It's become all about tying customers in and squeezing as much money out of them as possible—the opposite of value. I am happy to see so many non-Apple AirPods available for under £40. I know many people who, after several years of buying iPhones, have ditched them.

1.44

Value Is More Than
An Intellectual Pursuit
And Even More Than A Mind-Set

Being orientated to value and serving it is a state of being rather than just a set of actions. The same actions become stronger and more relevant if they arise in this state of being a *bringer of value* – impact. It becomes our essential make-up and resides in our psyche far beyond intellect and reason. This is a very tangible point and not a moral theory.

To be a *bringer of value* is natural to us all. After all, we are all takers of value, and therefore we can easily relate to it. In this case, we must also be bringers of value in our most natural state.

So, what's the problem?

Through our fears, expectations, ego, and desires, we become over-focused on our own wants and therefore distanced from being a value bringer. We become desperate.

In modern times people speak a lot about value orientation. Sadly, however, it's done with the prime motive of self-gain. It's over-intellectualised and processed and misses the feeling of genuine self-less care for the value-impact of whom we are serving. I'm not speaking against self-gain.

On the contrary, it's what we will achieve as valuepreneurs but, as a result, not as the motivation. Let's clarify this point with a famous once upon a time story.

King Solomon's Baby

Two women were arguing over a baby, each claiming to be its mother. With no resolution in sight, they were brought before the king to decide. It was long before DNA testing. The king said, that as nothing can be proven, let's just divide the baby into two halves and give the women half each.

The first woman agreed – *divide the child!* Neither woman should have the child. The second woman shrieked and pleaded with the king to give the baby to the other woman. The king judged that it was clear that the second woman was the real mother and gave her the baby.

(See I Kings 3:16-28)

Look at the difference.

The first woman was desperate to have the child for herself but didn't want the other woman to have the child. The second woman was only interested in the child's welfare and was prepared to sacrifice it to keep it alive. It's easy to spot the real mother. She wasn't thinking of value from an intellectual standpoint, and it wasn't a mindset. It was unconditional, selfless care.

And: who got the baby in the end?

1.45

Valuepreneurship
Is A Pursuit Of Care, Even Love

In the same way, in your work, profession and life, be unconditionally obsessed with bringing value.

I've used a highly emotive example to illustrate the point, and you are probably asking, *But that is a mother and child, Sanjeev. How can you compare this with something as ordinary as a seller/buyer relationship? As a seller, how can I care for a customer? I don't even like some of them, and you are speaking about care and bringing them value? Mothers love their children, which is a huge difference; it's nothing like that for customers.*

Well, think about this. What am I actually asking you to care for: the customer, the person? No! Not at all. You may never even have met them before. And it's ludicrous to compare the relationship between a mother and child.

So, care for what? Are you ready for it?

The answer is that you are caring for applying something you have, i.e., your talent, capability, product, or service, to *bring* success and a value-impact to someone.

We are not equating this to a mother's love for her child, but we are certainly drawing a parallel of how something profound, personal, and essential to you, i.e., your capabilities and the impact they can have. This, my friends even transcends care, and yes, even in business, we can call it love.

Again, it's not necessarily love for the other person, but for someone's value served through you. There is a valuepreneur within you – *a selfless bringer of value.*

By saying be selfless, I am not saying don't be successful – on the contrary, that's what this book and my work are all about – to help you be more successful. The point is to make success a result, not the driver.

Think of it in reverse. Who would you buy from, someone who is desperately selling to you with the sole objective of winning your business, or someone who is focused, even obsessed with your value, and only presenting their products as responses and nothing but responses to that value? And with whom would you argue more on price and negotiate harder? Of course, it's with the desperate seller. So, who becomes wealthier and therefore more successful?

Remember my chug-chug van, man? (See 1.35). It's the same point.

Being a valuepreneur makes you wealthier, more successful, and deeply satisfied, so it's worth it. And yet I say, don't let your mind tell you are doing it for that success; otherwise, you risk going back into your own desires. The ego, which fires wants, will definitely give rise to fears, i.e., the fear of not getting. The more you want, the more you will fear, the less likely you will achieve.

I recently asked a group of managers to write down a time in their professional life when they felt the most committed, engaged, creative, innovative, and loving their work. Surprisingly, no one wrote about when they got a pay rise or a promotion.

Everyone had written about an experience when their capabilities had been visibly applied to bring value to someone, a customer, or an employer etc.

So, don't just be a valuepreneur or do valuepreneurship but love revealing the valuepreneur in you and see how your creativity and productivity flow to lead you to great heights.

1.46

It's All About The Mind

If all of this is making simple sense, what prevents us from making it happen?

The state of our mind gets in the way, puts the brakes, interferes with our clarity. And yet the mind is a powerful engine that we can leverage to get us there and achieve great heights.

Explore the mind.

It is essential to understand it and ignite it in the right way to be in valuepreneurship.

We will discuss, understand, and shape the mind for stillness, availability, productivity, and brilliant achievement in Section 3.

Before that let's structure the value culture, we have explored in Section 1 and apply it practically to developing our work (whatever it may be), strategy, organisation, or business.

It's a method, toolkit, and full technique simply and step-by-step guiding you to your desired destination and well beyond. Throughout Section 2 please use you own project, business, work, or organisation and apply the method helped by the real examples given.

Section 2

The Method And Strategy
Of A Valuepreneur

2.1

Three Models To Definitively Set Or Reset Your Strategy For Your Business, Work, Profession Or Your Personal Life

- VORO© – Value Onion©/Response Onion© (covered in Section 1)

- CHRISTMAS TREE of Planning©

- SVOC Model©

The easiest way to describe strategic thinking and planning is through examples of businesses. But I must emphasise that these principles apply to you as an individual in any activity you do or are planning – be it professional, business, welfare/charitable, creative, sporting etc.. It also applies to all types and sizes of organisations – corporate, political, social/public service etc..

This is not a book about business; it's about work, activity, life, and personal accomplishment. We are applying it to business as an all-encompassing example.

Please take each model, technique and example and use it for your own activity, current or planned.

Having understood Value Culture in Section 1 together with full knowledge of what value and Valuepreneurship are, let's now turn it into our own individual reality.

In this section, we will take a step by step, simple, practical, and systematic technique to apply valuepreneurship. You will be able to implement it immediately in your work – whatever its nature, to bring you unexpectedly brilliant results, accelerate your progress and ease execution.

2.2

Christmas Tree Of Planning©

Method For A Super Strategic Mind And New Age Planning:

What Is It, And Why Do We Need It?

Imagine a practical method or framework which ensures that your business, organisation or indeed you yourself become distinguished, outstanding, respected, advocated and achieve results well beyond your objectives and even dreams. Well, here it is, and I call the Christmas Tree of Planning©, resembling a fir or Christmas tree. Essential to this method is the VORO, (the Value Onion/Response Onion model discussed (see 1.20).

In this process, we will also clarify and even redefine some regularly used and mostly confused terms like *strategy, objectives, missions,* etc.. which are over-complicated by academics – and managers – who at best, take a theoretical approach, and worse, make a hash of it by over-complicating it and missing out on real opportunities. After all, which business plan have you seen fully adhered to and then generating the forecast results? Despite this over-complication, we end up adopting an intuitive or hit-and-miss approach, which depending on the quality of the intuition or the luck of a hit, gives a level of success, or not.

It's Not Only About Business

While I am approaching the method from the business context, I'd like to be absolutely clear that this is done for comprehensive understanding. It is as applicable to any sphere of activity you are in – corporate; professional; artistic/creative; welfare/social/charitable; public service; politics; sport; campaigning etc..

No activity is excluded. It is a method to use in our lives.

The days of theoretical planning and heavy planning for planning's sake, have gone. The world is far more dynamic, with rapid and often irrational change as the norm. Look at what Uber has done to the taxi world and what Amazon has done to the retail world. Could traditional planning methods in supermarket chains like Tesco or Sainsbury's have coped with changes such as online shopping and customer behaviours shaped by the COVID pandemic? The number of store closures and job losses says it all. I was in India recently, and the taxi company I used was begging me to take their services at *half the price* as before – but Uber works better to my value.

We need a much more up-to-date, light, stealthy and flexible method to prepare our organisation for the incredible rate of change and opportunities that come with it and indeed the risks and inconveniences it throws at us. But don't be put off by words like *missions, visions, strategy* etc.. If done correctly, simply, and practically they will be great tools for your success.

In this section, we will redefine these in the new progressive, dynamic, useable way. I warn you, it will challenge past practices and even put off some academics, management consultants, and management who rely on these terms to propound their theories, or worse, use them to play organisational politics. Most often, however, it is done with good intention. Let's simplify it all and make it work for us with integrity and for immense success.

Hence the Christmas Tree model.

2.3

The Christmas Tree Of Planning Model©

The Christmas Tree is a tool and technique, which I invite you to use directly for your business/organisation. Please follow it step by step and at each step input your own information and parameters. By following these steps rigorously, you will not only finish up with an effective business plan, structure, strategy, and operation but also acquire a super strategic mind and thinking. This will guide you to success in your organisation, business unit, function, project or even day to day transactions and much further for the achievement of your own personal goals, destinations, and the realisation of your true potential.

With this model, I have had the privilege and joy of transforming companies and organisations globally in the last twenty years, be they small enterprises, charities, public organisations, or vast multinationals.

Any business – and by using this word business, I am referring to any enterprise, organisation, whether private, public, charity, government etc.., – needs to be designed and structured as follows. And I repeat: please don't be put off by words like strategy, objectives, missions, etc.. There is nothing wrong with them, but their interpretation, definition, and meaning has been at fault. We will blast the myth and re-configure them to the new reality, practical, applied and immediately useable.

THE CHRISTMAS TREE MODEL

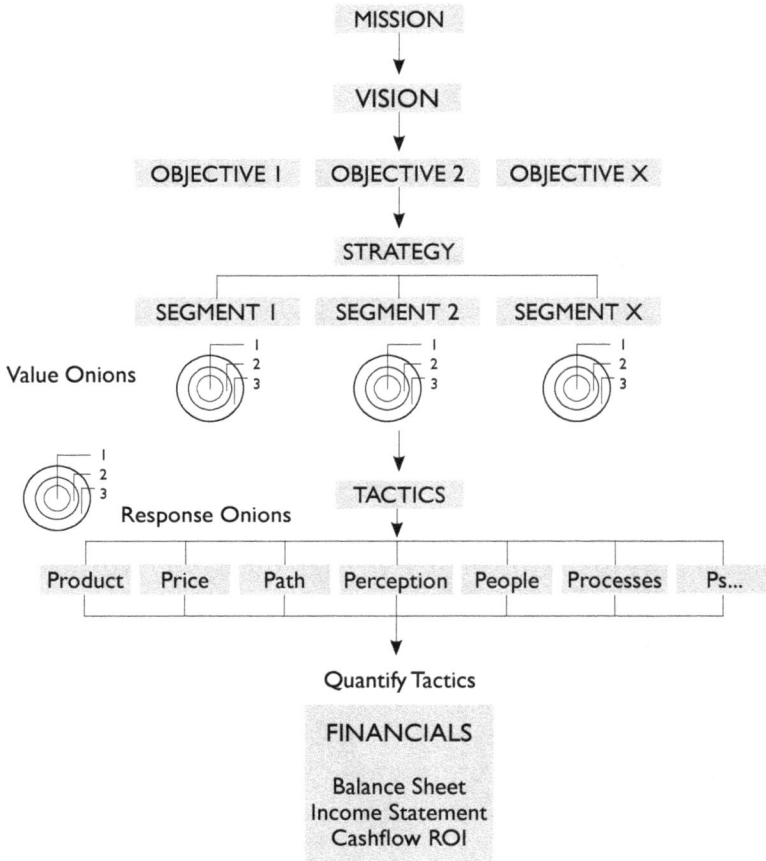

The Christmas Tree Model has six steps in developing a strategic and execution plan for your business, part of the business or a project, and it is a step-by-step linear linked process:

1. Missions
2. Visions
3. Objectives
4. Strategies
5. Tactics
6. Financials

The steps are abbreviated as M-V-O-S-T-F. Each step cascades into the next.

Please note that these same terms are widely used and defined in almost all strategy texts, and for consistency and collective understanding, it is wise to use the same terminology. However, their meaning and definition are about to change dramatically in the following few pages in the Christmas Tree Model and totally different to what you have known – yet their practicality and useability will be massively enhanced. I retain the terms for your ease of use.

Now to the model. I am going to work the model with you using a real and easily understandable business example. In parallel, I will also develop the definition of each step so that it will be crystal clear and useable. You will see how simple, practical, and instantly applicable it is.

Please refer to the diagram and follow my step-by-step guide on how to use it, detailed after the diagram.

2.4

The Christmas Tree Model: Definitions, A Story, An Example And A Users Guide To Illustrate The Model

Let's take a real business and work through it step by step. We will also define each step simply and clearly to leave no ambiguity, making it easily useable. The example I'd like to use is a UK mobile phone retail business. Let's just call the business *House of Phones* (HoP).

House Of Phones (HoP)

HoP has been a massively successful business in the UK ever since the advent of mobile phones back in the mid-1990s and grew exponentially to over two thousand shops. Each shop is well arranged with phones and offers displayed clearly. Recently however it's been facing a considerable decline; why?

Let's say you would like to get a new phone. You go to an HoP shop and ask the attendant to show the options in your range. He shows you working models of four phones - an iPhone xxx, Samsung yyy... Let's say that you settle for the Samsung.

Next, he shows you the different network tariffs on Vodafone, O2, EE etc.. You tell him the O2 offer seems best, for £65 per month.

The sales person says, 'You get the phone, 50GB of data, latest network across the UK… shall we sign you up?'

'Not just yet. Let me think about it for a day or two.'

You then go home and check directly on O2.co.uk and find exactly the same deal and phone, except it's £57 per month. HoP has become a costly and capital-intensive window shopping resource (two thousand shops) to help its competitors. Therefore, the business has been declining dramatically.

Got the story? Now, let's use the Christmas Tree model to plan ourselves out of this hole and into success. Remember the six steps M-V-O-S-T-F?

I will discuss each heading starting with strategies in two parts:

1. The definition and understanding of that element.

2. Its use in HoP's business to make it practical and useable for you.

2.5

Using The Christmas Tree Model To Plan HoP Into Success

The Starting Point

Where shall we start the planning process? Looking at the Christmas Tree Model, the temptation is to begin with missions, then visions, then objectives. Traditional wisdom goes this way, and often objectives are planned first. Does this make sense?

Objective is the destination. For example, increase sales by 15% or profits by 8% or market share by $x\%$ and so on. And, why not 20% or 10%?

But from where do these objectives come?

Sadly, they are a wish list, usually based on an improvement of history, which is probably irrelevant to the future in a rapidly changing world, or it's a wish list of the CEO or management or the owners.

We will definitely come back to missions, visions and objectives – simply and practically, which will make sense, but the starting point, my friends are none of these – it is *strategy*. We need a more robust basis for defining destinations. This is a radical departure from traditional practice, and it will be clear why.

2.6

Strategy

As seen on the Tree diagram, *Strategy* is the fourth step: when you present and layout your plan. But when you are creating your plan, strategy is absolutely and definitively the first step and the starting point. It is the centrepiece and driver of the whole program, and I know you have been waiting patiently for it, so let's discuss.

Understanding And Re-Defining Strategy

Firstly, let's not complicate strategy.

The Dubai Strategy Session

I was in Dubai training a group of twelve CEOs and senior directors from various corporations. I asked them to define strategy. They were exceptionally qualified and had studied in the top business schools of the world.

One by one, they gave fascinating, complex, and elaborate descriptions of strategy. I listened with keen interest and was massively impressed.

I then asked, 'Which of these definitions and descriptions of strategy can I practically and immediately implement in my business tomorrow and generate excellent results this year?'

A mixture of silence and over justification of their method told me the whole story.

It really isn't that complicated. If you are studying it in a top institute for two years, you have no choice but to subscribe to it. But how many MBAs did Steve Jobs have, or Bill Gates, Richard Branson, JRD Tata, or Mark Zuckerberg? None of course.

I have a lot of respect for the work of business schools and strategy experts. I have an MBA and even taught in top business schools early on. But this inspired me to move beyond it and develop simple, impactful, practical techniques and principles which have served me in turning corporations around and helping people to succeed - whether it was as a corporate leader or coach/developer.

Please understand I am saying this with all modesty, humility, and gratitude to have been fortunate enough to have helped organisation and implemented it consistently for success. I share this experience to help make it a reality for you.

So, what actually is *strategy*? Please follow this logically, step-by-step with me; the answer to this question is extremely simple.

Think about the word *strategy*, its sounds like *strata, street*, or *straat* in Dutch. In other words, *it is the route to our destination.* This is not the strict etymology of the word, which has its origins in Greek, but I am using a creative interpretive licence to enhance and underpin its practical application. So, if it is the route to our destination, it tells us how we will reach the destination.

If the objective is the destination – *where* we will get to, *by when* – then strategy tells us *how* we will get there. It's the route to the destination. OK, so far?

In business, there is one and only one set of routes that can take us to our destination. What do you think they are?

When I ask this question, people give me various answers.

It's a plan... the actions we need to do... how we structure the business to succeed etc.. These are all good answers, but they don't define strategy as the only route available to us. Are you ready for the answer? You will be shocked at how simple and obvious it is, and yes, it is the blindingly obvious which deludes us.

The only route or set of routes available to us in business – for absolute success – is the market, specifically, sets of customers called *market segments*; and their Value Onions. Tell me if there is any other route to your business destination? We exist; the business exists because and only because Value Onions of clients exist. If these Value Onions didn't exist, there would be no need for us or the business. Simple, isn't it?

Yet, the Value Onions of customer segments are what we miss in our strategic process. Or, if it is there, it is intuitive and incomplete. So, the ultimate, practical definition of strategy is:

Strategy = Market Segments + Their Value Onions

If you have five market segments then you need five strategies, each with its own Value Onion.

Further, remember that value is subjective, i.e., different customers will have different Value Onions – remember the airline example in Section 1? The Value Onion of non-resident Indians and Indian tourists was completely different even though the core (product or service) was the same – an eight-hour direct flight between London and Mumbai.

 Just to be clear, you will not find this definition of strategy in any academic text on management or hear it described in this way, but logically it can be the only definition. Having worked it through with arithmetical logic above, nothing else is needed. The point is that it works, and interestingly it's what the exceptions like Steve Jobs did intuitively. In this book, we are doing it with the same simplicity but in a more structured and planned way to make it useable across the organisation.

Let me tell you what I mean.

Billion Dollar Hippy

He was obsessed with his customer's value. There is a fascinating documentary on him called *Billion Dollar Hippy*. There is a scene - actual video footage of when Apple were designing the mouse in the late 1980s. It shows Steve Wozniak and the technical team standing at a whiteboard deeply absorbed in writing algorithms.

Alone, on the other side of the room, Mr Jobs. He's rocking in his chair, lost to the world, deep in contemplation and imagination, while playing with something imaginary on the thigh of his jeans (like a mouse). He was thinking, *Which problem of which customer am I solving here?* He was addressing the Value Onions of a specific set of customers. This is what set him apart, not only differentiated but distinguished the company to become the first trillion-dollar company.

This is strategy from a strategic mind. The outcomes are evident.

Summarising and defining strategy

- Strategy is the street, i.e., the route to our destination (objective).
- In business, only one set of routes can take us to our destination
  – the Value Onions of our customer market segments.
- Strategies = the Value Onion of each market segment to serve.

End of story. Now, let's make it real by applying it to HoP.

2.7

HoP's Strategy

On the Christmas Tree model diagram, let's say that Segment 1 for HoP is non-tech people aged over 60. On their Value Onion the core is simply the phone, 50GB of data etc...

Now, let's look at their outermost layer of the Value Onion – well, let's forget phones for a minute and ask an intelligent question – *What is the most important thing in these people's lives?* – I'm sure you'll say, *Grandchildren*. How do these youngsters communicate? With WhatsApp, Instagram etc..

HoP's Customers

Now imagine the grandparents live in London and the grandchildren in Sydney, Australia and the nine-year-old Katie sends a picture on her phone to the grandparents to tell them she has won the art competition at school. Grandma wants to open it and show it proudly to her friends – she can't because she is non-tech. Granddad wants to open it, print it, frame it – he can't because he is non-tech.

So, this is the outermost layer of the Value Onion. Having discovered it, we now need to create a matching response on the outer layer Response Onion.

Remember from Section 1 that Response Onions must come *after* the Value Onions. We need to develop matching responses layer by layer on the Response Onion to match and serve the Value Onion layer. Sadly, in most times, we respond without understanding or engaging with value.

Now, the perfect matching response to the most significant value of these grandparents (grand kids, photos, and videos) might be something called The Techie Squad. It's a new service, and it means that in selected HoP stores, there are a couple of young staff members dedicated to assisting you with your tech issues. They are not salespeople or have any other role. So, grandma or granddad can take their phone, as long as they bought it from HoP and say, *My granddaughter sent me a picture can you help me?* They will open it, download it, put it on your laptop, train you even print it for you, and you can go in as many times as you like. It's included in your contract. Wow, what a service!

Suddenly, by addressing the real value of that customer segment on the outer layers of their Value Onion rather than desperately trying to sell your phone and the contract, you have created a wow factor. Of course, the product will be bought. You need to sell nothing.

The second layer of value, moving inwards on the Value Onion, maybe that they are not very mobile, the third might be that they have sight issues etc.. This is all strategy.

It is important to note here that we are working down the Christmas Tree step-by-step and currently discussing the *Strategy* level, which comprises *market segments* and Value Onions. The Response Onion, which we have started to mention, is a part of the next level on the Tree called *Tactics*. We will discuss *Tactics* in detail in the next section.

Summarising the strategy, i.e. segment and Value Onion and the response to it:

LAYER	Value Onion	MATCHING Response Onion
1. Outermost	Love for and connection with grandchildren with photos, videos…	Techie Squad
2. Next layer in	Mobility issues – i.e. don't like to go out to the shops much.	Techie Squad on scooters
3. Next layer	Sight issues	We'll put a super magnifying film on your mobile
CORE	The core is the Samsung x; unlimited SMS; 50 GB data etc.., i.e., the actual product or service.	The same as the Value Onion, i.e. the Samsung x; unlimited SMS; 50 GB data etc…..

Table 2.7.1 Market segment – non-tech, over-60s people

A reminder of the core – it's the same on the Response Onion as the Value Onion. The customer will ask for a Samsung xxx with 50GB of data, and that is what you will give them. However, in the layers, as you can see in the table above, having grasped the customer's true value, the response to value must be developed, invested in, and worked upon.

The absence of this value understanding is the weakness in almost all businesses and their plans, but it is the true differentiator.

When you respond perfectly to the outer layers of the Value Onion, as shown above, you move beyond differentiation and into being *distinguished*.

At this stage, you are no longer worried about or over aware of your customers because you are blissfully in customer value.

This is where Apple (under Steve Jobs), Google, Amazon etc.., find themselves.

Their success is clear to see.

- Strategy 1 is over-60s, non-tech customers and their Value Onion (VO).
- Strategy 2 would be another segment, for example, university students and their VOs.
- Strategy 3 could be young couples and their VOs.

And so on – these are the routes to your destination, the *how* in your strategic thinking and planning.

2.8

Market Segments

Before we leave the strategy, level and move to Tactics, it is important to briefly discuss market segments which I have mentioned several times in the above discussion.

With our simple and powerful thinking now:

Strategy = Market Segments + Their Value Onions

We have discussed Value Onions at great length in Section 1, so the question is, what are market segments. Again, if you research this topic, you will find mountains of elaborate and complex information and may get lost in them. It's straightforward, and here is the only definition you need:

A market segment is a set of customers whose Value Onion looks very similar or almost the same.

And that is it. Notice I say *almost the same* and not the same. Because, as we noted in Section 1, value is subjective, and it belongs at the end to individuals, and this will rarely be the same. In that section, we also said that decisions are ultimately made by personal preferences, even in a B2B environment.

Using the COVs (Circles of Value) model (Section 1.39) to represent the Value Onion, the outermost layers are PV or personal value, which will be very individual.

So, going back to the definition, in my experience, 85% to 90% of similarity of Value Onions of customers will put them into the same market segment. Using the COVs model, we can say it as follows:

Customers will be in the same market segment if:

- 95-100% of EV is the same
- Over 85% of BV is the same
- Over 70% of PV is the same

These ranges are indications and not a precise science. However, if we have genuinely discovered the true Value Onion from the customer's perspective and not my selfish motives, you will get a very accurate indication of these percentages.

Traditional market segmentation uses strict and boring parameters that categorise consumers by *demographics* like age and income bands. They are called Class A (very wealthy), Class B, B2, C, etc. But the world, customers and their buying reasons and patterns are much more complex than that. This old-fashioned way is often inappropriate, although convenient for so-called marketing experts.

Our radical new way of classifying them by their Value Onions is much more relevant and robust. However, it relies on that critical step of understanding who our customers are and discovering their Value Onions.

Here is a hot tip to help you get segmentation right: ask the question *why*. In other words, *why do they buy the product or service?* It will take you instantly to *their* Value Onions.

Here are some examples:

1. In the Jet Airways example, by asking why people fly between London and Mumbai, we said one of the reasons is attending weddings, visiting family and friends etc. Then by asking *Who does this?* it gave us the segment – non-resident Indians. Now, the perfect response for them was 46kg of weight in economy class. Another answer to the *why* is – to experience multiple destinations in Europe.
Then the question, *Who's value is this?* gives us the segment Indian tourists, and their Value Onion doesn't speak of weight. For this segment a better response is offering deals to European cities like Rome, Paris, Barcelona etc.

2. In the House of Phones example, if the *why* was connecting with family, photos, videos – the segment was over 60s, non-tech people, and we build appropriate responses to them etc.

Why then is market segmentation so critical and central to strategy? – because value is subjective and by classifying our customers into sets by their Value Onions, choosing the most attractive segments to work with, we will develop the perfect Response Onions to serve those values, which will focus our energies, efforts, and resources. We will also develop the right processes, employ the right people and so on.

In summary, we will use our resources well and invest in the right response to the right market – success pretty much assured.

2.9

With Which Segments Should I Work? Attractiveness Of Market Segments

Strategy is as much about saying what we *should do* as what we *should not do*. Resources are limited, so we should apply them in a focused and most productive way. Therefore, choose attractive market segments to serve. But what makes a market segment attractive for me? Here are some practical points to make this decision. An attractive market segment is:

1. One which can generate more sales and profits.

2. One that is growing at a robust pace.

3. One where I am already known and have experience of serving.

4. One that has less pressure from competitors.

5. One that is a high-volume segment

6. One that we have access to...

7. Etc...

These are the obvious ones, and by analysing all segments available to you and scoring them against these parameters most relevant to you and your business, you will easily choose the best segments to serve.

I have one super parameter which supersedes these. If you use it, points 1-5 above will be met anyway. You will generate more sales, profits, brand capital and go beyond competitive pressure.

So, what is this super parameter to assess and choose the most attractive market segment for you? Shall I tell you?

It is very simply as follows:

The most attractive market segment to me is the one on who's Value Onion my skills, talents, capabilities, i.e., Response Onions can have the most significant impact.

I call this *Depth of Impact* when I develop corporations and their strategies. The more closely my Response Onion matches and overlays or serves your Value Onion, the higher my *Depth of Impact* on you.

2.10

Depth Of Impact

This makes you my most attractive market segment as you will gain most by my existence, which will distinguish me, build my brand at the highest and make me wealthier. It also means I can walk away consciously from segments where my *Depth of Impact* is low, and I am happy for my competitors to take it. I don't worry about my competitors; I care for the value of my customers - a desirable way to be.

Depth of Impact is much more important than the size or volume of the market segment.

Apple's Preferred Segment

Under Steve Jobs, Apple actively chose not to work in the largest volume market segment available to them globally. Still, it became distinguished and the wealthiest company in the world.

What was that segment? Corporations. Everyone who works in a corporation has a laptop and a phone. He had the guts to say we are not interested in this segment and instead focused on the segments where Apple's talents, capabilities and Response Onions had the most remarkable Depth of Impact —serving the values of music, videos, coolness etc. It destroyed the likes of Blackberry.

Apple didn't care or worry about the competition. They were just obsessed with the evolving values of their customers. This great legacy has sustained their brand strength even many years after Steve Jobs.

I believe that strategic mind has gone, and already Apple is sliding. They've changed from being an enigma to just another giant corporation.

I speak so much about Apple because it's an easy and compelling example for all. Intuitively and almost subconsciously, Steve Jobs did exactly what I am propagating.

We are just putting a simple structure to it all to help you make it happen and to sustain it into longevity.

2.11

The S-VOC© Framework
Quantifying Value
And Making Strategic Decisions

This model is the centrepiece of strategy. Why I call it S-VOC will become crystal clear later.

Remember that now our new, simple, clear, and practically applicable definition of strategy is:

Strategy = Market Segments + Their Value Onions.

With this in mind, here is a simple, powerful model to:

- Understand our market.

- Define our customers.

- Calculate customer's/market value.

- Rise above differentiation to become distinguished.

- Make excellent strategic decisions.

- Provide the platform for the best, innovative, creative solutions, products, services.

- Enable detailed operations and execution of the whole business.

- Resulting in growth and financial results and strength.

You are right to be sceptical. Is there such a simple magical solution? Read on, folks; you are in for a surprise and may I say, a treat.

Wide Application Of S-VOC

S-VOC is not restricted to customer-related organisations or projects. Before moving to the framework, I want to be very clear on this point. The S-VOC framework applies in any and every business, welfare, social, personal, or creative pursuit. It applies to:

- Commercial organisations – the whole organisation; each business unit each function or department; each project...
- Welfare, charitable or social organisations.
- Public, administrative, or political organisations.
- Professionals, creative people, artists, sportsmen and women...
- Individuals in any activity.

Using the method, I have had the good fortune of totally transforming and bringing vast success to many organisations and individuals in all the above categories.

The example I am using is in the commercial context, but later, I'll summarise its application and example of a welfare / charitable organisation.

2.12

The S-VOC Model©

The S-VOC Model© consists of three tables and several steps to constructing it and making it work. I will take you through these steps, and in parallel, we will take an example to illustrate each step so that it becomes practical and useable for you. To illustrate the Model, I have taken the example of an airline operating long haul flights, such as British Airways (BA).

Let's look at this as if we are BA. There are six steps:

- Step 1 – Select The Most Attractive Market Segments To Work In.

- Step 2 – Identify the customer values / potential values from your product or service offering.

- Step 3 – Evaluate the importance of each value to each market segment.

- Step 4 – Who is serving the market and how – including Competitors.

- Step 5 – Calculate Table 3 by multiplying Table 1 by Table 2.

- Step 6 – Make strategic decisions on the markets to serve.

- Step 7 – Innovative and Creative Responses to Important Customer Values.

2.13

Step 1 – Select The Most Attractive Market Segments To Work In

Identify the market segments served by you today as well as future potential market segments. i.e., groups of customers and customers you are serving today; and new ones you could serve.

Note: if you use the S-VOC process for a project not directly related to customers, replace customer/market segments with other stakeholders you are serving through your strategy. For example, if you are a charity, let's say for blind people.

Your end customer segments may be partially sighted people, elderly blind people living alone, university students with sight loss etc. Other important stakeholders whose Value Onion has to be served, may be donors, funding bodies, health and regulatory bodies etc.

	Segments	Segment 1	Segment 2	Segment 3
	Values	Corporate Board Members, VIPs	Business execs, Wealthy travellers	Families General travellers
1	Comfort	6	5	3
2	Food & Beverage	5	4	2
3	Economy	1	1	6
4	Entertainment	2	2	5
5	Flexibility	3	6	1
6	Friendly Service	4	3	4

Table 1 S-VOC Market Segments and Their Value Onions

In the British Airways (BA) example above), Step 1, the three market segments chosen are:

- Segment 1 - Corporate board members, VIPs.

- Segment 2 - Business Executives, wealthy entrepreneurs.

- Segment 3 – Families on holiday.

This is just a sample to illustrate the Model; you can have more segments.

2.14

Step 2 – Identify The Customer Values/ Potential Values From Your Product Or Service Offering

List all the values customers have within the context of your business. It is imperative to state these *from the customer perspective* and not yours or worse still from your products/services as is the natural tendency.

For example, as a computer manufacturer, you may say *the customer's value is to have a compact laptop.* It may be so, but this is expressed *from your perspective* because you make compact laptops. The customer's perspective and therefore value may be, *I want to be productive when travelling on planes, taxis etc.*

Our product response will then become a compact laptop, and if we don't have one and this is an attractive market segment, we will develop the product. So again, value must always *precede* response. The response must come *after* customer value has been truly discovered.

In Step 2, let's pretend that six values have been identified for BA customers. In my experience in doing strategy transformation programs is that we identify thirty to fifty! But there is no rule on this number – it will depend on *your* market.

In writing the values, it is essential to be clear of the benefit from the customer's end gain perspective, unambiguous and specific.

Look at value five: *Flexibility*. In itself, this is ambiguous and too general. But think of a business passenger who misses his flight because of a meeting overrun, who can easily switch to another flight on BA or even another airline. That might be *Flexibility*. But the actual value might be, *efficiently manage my meetings*.

2.15

Step 3 – Evaluate The Importance Of Each Value To Each Market Segment

Take a moment to look carefully at Table 1 again.

	Segments	Segment 1	Segment 2	Segment 3
	Values	Corporate Board Members, VIPs	Business execs, Wealthy travellers	Families General travellers
1	Comfort	6	5	3
2	Food & Beverage	5	4	2
3	Economy	1	1	6
4	Entertainment	2	2	5
5	Flexibility	3	6	1
6	Friendly Service	4	3	4

Table 1 S-VOC Market Segments and Their Value Onions

In Table 1, each value (*Comfort, Food & Beverages* etc.) has been given a number showing how valuable it is to each segment; a six representing the highest importance.

In Step 3, as you can see from Table 1, the highest value for Corporate Board members and VIPs is *Comfort*, and the lowest is *Economy* which makes sense and indicates their Value Onion.

For Business Executives, the highest is *Flexibility (6)*, then *Comfort (5)*. For families on holiday, *Economy (6)* is the highest value, and understandably they are willing to sacrifice *Flexibility (1)*.

So, under any market segment, the set of numbers is the Value Onion of those customers; and the Value Onion of each group of customers is different and individual to them.

Value truly is subjective.

To illustrate the model and make it simple to understand, I have ranked the values for each segment. However, when doing the exercise for yourself, please assign a score to each value against each segment on a scale of one to eight (eight being the highest). This will work better for you, and it will be easier to score.

Then you are not ranking the values comparatively, which will be difficult with so many values but looking at the importance of each value separately, evaluating its significance to that market.

Clarity On Values

For brevity, I have used these simple words, but the actual value-impacts need to be more specific and better expressed from the customer's end outcomes as follows:

1. Comfort = Arrive rested and fresh to work or enjoy.

2. Food & Beverage = Enjoy the journey with tasty cuisine; healthy; allergy friendly...

3. Economy = Take more holidays with a family of five; special deals...

4. Entertainment = Keep youngster occupied and happy on a long journey; catch up with latest movies...

5. Flexibility = Ability to change my plans without stress; get to my meeting despite missing the flight...

6. Friendly service = Pleasant experience on holiday; no-hassle journey.

2.16

Step 4 – Who Is Serving The Market And How – Including Competitors?

Now take a look at Table 2.

	Values	AIRLINE 1	AIRLINE 2	TOTAL
1	Comfort	4	6	10
2	Food & Beverage	6	4	10
3	Economy	3	7	10
4	Entertainment	3	7	10
5	Flexibility	8	2	10
6	Friendly Service	2	8	10

Table 2 S-VOC Understanding Our Position In The Market Today

Keeping the same values bring in a new element – a comparison between how well we serve each value compared to our competitors; let's say British Airways (BA) and Virgin Atlantic (VA).

For each value, assign a relative score to the competitor and us, adding up to ten. In the case of British Airways (Airline 1), we have chosen comparison with the competitor Virgin Atlantic (Airline 2). For example, on the value of *Entertainment* – VA is well ahead whereas in *Food and Beverage,* BA are better; and so on.

Important advice: If you are comparing several competitors, let's say four, there is no problem. Your spreadsheet will just be bigger, and instead of distributing the numbers out of ten, you will do it out of twenty-five (i.e., five points each). When I first devised the model, I used to do it like this.

Over the last several years using S-VOC to do complete strategy transformations on organisations, I find two columns are all you ever need; however, complex the competitive environment. The first column is us and the second column the competition, i.e., or all competition combined. It makes sense as we want to be the best of the best and well beyond to be distinguished. In one value, Competitor A may be the best, and in serving another value, it may be Competitor B. But stick with two columns for now.

Be aware of your competition but give them much less importance than you do. Most organisations are over-aware of competitors. Resultantly, at best, they can only be as good as the competitor and no better. Those organisations who focus obsessively on the customers and their Value Onions, almost to the point of ignoring competitors, are far more successful.

I repeat the example of Apple laptops. Dell, Sony, Toshiba, Acer, Lenovo, HP…. They are all competing with each other, and it's a desperate scrap. But if I say MacBook Air, can you name me a competitor? Maybe MS Surface but look at the market share; there is no comparison. This is what I call being *distinguished*, not *differentiated*. Apple are not concerned with competitors. They are even happy for competition to take the largest market segment, which for laptops is *corporations*. Apple has taken an active decision *not* to work with this segment, which takes guts, yet they became the first trillion-dollar company, globally.

It isn't by accident but design. Steve Jobs was obsessed with the genuine value of his customers, which is why he never made products. The iPod, iPad, iPhone, iMac etc.., are all Response Onions to perfectly discovered Value Onions.

Unfortunately, as things are going after him, Apple's future is less certain and less bright. It has become another ordinary corporation living on the strength of the brand and past glory. There is no innovation. My new MacBook Air looks and feels the same as it did five years and three laptops ago.

Don't drive your business cues from your competitors. Obsess with customer Value Onions. And having built the perfect Response Onions, look at the competition just to cross-check your perfection of response. It's not about desperately trying to beat competitors but caring for your customers to see how well they are being served. So interestingly, Table 2 looks as if it's about competitors, but it's more about customers and how they are being served.

2.17

Step 5 – Calculate The Value Of Table 3 By Multiplying Table 1 By Table 2

Table 3 (below) is very simply the product of the previous two tables and is calculated simply by multiplying Table 1 by Table 2.

Values		Segment 1		Segment 2		Segment 3	
Values	Airline (A)	A1	A2	A1	A2	A1	A2
1	Comfort	24	36	20	30	12	18
2	Food & Beverage	30	20	24	16	12	8
3	Economy	3	7	3	7	18	42
4	Entertainment	6	14	6	14	15	35
5	Flexibility	24	6	48	12	8	2
6	Friendly Service	8	32	6	24	8	32
		95	115	107	103	73	137
	Airline 1 as % Airline 2	83%		104%		53%	

Table 3 S-VOC Steps, Analysis and Decision

For example, in Table 1, the value of *Comfort* for Segment 1 had a score of 6. Multiply this by *Comfort* for Airline 1 (BA) in Table 2, which has a score of 4. In Table 3 above, and you will see the product of 24 in *A1/Comfort*.

Interpretation: On the value of *Comfort*, Segment 1 is served by BA at a level of 24 compared to VA at the level of 36.

How did we calculate Table 3? Again, Take Table 2, Value 1, *Comfort* (6) multiplied by Table 2, Value 1 *Comfort* (4). Equals 24.

Just so you are sure, here's the tables all together showing the workings.

Table 1

	Values	Segment 1	Segment 2	Segment 3
		Corporate board members, VIPs	Business execs, Wealthy travellers	Families General travellers
1	Comfort	6	5	3
2	Food & Beverage	5	4	2
3	Economy	1	1	6
4	Entertainment	2	2	5
5	Flexibility	3	6	1
6	Friendly Service	4	3	4

x Table 2

	Values	AIRLINE 1	AIRLINE 2	TOTAL
1	Comfort	4	6	10
2	Food & Beverage	6	4	10
3	Economy	3	7	10
4	Entertainment	3	7	10
5	Flexibility	8	2	10
6	Friendly Service	2	8	10

= Table 3

	Values		Segment 1		Segment 2		Segment 3	
	Values	Airline (A)	A1	A2	A1	A2	A1	A2
1	Comfort		24	36	20	30	12	18
2	Food & Beverage		30	20	24	16	12	8
3	Economy		3	7	3	7	18	42
4	Entertainment		6	14	6	14	15	35
5	Flexibility		24	6	48	12	8	2
6	Friendly Service		8	32	6	24	8	32
			95	115	107	103	73	137

	Airline 1 as % Airline 2	83%	104%	53%

2.18

Step 6 – Make Strategic Decisions On The Markets To Serve

Look again at the BA Airline 1 as a % or Airline 2 totals on Table 3.

Values		Segment 1		Segment 2		Segment 3	
Values	Airline (A)	A1	A2	A1	A2	A1	A2
1	Comfort	24	36	20	30	12	18
2	Food & Beverage	30	20	24	16	12	8
3	Economy	3	7	3	7	18	42
4	Entertainment	6	14	6	14	15	35
5	Flexibility	24	6	48	12	8	2
6	Friendly Service	8	32	6	24	8	32
		95	115	107	103	73	137
	Airline 1 as % Airline 2	83%		104%		53%	

Table 3 S-VOC Steps, Analysis and Decision

- In Segment 1, BA (Airline 1) is 83% as good as VA (Airline 2) in serving the entire Value Onion of customers in that segment.

- In Segment 2, BA is 4% better than VA.

- In Segment 3, it is just over half as good as VA.

In the initial look, we can probably say:

- We will work with Segment 1 and make improvements.

- We will definitely serve Segment 2 as well; however, we are highly vulnerable here. Think about it BA's most strategic market segment in the last decade has been business travellers, so it makes sense it's ahead of the competition. But here's the vulnerability – they have made the business segment their primary focus, yet they are only 4% better than their nearest competitor? It says that far from being distinguished, they haven't even built differentiated responses to the values of these strategic customers. We often say things and even plan actions to try and make it happen, but there is no real conviction behind it. It's a wish list, and worse, it's an advertising campaign with nothing really to show for it. We will examine this further in Step 7.

- On Segment 3, we have a tough decision to make, and at first look, it seems we shouldn't bother with this segment and let competitors have and enjoy it as they are twice as good as us in serving its Value Onions. Strategy is as much about saying what we 'should' do as much as what we 'shouldn't' do. Remember Apple's conscious decision not to serve the most significant market segment available to them for laptops, i.e., corporations. We can't do everything for everyone and must make the most of our resources. All too often, companies do things because they can, or serve markets simply because they are there. This will not differentiate us, leave aside distinguish us; it will only cost us and may even destroy us.

Strategic decisions are about:

- First, genuinely and caringly understanding values.

- Then innovatively and creatively developing Response Onions to that value.

- Then committedly serving those values with all other tactics and resources.

Tactics are elaboratively discussed later in this section.

So, at first look, we may decide to not work in Segment 3. But then look at the pairs of numbers in that segment. For example, if we can easily turn around *Entertainment* (15:35) and *Friendly Service* (8:32), then the bottom-line number goes to 126% in favour of BA – suddenly we are in business in this segment.

2.19

Step 7 – Innovative and Creative Responses to Important Customer Values

In Table 3, having looked at the total numbers and made strategic segment decisions, you now need to look segment by segment and the pairs of numbers. It will give you a diagnosis, analysis and platform to build excellent Response Onions. Choose the most important/attractive segments first.

Values		Segment 1		Segment 2		Segment 3	
Values	Airline (A)	A1	A2	A1	A2	A1	A2
1	Comfort	24	36	20	30	12	18
2	Food & Beverage	30	20	24	16	12	8
3	Economy	3	7	3	7	18	42
4	Entertainment	6	14	6	14	15	35
5	Flexibility	24	6	48	12	8	2
6	Friendly Service	8	32	6	24	8	32
		95	115	107	103	73	137
	Airline 1 as % Airline 2	83%		104%		53%	

Table 3 S-VOC Steps, Analysis and Decision

Let's run the analysis on Segment 2, *Business Executives and Rich entrepreneurs*. Look at the biggest and smallest numbers first.

- Flexibility – BA scores 48 to VA's 12. On the outermost layer of this segment's Value Onion, we (BA) are four times better than the competition. This is true.

Last year, I was speaking for a major pharma company in Paris, then going on to Dubai to do a program for them the following afternoon. They had booked all the flights on BA in Business. From Paris, I had to get a flight back to London and then connect to a flight to Dubai. I arrived at Charles De Gaulle airport in the evening only to discover that the flight to London was delayed. I panicked and went to the BA desk. They looked at my ticket and said, There is no problem. As you are in Business Class, we will pre-book you on a later Emirates flight. Further if you do make it in time for the BA flight, we will get you on to that. It really served my Value Onion, and I was impressed. Now consider this. Although BA is four times better on Flexibility, they will soon lose this advantage as Open Skies Policy has come in. Until now, only source and destination airlines can pick up passengers in any city. With Open Skies, any airline can pick up passengers anywhere and with airlines like Emirates gearing up as a multi-destination airline, BA will lose the advantage.

- Solution? Look for the next level of differentiator by considering the outermost later of the Value Onion of these customers and building innovative responses. How? Listen, listen, listen to customers and segments, and anticipate the changes on which to respond.

An example is Toyota Prius, conceptualised in 1991, when the environment was hardly spoken about. This is brilliant anticipation of upcoming changes in Value Onions, anticipating the change and designing responses to serve that change. This is what I mean by looking for the next level of differentiator.

Tesla is another example. Having found a new upcoming value, they had the courage to invest against the tide and make electric vehicles as advanced as they are in a short space of time. What is more alluring about Toyota is they innovated this significant new response despite being a giant company with the older technology.

- **Econom**y – VA are twice as good as BA, and the temptation is to work on this value, but I would tell my team in BA to forget about it altogether. It will do nothing for you. Look at the numbers – 3:7; they are tiny. In other words, it's an inner layer of the Value Onion, and therefore the ROI or impact of the effort will be very low. We have bigger fish to fry, so ignore this and don't even talk about it. Strategy is as much about what we should do as what we shouldn't do. It will keep our focus, energies and resources in the right place and not distracted by less important things.
- **Food and Beverage** is the next one to look at. BA) are in leadership at 24:16. But success is one of the most dangerous things to happen to us. It can make us arrogant, stagnant, and unsuccessful – think of Kodak, Blackberry and Nokia. So, what is the answer? Refresh your understanding of market segments and refresh your knowledge of their Value Onions.

Think about these two statements:

1. Today's market segments are not tomorrow's market segments for the same products.
2. Today's Value Onions for the same market segments are not tomorrow's Value Onions for that market.

Let's examine these one-by-one and then give the answers.

Today's Market Segments Are Not Tomorrow's Market Segments For The Same Products

Think about Blackberry. Who was buying these when they first came out? Businesspeople as a personal purchase. But then the market segment shifted – for the same product – to companies buying them for their sales force and management. They were for productivity (their Value Onion).

Two years later, and it now was teenagers, who were pinging each other on BBM (Blackberry messenger). The iPhone destroyed all of that.

You see, because the ultimate truth is that the market has its Value Onions, it will go looking for that value to be satisfied. I'm saying why let it happen by chance; go in reverse and understand the changing nature of those segments and design responses to their values.

Today's Value Onions For The Same Market Segments Are Not Tomorrow's Value Onions For That Market

Think about Kodak. What a gigantic global brand of the last century; but it was destroyed virtually overnight as the digital cameras on mobile phones came in. Kodak was caught napping. Their success had let them down. The Value Onions of the same segments were changing in the new world of snap and share instantly.

Kodak remained arrogantly stuck to their film and photo development fearfully, not acknowledging the change and thinking it was a just fad and hoping it would fade. As Value Onions of the same market segments change constantly, we need to listen, listen, listen and change Response Onions correspondingly.

Those organisations who see these two statements as inconveniences, as the vast majority do, will fear them, be in denial and before they know it, they will be surpassed, like Kodak, Xerox, Blackberry and Nokia. But suppose you see them as totally natural and logical. In that case, you will see them as an opportunity like Toyota with the Prius or Google or Apple under Steve Jobs, and you will ride the wave after wave of opportunity and success.

Getting back to BA and maintaining its leadership in *Food and Beverage* using the two statements above, we need to ask the following questions:

1. Which market segments are increasingly travelling in business?
   Let's say it is people from India and the GCC countries like Dubai.

2. How are their Value Onions changing? Maybe they want more eclectic international flavours and creative cuisine; may be healthier options etc..

Understanding this, we need to shift and build matching Response Onions – for example, a choice of Japanese, French and Indian, maybe pre-selected before the flight and have a sushi chef on board for first and business class. I'm dreaming this up, but do you see how it would swing the brand value and get people talking. Yes, it's an investment, but it's tiny compared to the return it will generate either through subtle pricing or occupancy.

I would now look at Comfort and Friendly Service and work on turning these numbers around.

Comfort, 20:30

Before attempting to turn this around, we first need to understand what comfort means for the customer – is it more leg-room, wider seats, wash room size, storage…

Leg Room

Let's say its legroom. The last time I flew in BA economy from Los Angeles to London, it was eleven hours of pure discomfort. My knees were touching the seat in front. I know I am now speaking about Economy class, but the principle is the same. BA argues that if we give more legroom, we will need to lose two whole rows of seats, which means less revenue. Is this a cost-driven mentality or an investment one?

Cost and value are direct enemies; price and value are best friends. This unfortunate cost-cutting mentality has hit BA badly – more on this below.

The answer is - for the comfort of a few more centimetres, most customers would be happy to pay a little more, maybe even 5 – 10%, to fly with a more comfortable airline for eleven hours. This is an investment-driven mentality. Investments generate returns, and costs generate pain.

Think investment, not cost.

I say to you there is no such thing as cost or expense; there is only investment. The accountants among you will be offended by this, saying they are two different things. Costs are in the income statement and investments in the balance sheet – I'm not speaking from the mechanics of accounting; I started my professional life as an accountant. I'm speaking from a business thinking point of view. When you understand customer value, then invest in serving it properly, the returns on investment are assured and much higher. A cost mentality will make you mediocre at best, as in the British Airways example, and building a loved brand with lasting success will be difficult.

Friendly Service 6:24

On the same flight, I got up in the middle of the night to get some water and got chatting with one of the flight attendants. He told me he was resigning. When I asked why he said that the working conditions at BA are the worst he had experienced on any airline, and cited gruelling work schedules. *They try and save so much cost that it compromises customer service and our motivation. Also, the pension scheme is a mess...* If this is going on in the staff's mind, how do you expect them to be friendly?

Friendliness is not something you can train people to do – then it is unnatural and counter-productive. Friendliness is one of the products of how staff are treated, managed, and inspired. But BA's mentality appears reactionary rather than innovative and proactive. In recent years, their significant losses or profit drops have been plagued by rampant strike action, and at times, they seem to be in battle with their staff – how can we expect friendly service? Just the strike actions have cost them hundreds of millions – it would be cheaper to put this into the pension scheme, sort it out and then ask people to smile. It is a test case of cost and internal problems rather than a value-driven mentality. I'm not a BA basher. I feel sad that what used to be such a solid and powerful brand has been allowed by its leaders to bring it down to this level.

Summary of this analysis – the above discussion is a way to analyse, interpret and diagnose the situation and issues in the customer's value and the opportunities to improve, innovate, respond, and invest. Look at the highest and lowest numbers first, and as you work on the pairs of numbers for each key value, a pattern will emerge. You will be much more robust in moving higher in your differentiation and, yes, all the way to distinction.

Once again, it's worth exploring the data on this table.

It tells a story; and it should inspire you to contemplate opportunities to deliver value.

That my friends, concludes our discussion on strategies, which is the centrepiece of my whole argument, this book and my method.

Let's move to discuss the next step in the Christmas Tree – *Tactics*.

2.20

Tactics
The Next Step On The Christmas Tree

After Strategies on the Christmas Tree come Tactics, which we can also call action plans, projects, programs etc.. They are the detailed activities and actions that need to happen in the business and the resources required.

Get this step wrong, and we are at best ineffective, and, at worst, hugely wasteful which can bring the business down, as often happens.

Before discussing Tactics, I want to make one clear and a forceful blanket statement.

All Tactics on this tree, as you can see from the diagram, are a function of the Strategy level. Strategy precedes Tactics. *Tactics* comes after Strategy.

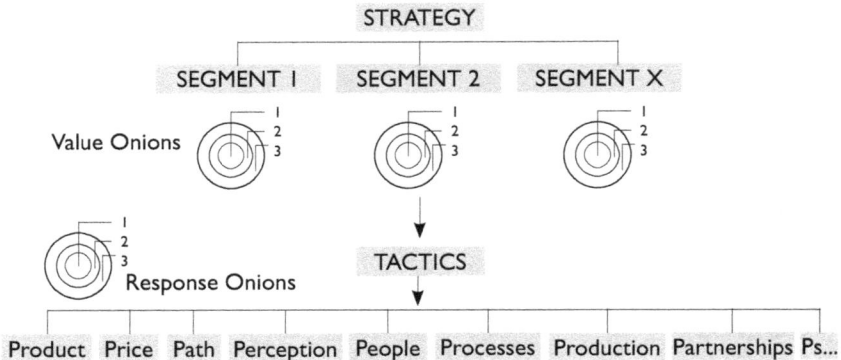

In other words, everything, every action, every penny spent and everyone in the organisation is linked to, because of and driven from the Value Onions of chosen market segments. It's critical to understand this point in our framework, and yes, it is a massive departure from current practice and theory. But it has massively benefited the hundreds of organisations with whom I've been privileged to work. And I say this with all humility and gratitude. It's radical, it's challenging, but it works. If it makes sense to you, especially after reading the *Tactics* section below, then it's yours. And I know it will make sense as it does to the thousands of managers, business leaders, entrepreneurs, and individuals I have worked with and developed. The ones that have implemented it and use it have generated much more significant business growth and created a far more engaged, responsible, creative, innovative, and motivated team of people and a culture of unity and collaboration. Sounds like unicorns in Utopia? I'll share plenty of examples and stories – it's reality!

The problem in most organisations is that they plan and decide on the objectives… and then jump to *Tactics*… and then start detailed planning of the activities, people, projects etc..

It's haphazard, not driven by a higher purpose of customer's Value Onions. All functions and departments run in their own directions based on their expertise rather than a common goal and purpose. Subsequently, we create vertical silos leading to a lack of communication, coordination, alignment and therefore lack of collaboration. It's confusing, wasteful, unproductive, and frankly dangerous. I describe the worst-case scenario, but it happens to a lesser or greater degree in all organisations. I am not saying that customer understanding, and value are absent, but they tend to be intuitive rather than structured and therefore opinions and interpretations and which not adequately used.

Our Christmas Tree process challenges and remedies this problem once and for all. By establishing a firm strategy, in the unique way we have defined it, i.e., market segments and their Value Onions - our Tactics line take on a much richer meaning. They are well planned, and resources utilised correctly. Everyone speaks to each other from a powerful common point - customer value.

The *Strategy* line forms the umbrella under which all tactics and activities will happen, setting up a common purpose. Every action in the *Tactics* line is driven from and cross-referred to outer layers of the customer's Value Onions.

What Are Tactics, And How Do We Plan Them?

Tactics are sequential planning, step by step, of all actions like what products/services we should design or improve. How do we market them, what people and processes we need, how we will sell or distribute, etc..

It becomes the complete operating plan.

If you follow the process on the Christmas Tree step by step, you will see just how easy and straightforward it is and much easier to implement. We tend to overcomplicate it. It is further exacerbated by the heavy-handed approach from many management and business experts and academicians. They gain a lot from this complexity but often mess up companies.

Before I give you the steps, let's speak about marketing, which will make this *Tactics* level smooth and easy. After discussing marketing, we will continue with the current question: *What are tactics and how do we plan them?*

2.21

What Is Marketing?

The usual answers I receive when I ask this question are... how I communicate with my customers, advertising, public relations, social media contact, how I sell to them, and how I become better known. The list goes on in this way.

Yes, this is all in marketing, but it is only a part of marketing. This narrow definition is no one's fault because this is what most marketing functions do. Marketing, in reality, is much bigger than this.

Think about this: everything we do in the business is driven from, because of and responds to our market. If our customers and their values didn't exist, we wouldn't exist. Everything we do is in marketing, and all of us are in the marketing function, not just the marketing department. After all, the drivers of all actions/ tactics are the Value Onions of our market segments and customers in them.

All of us – and all our actions – are in marketing.

With this in mind, I'd like to remind you of a concept marketers have been using for a long time called the marketing mix. We will then re-configure this to modern and future business and use it creatively to plan our *Tactics*, which is where this entire discussion leads.

2.22

The Marketing Mix

Neil Borden, was an advertising professor at Harvard University, popularised the idea of the marketing mix. His 1964 article titled *The Concept of the Marketing Mix* demonstrated the ways that companies could use *advertising* tactics to engage their consumers. It was actually E Jerome McCarthy, a marketing professor at Michigan State University, who refined the concepts in Borden's book and created the idea of *The 4Ps,* a term that is still used today.

The 4Ps include:

1. Product

2. Price

3. Place

4. Promotion

There is a fifth one and marketers do acknowledge this now:

5. People

But there are more Ps.

6. Processes

7. Production

8. Procurement

9. Partnerships (e.g., commercial partners like distributors)

10. …

In reality, there are many more than four Ps.

Let's understand each of these, re-configure them with our new methods in this book, and discuss the additional ones. I am not speaking against marketers. The 4Ps was a brilliant concept – but we are evolving and updating it in the modern context.

I am proceeding step-by-step, sequentially, and this is how you need to plan your tactics. It's a logical sequence, and you can only do Step 2 after Step 1 and so on. The current problem is that they are designed in silos and together. No wonder there is confusion, unclarity, non-ownership and commitment and wastage of resources and higher costs.

And it's unstrategic.

2.23

Tactic 1: Product
Which We Will Now Re-Define

By *Product*, marketers refer to the actual product or service being sold. For Toyota, it is the car itself. For Virgin Atlantic, it's the 11-hour direct flight between London and Los Angeles – and it will also include products like economy, premium economy, business class and first class.

Our new definition of product is far more accurate and up to date.

Product is the whole Response Onion.

Simple, beautiful, and complete, isn't it? After all, what is a product? A boring definition is: things we buy or make to sell.

A much better definition of a *Product* is - *something we have made or acquired to serve our customer's value.* It makes sense. If this is the definition, then the entire Response Onion serves value. We have developed it layer by layer to serve the Value Onion layers of the customer. Wow, it's compelling stuff.

So, product very simply is the entire Response Onion.

End of story.

2.24

Is There A Distinction Between Product And Service?

One further crucial point, I make no distinction between *product* and *service*. Making this distinction adds unnecessary complications. When I say product, I include service and vice versa. Think about it, if the definition of product is something we have developed or acquired to serve the values of our customers, then doesn't a service do this? And just like a product, don't we research and develop a service? Doesn't it have a life cycle, a unit cost and price? Don't we market it? Sell it?

Where is the difference?

I invite you to reject and move away from these complicated unhelpful distinctions between product and service. Think of your product/service as a composite Response Onion, responding to your customers' values. Some layers of the Response Onion will be physical products, and some layers will be service. And depending on your activity, one may be more dominant than the other. Managers and leaders innocently engaging in unnecessary distinctions and theories are often narrow in their market responses and not distinguished. Yes, there is one difference - products are made in a factory and ends up as a physical object you can touch and hold. Service is made by people on the spot. But then we can argue that a car, a table, a painting – all products – are made and sold in entirely different ways, so how can we lump them into a book on product marketing?

We must move on and modernise.

In fact, in the modern context, when value impact is the ultimate consideration, the distinction between product and service is totally blurred. The product is a composite of so-called product and service that serves value.

When you buy a car, there is the physical part to it; the vehicle itself. But then the warranty that comes with it and the three-year service included etc.., all form part of your total value of hassle-free uninterrupted motoring to get you to work or enjoy your family weekends etc..

Product in the Marketing Mix revisited is an aggregate of all layers of products and services, i.e., the entire Response Onion.

HoP's Product – Response Onion

What does HoP's Response Onion look like? What is the entire product in response to the Value Onion of over sixty non-tech customers?

The core of their Response Onion:

- Samsung yyy device (the only physical product element of the RO).

- Unlimited SMS.

- 50 GB data per month.

- Etc.

The layers of the Response Onion

- Outermost layer = The Techie Squad, responding to the value of love for their grandchildren, photos, videos.
- Second layer in = The Techie Squad on scooters, responding to the value of low mobility.
- Third layer in = Super magnifying film on their phones, responding to their value of poor eyesight.

This core and the layers now, i.e., the whole Response Onion, constitute the P of *Product* in the marketing mix.

Two further points:

- **First, develop the core.** The core is essential and indisputable and must be to the best level and second to none. Then move to the outer layers and create response layers going inwards.
- **Invest more effort, time, energy, people, money on developing Response Onion layers to the outmost Value Onion layers and less as you go inwards.** In fact, on the innermost layers, you may not invest in or develop at all. After all, the more you respond to the outer layers of the Value Onion, the bigger the Depth of Impact and, therefore, the higher your sales revenue, profits and return of investment. By the innermost layers, I don't mean the core, which, as I said above, is indisputable and must be excellent.

So *Product* or the Response Onion is the first *Tactic*. Remember, we are going step by step, and this is how you need to approach your business planning.

Moving across, let's now discuss and do the next *Tactic: Price*, the second P of the Marketing Mix.

2.25

Tactic 2: Price

Having created or bought in the product/service, i.e., the Response Onion, the next important step is to decide how to price it.

Firstly, please understand that pricing is much more of an *emotional* issue than a technical issue. Sadly, however, it is often set only from a financial perspective. All too logically we say the cost of the product is $10, and we want to make a 30% margin to cover the other expenses and make a profit so then the price becomes $13. This method is simple and safe, but only in theory. How do you know the customer won't pay $15 if it is of high value to them? And this is where it becomes emotional.

If you are only operating at the core, as most companies do, you are sadly obliged to set the price on the cost-plus method I described above. Then you test it against the competition to make sure you are not out of sync with the market. If, however, you take the VORO approach and are genuinely building excellent responses to the discovered value of chosen market segments, you can set price to value. And remember, the further out in the Value Onion you are responding to, the more comfortable the customer will feel paying a higher price.

Price then is a function of market segments and their Value Onions, which, if you remember, is the definition of strategy, and this way of pricing is strategic. When we genuinely serve outer layers of the Value Onions, pricing is not simply based on logic and financial calculations; it is emotional and much more potent. Undoubtedly, having set the price, cross-check that it is covering costs and giving us a good profit, but with this method, you will find you make a lot more money than the simple logic route. Let's take an example:

Apple MacBook Air

An Apple MacBook Air retails at around USD $1,500. Why in your right mind would you pay three times the price when you can get an Acer or Dell for $500? They are not pricing 100% or 200% above their competitors, but 300%. It's well beyond logic. The reason is that their Response Onion responds perfectly to the outer layers of Value Onions of their chosen customers, i.e., market segments.

Thinking about logical pricing - I was discussing with the engineering director of a company supplying the plastic for laptop casings. He told me that Apple is obsessive about the polymer quality to get the perfect finish and are prepared to pay 35% more than other laptop manufacturers for the materials. Now look at this, Apple's costs may be 35% higher than their competitors, yet they charge 300% more to their customers – where is the logic? Reason and logic will only get you so far, but, understanding Value Onions are principally emotional, pricing to that will take you much further.

Let's look at the price on the Value Onion. Price will always start as an outermost layer on the Value Onion. It makes sense. Let's face it everyone wants to buy cheaper to be human is to want to buy cheaper. If you offer a 10% discount to the wealthiest person in the land on their Maybach car worth $500,000, don't you think they would like it? It's nothing to do with how much we have or what we can afford; it's just a human condition.

When we get a 10% discount in a restaurant on an $80 bill, isn't it welcome? What's $8, yet it makes us happy. So, everyone wants to buy cheaper, and that's why price starts as the outer layer. However, the more you serve other outer layers of the Value Onion, the price starts to move inwards and where it ends up depends on how good you are building Response Onion layers at the outer layer levels. The better you are at these responses, the further inwards price will travel. If you are brilliant at it, price merges into the core and is no longer a big issue. For example, a MacBook Air – customers are prepared to pay 300% of the price they can pay for another brand, yet they became the wealthiest company in the world. Does it make sense? Per se no.

But approaching it from Value Onions, it only makes sense.

PRICE ON THE Value Onion OF THE CUSTOMER

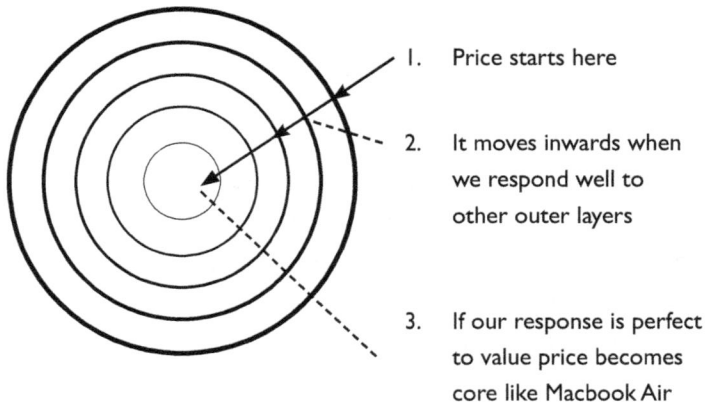

1. Price starts here

2. It moves inwards when we respond well to other outer layers

3. If our response is perfect to value price becomes core like Macbook Air

When you plan your business to the Christmas Tree, you can afford to price to value, which will be higher, and the customer will be happy to pay it. However, if you price to cost as we mostly do, you will always be in fear and customers will constantly try and negotiate hard.

From this discussion, here are three statements on price, which is all you need to guide you:

- **Everyone wants to buy cheaper** – it's our natural human tendency, by virtue of being human.

- **It's our business, professional, ethical, moral, integrity filled duty to serve the best value at the lowest price.** This statement makes sense because if we have maintained all along that integrity means serving Value Onions with genuine and matching Response Onions. Then if price starts as an outer layer on the Value Onions, it's our duty to serve it. With these two statements, you probably think that all I am saying is people want to buy cheaper, so sell it to them at lower prices. No, I am not. I am going sequentially because here comes Statement 3, which puts it into perspective.

- **Don't give value away.** This is the answer. In other words, when we price to value, taking Statement 2, the meaning of what is the lowest price completely changes. When we said the lowest price in Statement 2, the question is: in comparison to what? And it will usually be to competitors. But when we price to value, we are in a different realm, the realm of customer's emotional value, i.e., the outer layers of Value Onions. However, to not give value away, you have to know what value 'is'. This is the fundamental missing piece.

In any negotiation, if you don't know the genuine value of the other person, then go back to the drawing board, and first fully discover their Value Onion. The mechanics for doing this will be fully covered in Section 4 with techniques like *Spirit of Enquiry* and the four types of questions to navigate conversations.

This is the real strength of negotiation. It's what the ex-US President didn't do before jumping on a plane to North Korea with his misplaced bravado, and when it failed, and he returned with nothing, it was clear he hadn't worked out the dictator's Value Onion. When you know the total value, not from your perspective or what you want but what is value to them. Then price with confidence.

One further fascinating observation on price is that people are not really looking for a lower price (unless it is completely unreasonable, e.g., if the MacBook Air was priced at $5,000). They are actually looking for a discount regardless of the price, and whether it seems reasonable or not they want a discount or a special offer. Please understand this because our fears and worry of not getting the deal let us down, and we irrationally lower the price. There is a fundamental difference between lower prices and discounts. If the customer feels their value is met, they will accept a higher price, but a discount is that human emotion factor we discussed earlier: they want to buy cheaper.

So now the answer to excellent negotiation is simple.

- Understand the customer's true Value Onion

- Build perfect responses to that value and show the customer how you are serving their value – you are now holding the advantage. Not that it is a game but genuinely selling with integrity.

- If you would be comfortable selling at 100, price it to 112-115, depending on which part of the world you are in. They will want a lower price, and you will come down to 100. You will win the deal even though your competitor's price is 80. But then you are playing in the Value Onions of the customer, and the competitor isn't, so the customer wants you.

- Now they are happy at getting a discount or special offer; you are pleased to achieve 100. But don't go below 100, no way because looking at statement 3 above, at below 100, you would be giving value away. Your response to value is so strong you don't need to go below – you are not a desperate vendor; you're a valuepreneur.

Let me share my own experience. But firstly, I rarely get into tough pricing conversations with my clients, and I say this with all humility. The reason is that I am obsessed with *their value*, and genuinely from my heart, with a lot of care, I build Responses based on that value. And I never focus on or worry about my competitors.

Diminish Price Discussions

A giant construction company based in London was expanding across Europe. They wanted to strengthen their whole organisation, re-strategize and develop the management team and sales organisation involving around eight hundred and fifty people over a year. It was an extensive program. I worked on it for about two months to build the program in discussions with the senior leaders, HR head, country heads etc.. I understood the Value Onions of all stakeholders and created the right responses.

At the end of my presentation of the proposed program to the board, the CEO congratulated me, thanked me for understanding their priorities, and said, 'Just take 20% off the price, and the contract is yours.'

It was as cold and net as that. He thought I would succumb because it was a big contract. Something came over me, and I reacted in a way that still gives me the creeps when I think about what I said, but it taught me something.

I said to the CEO, 'Oh, I'm so sorry I completely misunderstood you. I didn't realise it was training you were looking for. I thought this was about expansion in Europe, opening up new markets and adding 20% to your EBITDA (profits) in the next two years. Sorry for getting it wrong. If it's just training you want to buy, I can recommend someone who can do it 20% cheaper.'

I closed my laptop as if to leave.

It was cheeky, risky, and fired by one of the worst emotions you can have, and that is anger. I feel frustrated that I've worked so hard with so much care for your success, and compared to the multiple millions you have to gain, you are arguing over a few thousand pounds of fees?

Now here's the question for you, did I get the contract? Yes, I did. But even now, I sometimes get a jolt thinking about what I was doing. However, it taught me that when you are holding the total value in your hands and have genuinely, with care and integrity, built responses to serve it - you can stand proud, confident yet respectful. And the only reason a customer can let you walk away is that they simply don't have the funds. That's OK; even if you lose 10% of business, the 90% you win will be more valuable and rewarding and, as a bi-product, make you wealthier.

So pricing is actually a function of the customer and their Value Onion. This makes pricing a strategic activity of marketing. Let's get back to HoP and look at their pricing of the Techie Squad.

HoP's Pricing

Here are two of the many ways to price to their customers the over 60s non-techs:

1. Dear customer, we know you can get the same deal for £57 by going direct instead of £65 with us. OK, we will align ourselves and price match and sell it to you for £57/month. Oh, and by the way, we have this unique service called the Techie Squad which will be an extra £8/ month. So, the total price remains the same, i.e., £65. Most of these customers, who may feel they are being sold extra things and they may also be budget-conscious, might well respond by saying, no thanks, I'll just take the phone contract for £57. They will have missed out, and HoP will have missed out. When a customer doesn't see value, then they go lower on price and compare with the competition.

2. Dear customer, we know you can get it for £57, we know we are £8 more expensive, but we will help you connect with the family and your grandchildren for free by solving any technical issues with our service, the Techie Squad designed for you. This is an entirely different and value/response approach and touches the Value Onion of these customers. They will undoubtedly go for it and tell their friends too – I got my phone from House of Phones they are a little more expensive but aren't they lovely caring people they helped me download and print Katie's picture when she won the art competition and didn't charge me a penny for it. Job done.

But remember, this discussion has been focused on Segment 1, which are over 60s non-techs. Segment 2 may be university students, who may view it completely differently and say I'll just get the phone. Some may subscribe to the Techie Squad for £8/month, and others may not. Their values are different to Segment 1 (over 60s non-techs). In this case, you may have a special pricing structure or special offers for students.

So once again, pricing is more of an emotional issue and driven by the values of the customer, so it is a strategic act of marketing and business.

Having discussed the second main Tactic, *Pricing*, let's move along the line to the next *Tactic*, which is *Place*.

2.26

Tactic 3: Place –
Which We Will Rename As Path

By this, marketers mean the Place where you sell your products. It is the *channel,* i.e., the *distribution channel* for selling your products and services. It is also called *route to market.* Examples of these channels can be distributors, direct online sales, franchisees, own sales force, retail outlets, concessions in other outlets, e.g., Estee Lauder have their own booth in Macy's or Harrods, or online portals or seller platforms like Amazon, eBay etc..

For example, Sony has a multiple channel strategy – they sell online directly and through computer retailers like PC World, online platforms like Amazon... Dell, however, used to sell only through their own direct channel and didn't use distributors; this is because their primary market segment was corporations rather than individuals. They have recently changed and are using multiple channels.

I'm not fond of the word Place. It was initially coined to suggest a marketplace, in other words, a *physical* place where you go to do your selling. It worked at that time, but the term considers the market to be static. In today's day and age, channels are much more dynamic, and thanks to ecommerce and platforms like Amazon, they are much more dynamic. We need a modern term for channels, and so we will rename it as Path. i.e., the Path to our market. It's more appropriate as we are speaking about route to market or channels.

The choice of channel will, yes, you've guessed it, be driven by the Value Onions of the market segment, so it is a strategic choice. i.e., we will select the set of channels that best serve the Value Onions of the market segment. Sadly, in reality, in almost all cases, it isn't done this way. The channel decision is usually based either on cost or to keep control, driven by ego or fear. Let me explain. In considering the channel decision, you may say we need to expand into Europe. Then someone will give you one of these two suggestions:

1. **Great, let's use distributors.** You ask why, answer: well because it's cheaper as distributors will take the major financial burden, so there is less risk for us. Quite logical, but is this a cost-driven mentality or a strategic mentality driven by market segments and Value Onions? The answer is obvious. Logic, as we have shown many times, not correctly contextualised in Strategy is frankly deluded foolishness.

2. **Great, let's set up our own outlets and sales organisation.** You ask why, answer: well because in that way we can keep control over the market rather than relying on distributors who may not give us complete information or even try and take business away from us. Again logical, but is it driven by fear, ego and need to control or a strategic mentality of genuinely serving our customer's values? The answer again is obvious.

So, choosing the channels, like all *Tactics*, is a strategic decision. As *Strategy = market segments + Value Onions*, we must select those channels which suit and serve our customer's values. If this means we need to invest, then that's what we must do. Because the return on the investment will be much more significant and surer than a cost or control driven decision. Further, remember the last step of the Christmas Tree is Finance which will check and confirm the viability of the decision and the risks. On the rare occasion that we have to go back and adjust the channels for financial viability, we can relook at it. But again, on the rare occasion, I have seen this happen. The analysis showed the fault lay in either poor selection of market segments or discovering their true Value Onions.

A simple model for making strategic decisions on which channels to use for your business. The structure of this model is exactly the same as the SVOC model earlier. Please refer to that model to these four steps in making great channel decisions.

1. Complete Table 1 as in SVOC – Include customer's values which are channel dependant e.g., product availability locally, fast repairs and maintenance, product advice, choice of brands etc.. Score up the table.

2. In Table 2 of SVOC, replace the two columns showing us and the competitor with the channel choices for example – own ecommerce site; distributors; owned shops; franchisees. Expand it from two columns for example if you are deciding between four channels then use four columns and distribute the scores for each value from a total of 20 rather than 10 as used in SVOC Table 2.

3. Multiply Table 1 by Table 2 to give Table 3 as in SVOC. Look at the totals at the bottom and choose the channels with the highest numbers. The higher the total in any column, the better that channel is in serving the full Value Onion of that market segment.

4. Look at the pairs of numbers of your chosen channels and develop action plans to support and help those channels to improve their responses for the outer layers of value. This is true building of collaborative partnerships for mutual success with your channel.

HoP's Channels or Path

The chosen market segment we are discussing is over 60s non-techs. Based on their lives, values, and preferences, we wouldn't exactly choose to sell the Techie Squad service online, would we? They are non-tech. So, we would prefer to have the Techie Squad in selected shops, and only those where these people live, so in shopping malls or streets of urban residential areas and not in the city's business district. Whereas for segment 2, university students, we would choose the online channel, university campus shops, etc..

So again, by taking a proper strategic approach to making the channel decision, we will achieve far greater success.

Having discussed the first three *Tactics* (Ps) on the Christmas Tree, *Product* (the Response Onion), *Price, Path*, let's go to the fourth: *Promotion*.

Remember we are planning *Tactics* sequentially. Which means you first need to plan *Product*, then *Price, Path, Promotion, Processes, People* and so on.

For clarity, marketers put *Promotion* before *Path (Place)* in the marketing mix. It makes sense to reverse that as your promotion actions will vary depending on the channel, i.e., the *Path* you choose.

2.27

Tactic 4: Promotion –
Which We Will Rename As Perception

By this, marketers are really speaking about marketing communications or trendily known as *marcoms*. It's a basket of methods for reaching out to the market and telling them how brilliant we are. This includes advertising, branding, PR, sponsorships, social media, blogs, seminars and conferences, exhibiting in trade fairs, mail outs, email out campaigns, and the list goes on.

I don't like the word *Promotion* as it is too narrow and refers to just one part of marketing communications - special offers. *Promotion* is, for example, *buy one get one free; get $10 off on your next visit etc..*

But there is a much better word to describe marcoms, and that word is *Perception*.

Think about it. This is what we are really doing through this *Tactic* or activity, building a perception in the mind of our customers of how well our Response Onion serves their Value Onion.

From now on, we will replace *Promotion* with *Perception*. Also, this is the fourth *Tactic* and must be planned after *Path* because depending on the *Path* (channel) we choose, e.g., online sales, distributors, franchisees etc.., it will change the *Perception* activities. For example, if we decide to sell through distributors, then we will invest in and manage the branding, and they will do the local promotions and advertising. In contrast, if we decide to go directly, we will do the advertising as well.

Getting back to HoP's business and plan, i.e. their Christmas Tree, let's speak about Perception.

HoP's Perception Tactic

Yes, you guessed it. It is the market segment's Value Onions that will determine the Perception activities we choose. As the customer segment we are discussing is over 60s non-techs, it would be inappropriate to advertise The Techie Squad on MTV. We have to choose channels or media which these folks use, like drama channels on TV in the evening. Far from stereotyping, I am looking for appropriateness.

For Segment 2, university students, you may well choose MTV, but the features you advertise and value highlighted would be different and relevant to those customers. So again, *Perception* is an activity decided on by strategic relevance.

Are there only four Ps in marketing/business? Not at all. There is a fifth and sixth, and more.

- **People** –who will be needed to do it; their recruitment, training, management.

- **Processes** – every process, e.g., IT, finance etc.. is only there to respond to the market; therefore, in marketing.

- **Production** – we make because and only because there is a market need of value for it.

- **Procurement** – Buying to deliver the perfect Response Onions

- **Partnerships** – collaborations for example with suppliers, distributors, advisors

Frankly, stick a P in front of any area of the business, and it will be in marketing. In other words, everything in a business/ organisation only exists to support our responses to the Value Onions of the market. It is therefore in marketing and hence a *Tactic* of the business. Any business element that can't be identified to the Value Onions of our segments - throw it out. To be fair, many marketers now include *People* in the Ps but once again not properly driven from Value Onions.

How Is This Marketing?

Someone on a program recently challenged me on this. He said, 'We have a customer credit receivables team. How are they in marketing?'

I said, 'Before I answer, let me ask you, aren't the receivables team members communicating with the client? Do they have an opportunity to discover value from a customer credit point of view and then propose a response solution to it?'

'Yes.'

'Then we have established they are in our new definition of marketing.'

Let's take an example. Understand the customer's Value Onion relating to credit lines. For example, a customer whose business is seasonal.

The Turkey Farmer

Let's say a Turkey Farmer pays large deposits in January, when he has high cash availability – due to Christmas sales – on the goods he needs in the rearing season in summer. A supplier might give him more extended credit facilities at other times and so on.

I'm not saying there aren't late payment issues with customers, and in some cases, you may well have to make tougher decisions. But looking at the issue – behind the issue – and building relationships with your customers, you will see more value than problems and be able to offer much more creative solutions to respond to their values, building trust and a lot more sales and profits.

Briefly, let's look at a couple of the Ps of *People* for HoP.

HoP's People Tactic

One question around *People* maybe what are the profiles of these techies in The Techie Squad? Given that we are discussing the market segment of over 60s non-techs whose outer layer of the Value Onion is about the love for and communication with their grandchildren, photos and videos, then the profiles of the techies need to match those values. For example, they need to be brilliant youngsters on technology but can express this simply in non-tech language and can communicate with a lot of patience and care. These become the qualities you would look for in the interviews. To serve Segment 2, university students, you may be searching different qualities.

So again, people across the organisation must match and respond to customer Value Onions. It's not just for customer-facing people but everyone without exception, as they are all working on some part of the *Tactic*s on the Christmas Tree.

All *Tactics* on this tree are a function of the *Strategy* level preceding *Tactics*, i.e., everything and everyone in the organisation is linked to, because of and driven from Value Onions of chosen market segments.

Conclusion on Tactics

- Tactics are a function of the Value Onions of the market segments with whom we have chosen to work.

- They are made up of the so-called Ps of marketing:

  Product (which we define as the full Response Onion)

  Price

  Path

  Perception

  People

  Processes

  Production

  Procurement

  Partnerships

  In-fact everything...

Plan these step by step in this order, and all your programs, projects, action plans will be well executed.

- The most radical departure in this method from current practice is the structural and newly defined line in our Christmas Tree called *Strategy*. All these *Tactics* and all their elements – projects, actions, resources, people, etc.. exist for one reason alone: to make a success of the responses to customer's value. If something doesn't trace back to the value, then throw it out – it's unnecessary and frankly a waste.

2.28

Financials –
The Final Step On The Christmas Tree

Having completed the planning of *Tactics*, our entire business plan will now be expressed qualitatively. Showing what we need to do with full execution details, people involved, resources required etc.. By using numerical estimations, we need to quantify the plan, giving us its viability and true financial potential.

Financials are made up of four main elements:

- Income statement or Profit & Loss account
- Balance sheet
- Cash flow forecast
- Return on Investment (ROI)

Discussing these in detail is out of the scope of this book. We will cover it in the sequel, where I will also simplify financials and break a lot of myths and complications. But even more importantly, you will see the financial numbers making incredible business sense within our revolutionary method of the Christmas Tree, tying every $ back to that indisputable point, the Value Onions of our customers. This is strategic business financial management.

We will take a few examples of this below but first, let's discuss the problem today.

In our planning process with The Christmas Tree, *Financials* are the last part to be developed. This will make more sense when we discuss it below. Yet too many organisations, in fact, almost all put it at the top. They set financial targets and then set about planning to justify them. In this desperation, they either miss the full opportunities or end up in trouble through wastage and misplaced financials. It also puts pressure and fears in the organisation and the teams who spend their lives in desperation of trying to meet these targets and the fear if they miss them, they will be reprimanded or thrown out. Is this an environment where creativity, initiative, taking responsibility, innovation, collaboration, motivation can flow with ease and beauty? How can it? I have seen many companies burn themselves and even blow themselves out because of this desperate target motive. Sadly, it's happening in most corporations right now, albeit to different degrees. In your own?

Just see how appropriately this analogy of the Christmas Tree is working. Where is any tree rooted? And from where it is nourished with vital nutrients? Of course, in the soil at the bottom and from this point, it is held solidly, upright against wind, rains and storms. That is the exact position of finance for a company, nourishing, nurturing, strengthening, and protecting it and not burdening it from the top to bring it down, as we described in the previous paragraph. But we must understand that finance is the enabler and one of the results of business success and not the driver. The driver of business success is single-pointedly our markets and their Value Onions and how well we can respond to those values and support that response.

Let's then look at this conversion of the qualitative plan to the financial one for HoP.

HoP's Financials

We will take a couple of examples from the *Tactics* line of our Christmas Tree for HoP.

In responding to over 60s non-techs with The Techie Squad, let's take the P of *People* from the *Tactics* line. If we plan to roll out the Techie Squad in two hundred HoP shops with two Techies in each shop, we will need to recruit four hundred Techies within six months.

- They will have a salary of $35,000 per annum, so the salary total of $14m will go into the Income Statement.
- They will each need a laptop costing $1,200, so $480,000 will go into the Balance Sheet as an asset. This is from the P of processes for IT.

These are just a couple of examples of the conversion of *Tactics* to *Financials*. In the same way, looking at this response of the Techie Squad to the Value Onion of over 60s non-techs across all the Ps, we will convert the qualitative tactics to financials.

Another example is running local promotions in the two hundred shops costing $20,000 per shop, looking at the P of *Perception*. Now $4m will go into the Income Statement.

Can you see that with this linear relationship M-V-O-S-T-F every step is linked, derived from and traced back to the top and most importantly, it is driven from and linked back to the Strategy (i.e., customers and their Value Onions).

The $14m in the salary line of the income statement in the financials is due to the four hundred Techies needed to launch the Techie Squad in two hundred shops in four months responding to the outer layer of the Value Onion of over 60 non-techs, i.e. love for and communication with grandchildren with photos and videos on WhatsApp etc.

2.29

Objectives

Having discussed *Strategies, Tactics* and *Financials* on the Christmas Tree, we now speak about *Objectives*.

If you remember, we said it doesn't make sense to start the planning process with objectives. To do so would be an expression of desire rather than an outcome reasoned through strategy. Reasoned here means going via a strategy and finding the destination. In business, don't set your destination – discover it through *Strategy*. This is a radical departure from traditional practices.

Definition: *Objective* is the destination. It tells us where we will get to by when. It doesn't say anything about how we will get there or what we have to do.

I am a simple person and work in straightforward terms like where, when, how, who, what etc.. And that's what we need. It has worked for all organisations I have had the good fortune and honour to transform to success. We are distanced from the over-complex definitions and elaborate theories that may be intellectually stimulating, but at best, get you nowhere and at worst create a mess, conflicts, and divisions.

2.30

Smart Objectives Revisited And Adjusted

Before speaking about the objectives for HoP, let's explore a famous old, globally used and handy acronym to test the strength of our objectives – SMART. All objectives need to be SMART, and frankly, any discussion of objectives without speaking about SMART would probably leave you frustrated. So here is a reminder of what it stands for currently.

Objectives must be:

S = Specific

M = Measurable

A = Achievable (or Attainable)

R = Realistic

T = Time-bound (i.e., when is it expected to happen)

It's a five-part test and having set your objectives, you need to check that these five elements are satisfied in your objectives. It's excellent, but two vital elements are missing for me, so let's adjust it without destroying the acronym.

Firstly, correct me if my English is weak, but how can something Realistic not be Achievable? And if it is Achievable, it must, by definition, be Realistic.

So, let's replace the A with the word *Ambitious*.

Now an objective that is Ambitious and Realistic will make it much smarter. Why do I say this? Time and time again, helping organisations, I find they tend to under-set the objectives. It's just human nature and almost driven by a subtle and subconscious fear of failure or non-achievement. We are not even aware of it. You will see later in this section the best way to set objectives beyond fears and yet be realistic. So please don't fear making your objectives Ambitious. The fourth test, Realistic, will ensure it remains achievable. How will this happen?

Secondly, on the S and M in the acronym, have you ever tried to measure something not specific? If something is Measurable, it must be Specific; and if it is specific, it will be measurable.

So now we are wasting one of these letters.

Let's keep Measurable and replace the S. I'll use a little artistic licence, but you'll get the point, and it will keep the integrity of SMART.

Let's say you are heading to a destination with a group of friends. You must all agree on that destination; otherwise, there will be arguments, disagreements, conflicts, and dissatisfaction, resulting in the destination never being achieved. This is the sad reality in most organisations. It is why we say there must be a collective buy-in to the objective, and all are agreed on it.

So, let's replace the S (specific) with the word Sellable. i.e., an objective must be one we can sell to everyone to get the 'buy-in'.

With these two changes our SMART acronym becomes:

S = Sellable (getting buy-in)

M = Measurable

A = Ambitious

R = Realistic

T = Time bound (i.e. when is it expected to happen)

Now that's a super-smart objective. How to get to it? – I'll make it clear and straightforward for you later in this section. It's a promise.

HoP's Objectives

Having defined objectives and the five-element test to make it smart, let's say that one of HoP's objectives is to increase its subscribers (customers) by one point one million in eighteen months from now. So doing the SMART test:

- Sellable – it's based on market surveys and what we can do for the market.

- Measurable – 1.1 million is a specific target and thus measurable.

- Ambitious – it's an aggressive target, but with our Christmas Tree to serve our customer's value, there should be no fear to achieve it.

- Realistic – the Christmas Tree shows us it is entirely attainable.

- Time-Bound – 18 months from now.

This is one of the objectives by way of an example. They may have four or five more (not too many) like revenue and profits, market share, brand expansion etc..

2.31

The Linear Relationship

Summarising HoP's planning of *Strategies > Tactics > Finance*

STRATEGY

*   Customer/market segment = Over 60s non-techs
*   Value Onion (outer layer) = Love for and communication with grandchildren with photos and videos on WhatsApp

TACTICS + FINANCE

1. Product i.e. Response Onion (outer layer) = The Techie Squad
2. Priced at $65/month for 1.1m customers = $858m in the sales revenue line in the Income Statement for the year
3. Promotion - $20k/shop = $4m in the Income Statement
4. People – two hundred shops, four hundred Techies at a salary of $35k = $14m in the Income Statement
5. Process (IT) – a laptop each at $1,200 = $480,000 in the Balance Sheet as assets

The 60 Seconds Rule - To ensure this linear relationship is working, I use the 60 seconds rule as follows. In organisations where we have fully installed the Christmas Tree, I can walk down the corridor in that company, and the first person I see, I ask the question, *What are you working on?* (i.e., the *Tactic*). It could be the CEO or a secretary in the accounts department. If within 60 seconds they can tell me, then all is well:

> I'm working on XYZ project.
>
> Which helps to make the response to that Value Onion of those customers.
>
> Which will make us reach that objective by then.
>
> And this is how it achieves our Vision and aligns to the Mission.

If not, it's back to the drawing board. The beauty is that where they have been committed to and diligent in making the Christmas Tree, we get the answers and don't need to go back to the drawing board. It's powerful, clear, and satisfying.

Cost Appropriation V Cost Reduction

Here is another fascinating observation I'd like to share with you. Having completed the entire Christmas Tree exercise, planning all the Tactics and then down to the Financials. We then take a step back and look at all of the processes in the organisation. Each business unit, function or department lists and considers every single process. Then for each process, we ask the simple question: *which layer of which customer's Value Onion is this process serving?* If they can identify the process as helping serve the important Value Onion layers of strategic customers. If not, then it is unceremoniously and surgically removed. By doing this, every time without exception, we can eliminate between 20 and 30% of costs. In other words, we achieve absolute relevance, and irrelevant costs stand out, identify themselves staring you in the face and flashing themselves saying, remove me. Can you imagine how much anxiety and trouble we face desperately having to cut costs. How do we know they are the right ones to eliminate and what damage will be caused by their removal? Our newly defined cost appropriation beats cost-cutting hands down, no contest.

There Is No Such Thing As Cost

Any process and therefore the cost associated with it exists and only exists to serve the Value Onions of our chosen customer segments, end of the story. But the key point here is that we need to identify and link the cost to the Value Onion layers. The Christmas Tree Model protects us, enriches our actions and makes us more profitable.

With this in mind, I'd like to tell you there is no such thing as costs or expenses. Perplexed? I can understand.

There are no such things as costs or expenses; there is only investment. If the marker pen on this table in front of me costs $2, I say that's an investment. I know the accountants among you will correctly say, *No, no, the pen is an expense in the income statement and not an asset in the balance sheet; therefore, it's not an investment.* Sure, I fully agree from an accounting point of view, but we are not speaking of accounting mechanics but business reasoning.

When you reason in costs and expenses, it feels like a negative thing, sunk, gone, and reduced profits. When you reason in investments, you automatically reason in that 'R' word, *returns.*

Expenses cost and reduce profits, but investments are great as they serve values and, as a result, generate more profit as more is bought at better prices. If the marker doesn't work and we have to stop the meeting to get a fresh one, it's not just the $2, which is the real cost, but the time wasted for the twelve people in the meeting. They could have used that time to make valuable business decisions that would return strong results. We can also call this opportunity costs. The focus here is that in real terms, that marker is serving vital value and is returning results, so it is an investment rather than cost. I'm speaking of a mindset, a way to think and reason in business rather than an accounting mechanism.

In the Christmas Tree Model, every dollar is associated with value, and every value has the right amount of dollars assigned to it. It's a fail-safe, cost preventing, value serving and profit increasing methodology which is working today in the many organisations where we have installed it and bringing significant growth and strong results.

Costs Relevant To Value = Investment

To nail this point, here is a fun example.

The Green Sofa

Vijay, is the CEO of an IT company that exclusively handles the IT of one of the biggest retail organisations in the world.

When I visited him, Vijay was in a rage and very upset. I asked him what was wrong, and he said, 'Just look at these guys, speaking about his directors. They aren't serious and behave unprofessionally, bringing up petty issues. Please do something with them, coach them, train them, whatever you need to do but shape them up.'

I said, 'Relax, Vijay and tell me what happened.'

'Our mother company has given us the mandate to do business with other customers in the open market, which is a great opportunity. We have a strategy to build, and these guys are concerned with petty issues. Rakesh was in my office just before you came, and he complained that the sofa in his office isn't big enough. I'm so upset.'

I said, 'Call Rakesh and ask him to show you which sofa he wants? Oh, a Roche Bobois? The dark green one with a yellow pattern? How much $15k? No problem at all. I'll get it ordered.'

Now Vijay is looking at me perplexed, thinking I've lost my senses, too.

I said to him, 'As Rakesh is leaving your office, just ask him, 'By the way, which Value Onion layer of which customer segment is this sofa serving'?'

It's a simple question.

'If he can answer that going out on the open market, there is a tremendous opportunity with media companies; and from an $100m market this year, we can win a 4% share, i.e., over $4m, as media companies are impressed with designer sofas – it's their value. 'Then dear Rakesh, have two sofas and a bigger office too!

However, if he can't identify that outlay of $15k to a viable return via the serving of Value Onions, the answer is simple. When we inculcate this thinking, Rakesh himself would accept the *no* happily. Frankly, he would never bring that expenditure to Vijay in the first place, knowing it's not an investment with returns.'

Do you see how simple it is? In all organisations where we have implemented the VORO, SVOC and Christmas Tree models - their thinking, planning, conversations, and execution have been simplified. Conflicts are significantly eliminated, and we move forward constructively and collaboratively to success.

Linearity Is Vital

That linear link M-V-O-S-T-F in the Christmas Tree means that everything we do, spend and even think is crystal clear and makes sense.

Sadly in most organisations, most of the time, it doesn't work this way. Top management go on Mission and Vision away-days; Directors write the Strategy - complicated and not through Value Onions. Across the organisation, managers write tactics and implementation plans; finance people develop budgets with wishful inputs from managers and so on. It's all disjointed, confusing, and at best complicated, at worst hap-hazard and damaging to the organisation. It's no one's fault, and the intention is mostly excellent. However, what is missing is a shared language, thinking and practical framework to make it happen.

Thankfully that's what we now have.

2.32

Missions And Visions

Having discussed *Objectives, Strategies, Tactics* and *Financials* on the Christmas Tree, Let's now go back to the top and discuss the first two steps, *Mission and Visions*.

Why are we talking about this at the end? I'll explain it later in this section with a fascinating insight.

First, let me ask you this question, do you like Missions and Visions?

Most people reply *No*. Others say *Yes* because they can unite everyone behind a common goal. Yet even those who say *yes* will add a *but*. They say *yes... but...* they are often too long, confusing, insincere, slogans, textbook-style positive messages with no substance behind them and even lies because we are saying one thing but doing another.

Most political leaders and parties are perfect examples of this insincerity. Their manifestos – which are similar to *Mission and Visions* – are clearly constructed for the self-interest of being elected to power. There is little care for the Value Onions of the electorate. In power, they are obsessed with protecting their position, reputation and retaining control.

This is not a political message but an analysis of the dis-ingenuity of our messages and behaviour, which is a counter-indication to the integrity of bringing value and being a genuine valuepreneur. But I want to emphasise that by taking this example, I am not saying that all *Missions and Visions* are written with a lack of integrity. I am just taking an extreme case. Most people are well-intentioned, but they just didn't have the clarity of simple thinking and framework to make it happen well.

The valuepreneur will be better equipped.

We can conclude so far that *Missions and Visions* are a great thing, and if done well, they have the power to unite everyone on a common destination and inspire the people in the organisation. The issue then is what is the meaning of *done well*, and how can this happen? There are many fascinating intellectual definitions but rarely practical and implementable.

With our new thinking through The Christmas Tree, let's re-define *Missions and Visions* conclusively, remove ambiguity and use them for excellent outcomes.

2.33

Definition of Missions and Visions

Firstly, what I am calling *Missions* others may call *Visions* and vice-versa. It's not important, and frankly, you can call them apples and pears, but what is important is that they are linearly linked through M >V > O > S > T > F and in *The 60 Seconds Rule* can be easily traced back from everything we do.

So here goes.

Mission

The big picture is the reason for our existence, our raison d'être. What is our reason for existence as an organisation or through the work we do as an individual? Of course, it is to serve the value of our customer, and remember I'm using the word *customer* liberally to mean anyone whose value we serve with our skills, knowledge, and resources.

It's clear that our Mission in life is to bring value, and it's the same for any organisation.

As a doctor, it is to help people live longer and enjoy doing what they do. As a road sweeper, it is to help people live life with sanitation and enjoy living in an aesthetically pleasing environment.

This is our *Mission* and, therefore, the reason we exist, our raison d'être. So, *Mission* in our Christmas Tree doesn't speak about me. It shouldn't say who I am and what I do. It is about someone else, i.e., who's value I serve.

Keep to this simple path of thinking. You will avoid the constant muddle people and organisations get into and say ridiculous crass things like we are the best in the world etc.. – it's meaningless, probably untrue, and misleading to people inside and outside the organisation.

Anything we do must begin from the outside.

Think about what you do, this could be your work, charity, activity, and in all cases, someone will somehow benefit from it. Ask yourself who and how.

Remember the janitor in NASA who was asked by the US President, *What are you doing today?* He answered, *Putting a man on the moon, sir.* It was his *Mission.*

Remember Klara, who was developing digital applications? She didn't even realise that her work's end outcome was to protect and improve the livelihoods of poor farmers in rural Africa. It was her *Mission* in this project. Think of your work, your talent, skills and the true impact it brings to whom and their value? This is *Mission.*

The Final Definition Of Missions

The big benefit brought to whom by my existence on a broader time scale. It doesn't speak about me but their values. We will take a couple of examples after discussing *Visions.*

Vision

In the big picture, this is the look and feel of what I/we will be and look like in the medium to long term to serve that Mission. So unlike *Mission*, the *Vision* talks about me and what I need to be and have. It's my *Vision* of me to serve the *Mission* of others' values.

Linearly, this is making so much sense, especially to a true Valuepreneur. Again, this is a departure from most straight entrepreneurs who first think about what it will bring me, and then to whom can I sell it to make more money. Yet valuepreneurs are wealthier. No wonder there is confusion over definitions and the usage of *Missions and Visions*. They tend to be poor, counter-productive, and disliked due to the self-motive and the diminished integrity as a result.

I am not saying that all entrepreneurs lack integrity. What the best ones do intuitively, i.e., serve value, is what I am making sure of by this framework of the Christmas Tree.

Entrepreneurship is excellent because it shows comfort with risk, taking opportunities, creating and financial success. Valuepreneurship is all that and much more because it drives from the position of bringing value and generates greater outcomes and results for all.

Suppose Klara's *Mission* in her current work is to improve the livelihoods of poor farmers and small businesspeople in rural Africa. In that case, her *Vision* may be to become a leading expert in designing digital applications for the banking world, work for an organisation specialised in developing digital apps and build a team of programmers with digital skills.

Again, it always starts with what value of whom exists within the context of my work, which becomes my *Mission*. Then comes what I will do and be to serve this *Mission*, and this is our *Vision*. In other words, what I will look like to serve the *Mission*.

Now, look at this fascinating observation – on a macro level which onion is the *Mission* representing? That's right, the Value Onion. The *Vision* represents the Response Onion.

Just look at the consistency of our approach and framework. The Value Onion precedes and determines the Response Onion. We have maintained this theme from the beginning of the book, and it makes excellent sense. Further down the Christmas Tree, we find the same order at the micro-level.

On the *Strategy* level sits the Value Onion of specific customer segments. After that, the Response Onion sits at the *Tactic* level as the first P (product) and corresponds layer by layer to the Value Onion. It's simple, it's logical, it's magical. It is even more magical as I have had the privilege of implementing it in many corporations and organisations around the globe. Their results are spectacular, as shown in the many examples I have shared with you. These results are not only financial results but uplifting and inspirational for the people in and out of the organisation.

HoP's Mission And Vision
In The Context Of The Techie Squad Project

These are just examples of the kind of statements we can make, and they are within the definitions.

The Mission

Help people unfamiliar with technology to easily connect with younger family members like grandchildren with photos, videos and messages with modern methods without an expert.

Mission Definition Reminder

The big benefit to whom by my existence in the broader time frame. It doesn't speak about me but their values:

The Vision

Provide full technical support to 2.5 million senior users by 20xx included in the contract price. A support organisation for non-tech seniors, the Techie Squad in seven hundred shops in three years.

Vision Definition Reminder

The big picture look and feel of what I/we will be and appear in the medium to long term to serve that mission.

Can you see the linearity in these Mission and Vision statements?

They could be written in many different ways, and I'm sure you are thinking of some as you read it. That's fine.

The main point is the simple definition and logical flow starting with the external world whose value we are serving, followed by what I will be to serve it.

2.34

Five Further Key Points On Missions And Visions

It Can Be A Combination Of Two To Three Statements. If they are long and complex, which is often the case, they will be counter-productive. At the same time, you may need two or three short statements to be complete, don't be scared of that, and so long as you are in the definitions, they will be concrete.

Where do you practically see *Missions and Visions?* Through the whole Christmas Tree and especially throughout all the *Tactics,* i.e., in the *Product* (the Techie Squad for senior non-techs), *People, Processes* – they are all designed to, and only to bring value.

Value Statements speak about the moral, ethical, and behavioural values that we need to have as an organisation. They are not to be confused by the word *value* we have used throughout this book, i.e., the Valuepreneur.

Examples of points in value statements: We will:

- Conduct business with honesty and integrity

- Protect the rights of all stakeholders we interact with

- Be a listening organisation respecting each other's views

- Deal with suppliers with fairness, for example make timely payments

These value statements are not in the linear relationship of M-V-O-S-T-F but sit alongside *Missions and Visions*. They are practical and real, and you should see them in all *Tactics*. For example, if you say you are a listening organisation – then in the P of *People*, are you recruiting people who listen well and do you genuinely encourage the flow of ideas and listen to them. Let's say you have five values in your value statement in all actions and projects at the *Tactic* level, do a five-point check that you are keeping to and not breaching any of the five values in all tactics.

Who Are Missions And Visions For And Used By?

Missions are for stakeholders external as well as internal to the business, that is:

- Customers – who will clearly understand how their values are served

- Suppliers – who are clearer in supplying the most appropriate goods and services to the company to in turn serve its customers better,

- Financiers – to understand the business plan and have confidence in its strength and viability.

- Employees will gain the clarity of common purpose and be inspired to serve, innovate, and collaborate.

- Shareholders – ensuring the business is on track keeping to their mandate.

Visions are principally for internal stakeholders – mainly the people in the organisation to be clear on and contribute to the direction of travel and destination to reach.

Externally, *Visions* can help investors and financiers to understand the plans and resourcing requirements. They are not intended, however, for customers.

Are They Changeable?

What do you think? Should we or should we not change them?

The answer I often get is *no* because if we do, people will think the management is out of control and lose credibility. Well, here lies the problem, is this a valuepreneurial logic or self-preservation like many Prime Ministers and Presidents? Too many so-called leaders sadly think and work in this way. They only change Missions and Visions when they are newly appointed to stamp their presence, *I* have arrived, *it's my way*. They force their authority and want everything in the organisation to change even if the previous regime worked well.

Is this valuepreneurship? Or the worst of personal egos?

For example, a US President who reverts the Climate Change Accord already set, or the Nuclear Agreement or Obamacare. Yet, I have seen the rare courageous leader who works in the interest of the company and the customers and is happy to preserve what works and change what needs to change to serve customers' value with integrity genuinely.

Martyn D, is one such leader. As the new CEO of a business, he asked me to help him strengthen the team and company. He worked strategically and valuepreneurially and first looked to preserve the team and keep the projects which were serving value instead of just replacing them to stamp his presence. Five years down the line, 85% of people are the same, but the business has shaped up and grown exponentially and is much more profitable. People in the organisation feel valued, attrition is negligible, and satisfaction high. Creativity and innovation flow with excellent collaboration.

So, the answer to whether we should change Missions and Visions is a resounding YES. Why? Because the market and customer Value Onions are constantly changing and evolving. This is the only certainty we have, and not changing our Response Onions will mean we are not serving true values and suffer. Changes to the Response Onion, keeping linearity and the linking through the Christmas Tree, will then necessitate changes in all the *Tactics* – *People, Processes* etc..

Organisations who did not change their *Missions/Visions* and hence *Strategies* got into serious trouble.

Think about Kodak, who doggedly stuck to film when the world was going digital. They were destroyed. The same with Nokia, Blackberry, Woolworths, Xerox, even the United Nations – the list goes on.

People say it was competition that destroyed them. I disagree. New companies will see a need and respond to it.

So yes, although the market gets taken away from the existing company, the problem remains with the current company for not keeping up with the changing nature of the customer segments and their Value Onions, shifting their M-V-O-S-T-F accordingly.

Toyota is one such organisation with moves in line with and a little ahead of Value Onions by listening and anticipating the changes. Google is another one. Apple used to be, but the future is questionable. The recent announcement from a hardware focus to being a media platform for videos and news is yet to be seen as a good or bad idea. It could be a masterstroke if it has found gasping unserved Value Onions of key market segments, but if it is a desperate knee jerk competitive response to Netflix, then it could be a disaster.

2.35

Don't Change Your M-V-O-S-T-F At Your Own Peril

The IT Company That Decided It Didn't Need To Change

Back in the 1990s, as CEO of an Europe-wide IT company selling huge software and building applications around them, I realised a sudden and significant change in the market. It was called downsizing for those of you who remember. We took a $95m cheque from our investors, a major venture capital organisation, to build a business based on MVS (old mainframe platform). Suddenly, the market was downsizing to the new technology called Unix. I spoke to Chairman Leon and said, 'We need to completely re-strategize the entire Christmas Tree (this was the company where I had first developed the method) and move to the new platform.'

Leon said, 'I get it, but frankly, my neck will be chopped off if we go to the shareholders a year after taking that cheque.'

'Leon, your neck will be chopped off much harder by the market, which is unrelenting. At least with the investors, we have a chance to show them that we are protecting their interest, investment, and money.'

This made sense to Leon, and he said, 'Let's do it.'

It took me six weeks to completely reshape the strategy on the whole

Christmas Tree. Two days before the board meeting, I remember sitting in our head office on the twenty-fourth floor in La Défense, Paris, putting the finishing touches to the presentation with a glass of excellent red wine. It was around midnight, and Leon took a deep sigh and said, 'Sorry, Sanjeev, I can't do it.'

This is what fear does.

I said, 'Leon, my professional integrity doesn't allow me to crash the investment for people who have trusted us or work against the values of the market.'

To be fair to him, he understood and didn't stand in my way of resigning and wrote me a cheque. But it took exactly six months at the hands of the market to destroy that fantastic business – personally heart-breaking.

The moral of the story is that when you plan to the Christmas Tree as the method for planning and running your business, you will keep ahead of the changing values of the market. Then you can have the courage to shift and change the Missions and Visions and, as a result, the Objectives, Strategies, Tactics and Financials.

2.36

Who And How?

In Corporations – who will execute the Christmas Tree plan; how will they interact; how can we crucially ensure everyone is aligned? The question is essentially one of organisation structure and interaction between functions.

Here's what typically happens in most organisations – people work in functional silos. They are mis-aligned and often wastefully pulling in different directions. Parts of or most of the plan is disjointed, not adhered to and has to be constantly adjusted, costing, time, effort, money and lost objectives.

In the planning process typically, management agrees on a set of Objectives, then they think of the actions which need to happen to achieve those objectives, called programs, projects, action plans or indeed tactics. Can you already see the critical layer of the strategy, in the way we have defined it, (customer segments and their Value Onions) is missing? I'm not saying that they don't consider market segments and values; every business does, one way or the other. But either it is intuitive, therefore not robust enough in the way that we have discussed above, or it isn't planned sequentially with linearity and link between the market values and our actions. Therefore, our actions are nowhere as relevant as they can be, resulting in wasted efforts and resources.

Having stated the actions needed, they then naively set about saying who will execute them. They jump to an organisation structure around the actions or fit them into an organisational structure which is often a political exercise rather than a strictly strategic one. I see this all the time in the vast majority of the many corporations. The resulting problem? Yes, you guessed it, functional silos. They are only working through their functional roles and departments. They rely on and are defensive of their subject expertise, not questioning what value this expertise serves and how. They communicate poorly, not collaborating but justifying their position or pushing their methods and ideas forward. Conflicts arise, and the business, its customers, and shareholders, suffer. The only winners are competitors.

The diagram below shows this unhappy but accurate picture of most organisations:

Notice the missing *Value Onions + market segments* stage, which you and I now call *Strategy*.

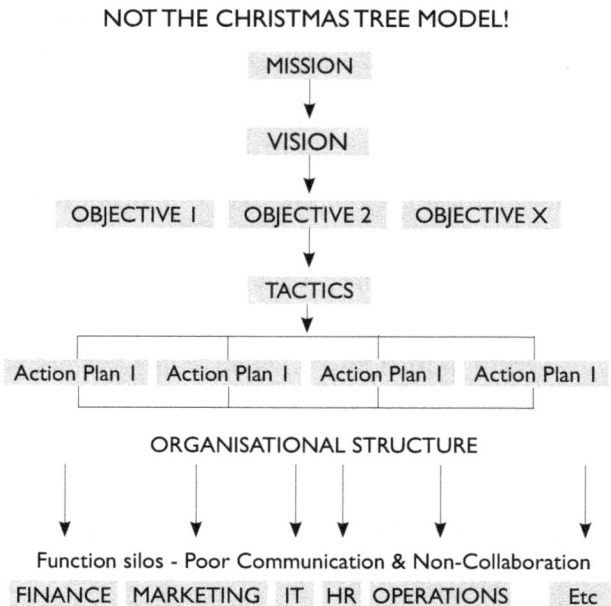

NOT THE CHRISTMAS TREE MODEL!

MISSION

↓

VISION

↓

OBJECTIVE 1   OBJECTIVE 2   OBJECTIVE X

↓

TACTICS

↓

Action Plan 1   Action Plan 1   Action Plan 1   Action Plan 1

ORGANISATIONAL STRUCTURE

↓   ↓   ↓   ↓   ↓   ↓

Function silos - Poor Communication & Non-Collaboration

FINANCE   MARKETING   IT   HR   OPERATIONS   Etc

Before giving you the answer, I want to highlight this problem with an example:

The French Cardiologist Device Company

I was recently running a strategy workshop for a huge medical device company in France, and they make clever machines in electrocardiography, a vital treatment for heart patients.

The marketing director (CMO) and the finance director (CFO) had a big disagreement. The CMO said, 'I want to recruit an extra twenty-five maintenance engineers.'

The CFO said, 'No way.'

What do twenty-five additional maintenance engineers represent to the CMO in this story? Faster response times, better customer service, stronger brand, more sales, market share, something great, right? What does it represent to the CFO? – cost, expense, i.e., something horrible.

One simple reality, which is: twenty-five maintenance engineers. One sees as something beautiful and positive; and the other's perception is of something horrible. Each has a good point from their own knowledge and expertise, but they are working in functional silos of their expertise. They conflicted, and frankly, it was getting unpleasant as the disagreement continued. So, what's missing and what's the answer? That there was no common point aligning them. This is a familiar story, and you see it all the time.

I asked the CMO *why? Why twenty-five more maintenance engineers?* That simple three-lettered question which deludes us.

He said, 'So that we can give a better service and grow the business.'

'How do you mean *better service?*'

'We could reduce the time to repair a machine when it breaks down in a hospital or clinic by half.'

'How long does it take now?'

'Nine hours... So you mean you can repair machines in 4.5 hours?'

He said, 'Four to five hours would be guaranteed. Mostly it will be repaired within three hours.'

'Wow, so how important is that for your market and to whom?'

'Well, for State hospitals in Germany, it has no impact because the way devices are funded, you can have a spare one. However, for private cardiology clinics in France, it is critical.'

'OK, and what are your competitors doing?'

'Nine hours.'

'So, it is a major point of differentiation with our customers, and if you said to the private cardiology clinics in France that we can repair in three to four hours, what would it do?'

And out came his laptop.

He named six clinics, Nantes, Paris, Lille, Toulouse, Marseilles and Rennes and said, 'For these six, this is the main problem of value, and if I can solve that, I can close the deal tomorrow.'

'Wow, at one point two million Euros each, that's seven point two million Euros straight away and a lot more behind it. And just with these six, two point five million Euros profit against twenty-five salaries just in the first three months and maybe ten million over the year.'

Then I turned to the finance director and asked, 'Would you like that?'

And suddenly, we're all on the same side. Neither was wrong. Both were right in their own way and their own context, but they were in opposition without a point of alignment.

The answer came from going back to the Value Onions of the customer segment, that is, the French private cardiology clinics and their need to have the machine operating at maximum level to provide patient treatment and save cost. In other words, if they had planned to the Christmas Tree, this argument would be most unlikely. All decisions would be driven from that ultimate point of alignment which I call the 'Point Of Zero Conflict' (Section 5), the Value Onions of our customers, i.e., the Strategy level in our Christmas Tree.

Having discussed the problem in current practice, let's go back to the original question:

Who will execute the Christmas Tree plan, and how will everyone interact? The answer is as follows:

Please look at the illustration below, entitled *Not the Christmas Tree*). Look at the bottom right of the Diagram which shows different functional departments; and follow the steps with me.

NOT THE CHRISTMAS TREE MODEL!
Most Current Practice

```
                        MISSION
                           │
                           ▼
                         VISION
                           │
                           ▼
   OBJECTIVE I       OBJECTIVE 2       OBJECTIVE X
                           │
                           ▼
                        TACTICS
                           │
                           ▼
   Action Plan I   Action Plan I   Action Plan I   Action Plan I

            ORGANISATIONAL STRUCTURE

      │         │        │   │        │              │
      ▼         ▼        ▼   ▼        ▼              ▼
   Function silos - Poor Communication & Non-Collaboration
   FINANCE   MARKETING   IT   HR   OPERATIONS        Etc
```

This is typically the way most organisations plan, the departments at the bottom show how we end up in functional silos, not speaking as one collaborative team - each pushing their own expertise and perspectives.

In our version, which is the right way and fits with the Christmas Tree, the organisation structure is more of a matrix.

Each function contributes to the *Tactics*, which have been so beautifully planned as described previously in this chapter and crucially driven from and determined by the Value Onions of specific customer segments.

So here is the magic of this whole process – 'we are aligned'.

Yes, I will repeat it loud and clear we *are* all aligned to each other by the Value Onions of customer segments, i.e., the *Strategy*. In turn, this gives us the activities or Tactics on which we can collaborate and contribute to serve responses to those Value Onions. It is indisputable, compelling, and extremely simple, and this becomes what I call the *Point Of Zero Conflict* covered in Section 5.

Now let's examine this further, applying it back to House Of Phones (HoP).

2.37

Every Function's Alignment To The Whole Business

Firstly, *all* functions and everyone in each function will align to the *Strategy* of serving the segment of Over 60 Non-tech people communicating with their grandchildren with photos, videos, WhatsApp etc.. Next, we will all align through the *Tactics*, of which the first one is the product, i.e., the Response Onion of the Techie Squad.

Each subsequent tactic – price, path, perception, people, processes- will now be planned and executed by all functions in a collaborative way aligned with that ultimate common point of alignment, the Value Onion of those customers.

For example, let's take the *Tactic* P of *People*. Who takes the lead on this? Yes, the HR function. Now all functions will align with HR as follows:

HR says here is my contribution to making the Techie Squad a successful response to this segment. And my plan is as follows:

- Objective – recruit 200 Techies in four months

- Strategy – who are these Techies, and what is their value?

They are 22-25-year-old youngsters who are technically brilliant but communicate in regular English, as customers are non-tech. Their value is that they are on social media and enjoying music and fun with others in their age group.

- Tactic – The Path to recruiting these youngsters will not be a recruitment consultancy but a fun website or Facebook page with music and competition to recommend their friends etc..

- Financials – each Techie will have a salary, let's say £20,000, so £4m (£20,000 x 200) will go as an expense in the Income Statement. Each Techie will be equipped with a laptop for £1,000 - so £200,000 will be an asset in the balance sheet and so on.

As you can see, HR's O-S-T-F is perfectly aligned to the whole company's O-S-T-F, and every individual within HR's O-S-T-F will be aligned to HR's, which is aligned to HoP's Value Onion. This is clarity, visibility, simplicity, coherence, which will generate commitment and engagement of every individual.

2.38

Cross-Functional Alignment – Perfect Communication And Conversation

Now let's consider the other functions and how they align through the people tactic. Look at diagram B below – now Finance come to HR and say dear HR in serving the value of Over 60s non-tech people through the Tech Squad we can help you. Let us know the pattern of recruitment, and we will make sure we have the budgets, cash flows, salary admin set up etc.. Marketing says, dear HR, we will help you by defining the job descriptions, as we know our customer's values and what profile of Techie is needed. IT says we will help you, dear HR – let us know the recruitment pattern, and we will ensure that as soon as a Techie is on board, we will have their laptop ready and networked…. Operations say we will help by ensuring that when a Techie joins, they have a desk, the banners, the training, etc..

So can you see every function and everyone in each function is perfectly aligned through the activities, i.e., tactics to that ultimate point of alignment, the Value Onion of the customers in the market segment served. And because of this, each one is dedicated to making the response of the Techie Squad excellent.

Another fascinating thing is happening –we have created the perfect conversation and communication between all the functions and within each function via the activities (in this example, recruitment of Techies) to serve the customer's value. This is what we call working to a common goal. Unfortunately, these terms are used as a high moral position without any substance, method, tool or practicality behind it. So now each function and person is working to a common purpose and goal, perfectly aligned, clear and in no doubt.

PRICE ON THE Value Onion
OF THE CUSTOMER

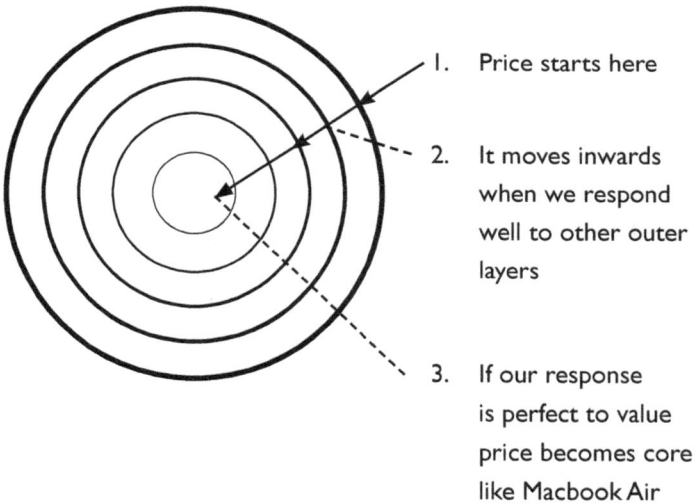

1. Price starts here

2. It moves inwards when we respond well to other outer layers

3. If our response is perfect to value price becomes core like Macbook Air

2.39

The Order Of Planning In The Christmas Tree

Big tip: *Don't set your destination, discover it.*

I will share a fascinating and valuable insight that goes against all received wisdom, but it will make sense. When you present your plan, you will first give the Mission, then Vision, Objectives, Strategies, Tactics and Financials. This seems quite logical and would make sense to the audience.

However, when you are actually developing the plan, what is the order; what is your starting point? I hear you saying, as most people do, the Objectives. Really? So, for House of Phones (HoP), can you really say that our objective is to increase our customer base by 1.1 million in 18 months? From where does this number come? Plucked out of the air? An extrapolation of historic growth? But how relevant is this to future conditions? Some ordinary market research and market shares etc..? The truth is its poor guesswork, a wish, maybe a dream. Why shouldn't the figure be one point five million or two million or half a million for that matter? So objectives can't be the starting point.

The starting point is not Missions and Visions either – which I know seems most strange. Of course, a quick initial thinking on Missions and Visions is important at the beginning only to contextualise our business and keep under a broad umbrella of the scope of our business or project. The proper Missions and Visions will be finalised at the end.

So here is the fascinating insight and radical departure from traditional wisdom:

- The starting point, my friends, is STRATEGY and therefore S-VOC. In other words, we start by saying who is out there (segments) and then what are their Value Onions. Putting these two together, if you remember, is strategy. You see, it always starts from understanding who we exist to serve and their values. The next step is to plan the *Tactics* – all the Ps in the order – *Product* (Response Onions), *Price, Path, Perception, People, Processes etc..*

- Next, we plan the *Financials* by forecasting the income generated from our strategies, segment by segment. Then the resources required and therefore costs to serve those strategies.

- From a financial standpoint, the result of these financials actually *become* your objectives, and most objectives have a financial dimension to them such as EBITDA (profits), Sales increase etc.. So, by starting with strategies, we discover objectives much more strongly than we can plan them. Also, your non-financial objectives, or those that aren't directly financial, will be clear outcomes of the S-VOC process, such as new segments to open up, market share growth, new products to develop and launch, etc..

I repeat –- in life, we can set goals and objectives, but in business: don't set your destinations, discover them.

In almost all strategy development programs of companies I have worked on, the business heads request that I start with objectives. I comply and say OK, and we spend an hour or two and come up with a set of SMART objectives. Then I say let's put that to one side and go through the whole S-VOC and Christmas Tree.

On completing this plan, I remind them of the objectives we had planned initially, but 100% of the time, the objectives which come out of the S-VOC are far greater than what had come out of their wish list at the start.

These objectives are also far more objective and reasoned against solid parameters and not just subjective guesswork. As a result, management and teams have much more confidence in them, and their commitment to the destination is much stronger. Most objectives, set as subjective guesswork, are heavily influenced by or even stipulated by the business head who is desperate to drive a result. How can we get buy-in and therefore commitment and engagement from all to achieve it. If the commitment is low, they can never take responsibility, and we all end up working for destinations we can't see or believe in, or we work towards them for fear of the boss.

Proper commitment can only happen with genuine inclusion and contribution in setting our routes to the destination and finding those destinations ourselves. Working together as a collaborative team, we achieve engagement, acceptance of and taking responsibility with pleasure, and, yes, passion.

Missions and Visions

Now, having discovered the objectives or destinations through S-VOC, you need to go back to the Missions and Visions and redefine them. Not only will they be clearer and more robust, but they will not be nebulous bland statements like we will be the best company in our industry…. Also, they will fit perfectly and linearly in the Christmas Tree.

Remember *The 60-Second Rule*?

Every step of the Tree is linked to the previous and defines the next. It is a linear link and makes perfect sense from Missions to

Financials and back in the loop again. As a reminder – the problem is that in organisations, this linear link is missing. Someone develops *Missions and Visions,* someone else the strategies, someone else the tactics and someone completely different the financials and budgets. No wonder most plans are a mess and never indeed implemented.

Most successful plans have been simple and intuitively followed a similar path to our Tree, but now we have a proper framework and can use it practically for tremendous success.

Summarising the steps in sequential order:

Presenting The Strategic Plan	Planning The Strategic Plan
• Mission	• Strategies (S-VOC)
• Vision	• Tactics (Ps)
• Objectives	• Financials
• Strategies (S-VOC)	• Objectives
• Tactics (Ps)	• Mission
• Financials	• Vision

Section 3

The Psyche And Mind
Of A Valuepreneur

3.1

A Powerful Friend or Foe

Our mind is an invaluable friend or a venomous enemy. Managed correctly, it liberates the intellect, and therefore, our creativity, application and success. Poorly handled, it will obscure our intellect, pushing us into mediocracy at best. At worst – underutilised intellectual potential, waste, missed opportunities and even failure. Let's choose a better way.

Understand the mind. Understand the nature and the working of the mind, and there's little else to understand. It obscures. It agitates. It makes us regretful, fearful, defensive, and above all, it makes us miss out on the best of us. We mostly remain hidden behind the mind. It's time to raise this veil, this curtain if we want to genuinely understand, appreciate and realise our true potential. We need to turn the mind into our invaluable servant and not remain in its servitude, subservience and be limited by it.

For example, let's imagine you're being interviewed for a big job or promotion. It's the one you really want, and you're convinced that your skills and capabilities truly merit you getting this role. But you also know you are up against tough competition. Two other colleagues are also being interviewed. But the decision-makers are also looking to hire someone from the outside. You get the scene? Now, you're preparing for the interview.

What's going through your mind? What is it saying? *I hope I get the job; I hope they understand that recruiting internally will be better than going outside; And that internally, I am the best candidate. I hope the decision-makers don't pick up on the mess made by my department last year; I'll be prepared to compromise on the salary level to get this job,* and so on. Sounds familiar?

And to a greater or lesser degree, in all situations, it's the same story. You might be asking for funding or updating your low-performing project, or asking your team to take on an unpleasant task. The mind chatters. It is agitated.

In other words, with this subjective nature of the mind, I make every situation about me. It takes me further away from objectivity, the actual situation. I'm emotionally engaged, entangled, distracted from the task at hand and the simple reality of that situation. In this interview, the best way to succeed is not to make it about me. This interview is frankly not about me. It is about the value, the success that this role will bring to the company. That's an objective direction. The mind comes in the way.

Job Applicant Interviewees

I recently visited the CEO of a major IT company in India, a client of ours, along with my Sales Head, George. As we waited in the lobby to meet the CEO, I saw ten youngsters sitting in the lobby, all looking very nervous. I turned to a young lady (Nina) and asked, 'Are you here for an interview?'

She nervously said, 'Yes Sir.'(In India, people are very respectful to grey hair!)

'Are you prepared?'

'Yes, Sir.' *(Nervously)*

'How will you handle it?'

'I've had my CV prepared professionally. I will tell them all about my experience, my skills, my education.'

'Really? And that's going to put you ahead of these other nine, is it? Do you not think they have all done the same?'

Now getting a little more nervous, which I felt terrible about, she said, 'No, Sir, I guess they will all do the same.'

So, here is the fearful, nervous, expectant mind, justifying itself, reasoning with itself, defending itself. And it's become a dangerous hindrance to getting that job. So, now what was the answer? And I knew I had disturbed her peace of mind. But what I was about to say would help her immensely. I asked, 'How many interviews are you going to this week?'

'Fifteen.'

Remember, this is the IT industry in India. People move around constantly.

Me: Out of these fifteen, you can afford to mess up one, can't you? You'll still have fourteen.

Perplexed and hesitantly, she said, 'I suppose so, Sir.'

'For your success, for your real success, make this that one.'

'What shall I do?'

'In the interview, take a genuine interest in the interviewer, the company, and what value does this job translate into - growth, the success of the project or the business. Respectfully and with determination, ask them questions and understand why – this job, this recruitment? Then and only then, talk about your experience and capabilities and CV.'(In other words, first the Value Onion, then the Response Onion.)

This approach was a massive departure from what she had known. And frankly, everyone being interviewed for any job around the world thinks in the wrong way. Their minds are preoccupied with the *me, my job, my CV, my success* rather than the *you* - your project, its success, your recruitment etc.

Can you see how this shift from subjectivity, which the mind has imposed on us, into the objectivity of their value gained, will significantly increase the chances of getting the job?

I knew I had disturbed her. But not as much as she had disturbed herself until now. And yet, she saw a ray of hope. Saying to her you can afford to mess up one of the fifteen interviews was not because she should or would mess this one up, but it was done to remove the futile, unnecessary, dangerous fear. That's all. When you play without fear and have an *I have nothing to lose* attitude, that's when your confidence is at your highest, that's when you shine and succeed.

I went into my meeting with the CEO, and I requested George to speak to Nina when she comes out of the interview and ask her how it went. George told me she came out with a big smile on her face and said, 'Please thank Sir.'

We don't know if she got the job, but she said she had never felt more confident in an interview or any testing situation. Nina mentioned that they were very open with her and showed a lot of interest in her profile. She even said, 'I think I'll get it.'

It's the mind, my friends. It's nothing but the mind. Don't allow it to suppress the best of you. Leverage it as a powerful tool, a friend and, as we've said before, an invaluable servant. Don't be a slave to it.

3.2

Three Conditions Of The Mind

1. The Mind Obscures Reality And Makes Us Presumptive

This is the first condition of the mind. It keeps us hidden from reality. It is always judging - ourselves, situations, people before and often without a proper objective understanding. We can say it is in prejudice. Look at the word *pre -judice*, i.e., judging before something. Judging before an objective analysis and intellectual understanding and seeing simple reality in its raw, absolute form without assigning values, worries, concerns and self-motivations.

It reaches conclusions with such ease and agility that there is no time to reason with it. We just react. And this is the root of conflicts. Within us as individuals or society as a whole. Israel was established. Good or bad? It depends on who you ask. It's a matter of judgement and personal perception. One person will call it an acceptable reality, and the other calls it a blunder.

A lake to someone represents beauty, pleasure and inspiration. And to another person misery because they saw someone drown. The lake is still the lake. The day that we see it without perceptions, misperceptions and complicate it by assigning values to that reality through our mind, we will derive the real benefit from it.

The mind is constantly engaged in some perception or the other. It is the source of perceptions and, therefore, often misperceptions. It sees what it wants to see or even what it fears most.

The Lost Earring

Recently, we were invited to a wedding, and close family and friends were staying in a huge mansion.

One evening, a friend of ours, Sonia, came rushing down in a panic saying, 'I've lost, I've lost it!'

She had lost a precious diamond earring. Now the search begins. Everyone is rushing around trying to find this earring. And amidst this commotion, Sonia said to me. 'Just look at the maid. I know she's done it. She stole it. And everything about the maid showed that she had stolen it. Look at her shifty eyes, she said, and the nervous look on her face.'

Ten minutes later, my niece came rushing down, saying, 'Aunty, I've found it, I've found it! It had fallen behind the sink in the bathroom'

Panic over. We settle down to tea.

Now Sonia said to me, 'I feel so bad. I am horrified with myself. Just look at the maid. She looks like an angel. The picture of innocence, how could I have blamed such a lovely person? It must be me.'

Yes, my friends, it was her. It was nothing but Sonia's mind. The girl didn't change from a thief to an angel or vice-versa. It was the misperception and misconception, fired by her agitated mind in the worry, concern, sadness of having lost a valuable object. In this misguided state, we end up taking wrong decisions, wrong actions. For example, we may want the girl searched or even call the police. But, the objective reality is that it had fallen behind the sink. The subjective misperception or prejudice that the maid stole the earring would lead us to wrong actions.

Do you see the sequence? The biases born from negative emotions of the mind lead us to wrong actions, which generate more anxieties, stresses and disharmony in the mind. Let's not disturb ourselves. Let's see it as it is.

We are victims of this presumptive condition of the mind in most life situations.

The Busy IT Team

The Director at the client asked the IT Team Manager to urgently provide a workload optimisation report – which is simply a full analysis of who was doing what and how much spare time they had. The manager and the team became very nervous as they felt certain that the client was checking on them and thinking that they were not working hard enough. Fearing the client would reduce the size of the team, they went out of their way to show they were working at over 100% occupancy, whereas the reality was close to 80%.

So again, here is the mind, jumping to conclusions, misperceiving and pre-judging. It is prejudiced. And in this presumptive, emotional reaction, they had missed the reality, which was the client had another urgent project to do. The contract for this project would be awarded to the IT team with spare capacity. But it wasn't to be, and they missed the opportunity. It was awarded to another IT company altogether because the workload optimisation report showed no available capacity. So, who lost out? And who was the architect of this loss? Yes, none other than the IT team and their manager. We cause our own downfalls, folks - don't blame it on others or situations.

Our prejudicial misperceptions, which is the first condition of the mind, not only end up with wrong conclusions and decisions, but the outcomes can often hurt us and cause damage.

Why do we inflict these wounds on ourselves?

Not looking at the mind, observing it, understanding its workings, and missing reality and objectivity is nothing short of masochism and self-inflicted harm. Get out of your way. Turn the mind away from the *me*. See reality for itself. Ask the question why. Then objectively, with a stable and fearless mind, take decisions to bring success.

A quietened mind is a magnificent mind, which will capture opportunities and utilise your intellectual potential with clarity, objectivity and completeness. In that state, you are unstoppable. How can we achieve this? – Many practical methods and techniques to follow in this Section.

Everyone Can Sing

My wife and I were running a workshop in France on music and meditation. We were teaching them to sing and use music to balance the mind and make it more available to ourselves. They were not singers per se. We started the session by asking them to sing a note I was playing. I could see hesitations, lack of confidence and to differing degrees, they were out of tune.

I said, 'Stop.' Then asked each of them to say what was going through their mind. The responses were varied and as follows:

- I'm tone-deaf

- I can't sing in front of others; I'm feeling too self-conscious

- My school choir told us people can either sing or not, and you fall in the latter category.

- I don't want to make a fool of myself.

- I'd love to be able to sing.

- Others are singing better than me.

... and so it went on.

If this is the kind of nonsense distracting our mind, we will certainly be blocked, and the reality is obscured. My presumptive nature is hyperactive: how can I ever hope to hit the note with the right tone?

I said, 'I can prove to you logically and conclusively that there is no such thing as tone deaf and that everyone can sing. You *can* sing.'

They were relieved, somewhat excited but sceptical.

I asked them, 'Has any one of you been very angry with someone recently?'

One lady put her hand up and said, 'On my way into the workshop this morning while waiting for the traffic light to go green, someone bumped into my car from behind. I was furious, it's a new car, and it was their fault.'

I asked her to re-enact what she said to the other driver, and in the exact tone, she had used. Apart from anything else, this worked out as a mini-therapy on releasing her anger! The experience of the accident was fresh and raw, and her feelings were rife, and she went for it with a full-throated expression saying, *'What the hell are you doing? Can't you see the light was red and I was stationary? You've made a dent in my brand-new car. You shouldn't be driving..........'*

She used many expletives I can't mention here. I said to everyone, 'Now listen to every syllable Florence just said. Each syllable was on a different note, musically.'

Was it monotone? Was it out of tune and awkward in sound? *'Not at all,'* they remarked. *'It was perfectly in tune!'*

Try it for yourself. When we speak, we actually sing. Intonation is singing. Choosing a situation of anger was just to get a more extreme expression to prove the point, but every conversation of ours is musical, tonal and in tune. Who says you are tone deaf? There really is no such thing. If you can speak, you can sing. Who told you that you can't sing or that you are tone deaf? Turn your back on those naïve people.

This was a revelation to the group, and the self-imposed blocking started to un-block.

To those who said they were conscious that others were observing them, I asked, 'When one of the other participants in this room was singing, were you judging them? Or looking at them negatively?'

The answer was no.

'Then why would they judge or think badly of you?'

These are the unfortunate errors of the mind which are self-created and obscure the reality from us.

I asked them to reflect on and discuss their thoughts with each other deeply. The process was a realisation of the reality which was being obscured by our minds.

Now, we asked them to hear the note again, and because the mind had been cleared of the nonsense blocking us, they could genuinely listen to it.

Our problem is that we hear a lot but listen to nothing real. We are listening to ourselves, not reality or the other person. Worse, we are listening to our own fears, worries, concerns, presumptions and manufactured falsehoods. We are subjective, i.e., distracted by distorted but powerful emotions which shape the mind and not objective, i.e., seeing reality in its' raw, naked, natural, actual form.

I recently heard a brilliant acronym for FEAR:

False

Existence of the

Appearance of

Reality

Let's examine this for our music workshop participants – that they can't sing or tone-deaf or people are judging them was FALSE. It's they who made it EXIST. The more it existed, the more it grew, snowballed, multiplied by the power of the mind, and the mind is all-powerful. As a result, it started to APPEAR as REALITY which we then owned. Things we own, we hold on to and find difficult to release.

More on this later when we discuss how to deal with difficult, angry people and harsh attitudes.

So, the secret to singing and therefore work and life itself is:

1. **Listen to the note** – the note is a vibration, a sound frequency.
   The note 'A' resonates at a frequency of 440Hertz. It's there, whether you are there or not; whether you can hear it or not. The more your mind says *I can't hear it, can't sing, or even I want to hear it,* you are over-occupied with your mind and not with the note, you will not hear it. The note here represents every simple reality, existing daily in our lives and work. Release yourself from the apparitions and obscurities of the mind. As we did for those people in the workshop, or Sonia or Anita or Andy and the many examples we have already had. Then you will engage with the frequency, the real one.

2. **When you can hear, listen to and realise the actual note,** the reality, you have a genuine chance to accord with it. Now you can produce the note as everyone's vocal cords (unless there is a medical condition) have all the frequencies needed.

Hence meditative people are better musicians. We proved that with the angry lady's expression above. Being a better musician here represents our efficiency and brilliance in everything we do at work and indeed in life.

3. **Meditate to take control of your mind** (see later on the technique). With this, you will be in charge of producing the note whenever you want, not when the mind allows it.

4. **Practice.** A young cellist was walking on a cold, dark wet evening in New York, going to play at the famous Carnegie Hall. The cello was heavy on his back, and he had been walking a while. He was lost and saw a wise old man walking past and asked, 'Pardon me sir, do you know the way to Carnegie Hall'? The wise old man said, 'Young man, practice, practice, practice!'

This story is not relevant to our topic here, but I thought you would like it anyway. I have used these four steps to singing.

Still, I hope you can see that it is parallel to show that it is precisely the method we need to adopt to do our work, live life, interact with others and ourselves. Un-obscure the mind, take control of it, see reality objectively, not subjectively, through the discomposures and turmoils of the mind, and then you will make the right decisions and follow the right actions.

3.3

Expectation Is The Killer Of Man

The mind is always wanting, which then gives rise to expectations, which then gives rise to fears and therefore, it is constantly agitated.

A mind in expectation will always be weaker, lacking confidence and is underpinned by fear. Have you noticed that our minds are always in one of two states? We either fear the future or regret the past. We are always wanting something or desiring something to happen. In this state, how is it possible to be strong?

But a giving mind, which focuses on the value that it can bring, sits in the present and its valuepreneurial. Yes, you can learn from the past. You can plan for the future. But the power of now is what makes actions the strongest.

Super Frank

In August 2005, the English football season started, and three months into it, the highest scorer in the English premier league was a mid-field player called Frank Lampard, not even a striker. He played for Chelsea.

For those not interested in football, this is not about football, but a simple human understanding. And then on the 15th of November, it was as if someone had turned a switch off and Frank scored hardly any goals for Chelsea or his country England in the following World Cup in Germany in 2006.

So, what happened? Did someone take a skill away? Can you suddenly lose your technique, your mojo! No. You're a practised, rehearsed, top expert in the sport.

So, what went wrong? It was that the mind had darted into expectation.

Now, every match when Frank comes into the field, 45,000 people are shouting, *Super Frank, Super Frank, and the headlines read, The Boy In Blue Does It Again, Frank The Golden Hope For England In Germany, Super Frank Does It Again*. It's turned into an expectation. And that expectation turns into a fear of not scoring in another match.

Now, on the pitch, hearing the *Super Frank* chants and the headlines in the newspapers resounding in his head, his mind says, *I've got to score, I've got to score.*

The *I* has become so big. Inadvertently, subconsciously, through no malintention, but look what it does. Every single shot is going above the goal or on the side of it, just not in it. The expectation of scoring and the fear of not is making him miss the target. Expectation kills.

It's the same when you are sitting in front of a customer and feel, *I've got to win the contract.* Or with your boss asking for a budget for your project or your team hoping they will respond positively to you, or indeed your life partner.

It's the same thing. Don't hope for anything. Understand the value that you can bring, know your strength in responding to that value, and you will deliver without worry.

So, what should be Frank's approach? Don't worry about scoring a goal? Notice I am not saying don't score a goal. I am saying, don't *worry about* scoring the goal.

On the contrary, by not worrying about scoring the goal, your chances of scoring are going to skyrocket.

You see, these two words, expectation and fear, are directly and linearly linked. Because what is fear? Where does it come from? It is the emotion of not getting what you want.

You want to be healthy, but the fear is you will fall ill. You want to win; the fear is you will lose. Wherever there is an expectation, the emotion and the concern over not getting it puts you in fear. Said differently, expectations will always generate fear. So, don't fight fear. It is a symptom. Fight the source, which is our expectations.

And how do you do that? By shifting from a *receiving* mode to a *delivery* mode. As we said in Section 1, be nothing but a *bringer of value*, which was extensively defined and explored.

Remember Andy? He was trying to score. He felt he needed his boss to sign his project. And in that expectation, the fear of not getting it signed put him in his own sphere (see below *Me Sphere* and *You Sphere*) and in the *receiving* mode. Why would it get signed?

Let me be emphatic on this point. By saying don't be in expectation, I am certainly not saying don't succeed. On the contrary, I say win, score, become wealthy, be famous, rise through the ranks, win the contract, whatever success means. What I am saying is don't *worry* about achieving it. Don't expect, just do. Work objectively with a mind in stable equilibrium, with clarity and insight, not fears, concerns and doubts.

I hear you say, *I get the point. But how do I put it into practice?*

We've already answered this briefly above by saying shift from the *receiving* to *delivering* mode. But let's expand on this question – how do we do it?

3.4

Which Sphere Are We In And To Which One Should We Move?

Me Sphere – You Sphere

There are two spheres in communication, business, and life itself: the *Me Sphere* and the *You Sphere.*

What is turning in the *Me Sphere*? Me, my job, my work, my objectives, my salary, my bonus, my career, my project, my boss, my team, my success, my promotion, my family, etc.. Do you recognise this?

So, what's turning in the *You Sphere*? Precisely the same things. Me, my customers, my project, my salary, my commissions, my boss.

Which sphere do you need to be in to get the most remarkable success? Of course, it's the *You Sphere.*

So, you need to walk into the *You Sphere* and walk out from the *Me Sphere* to generate success, and I will give you an example. But before that, I want to be clear that the last thing I am saying is that the *Me Sphere* is unimportant.

On the contrary, it's fundamentally important. Becoming personally successful is the ultimate reason we are working, doing business, or playing the game. However, I am saying make this *Me Sphere* the result and not the driver of the process. The more you walk into the *You Sphere,* the more the *Me Sphere* will become abundant.

Let's illustrate this point with Andy's story (see 1.13).

Reread the first conversation that Andy had with his boss, George. Which sphere was he in?

He talked about my project, my idea, please give me a budget; *I have a good idea for you.* Andy was in his own sphere. However, as George couldn't feel the value, he instantly brought Andy down to a mundane discussion of project and price rather than benefit and value. The conversation ended.

THE RIGHT SPHERE

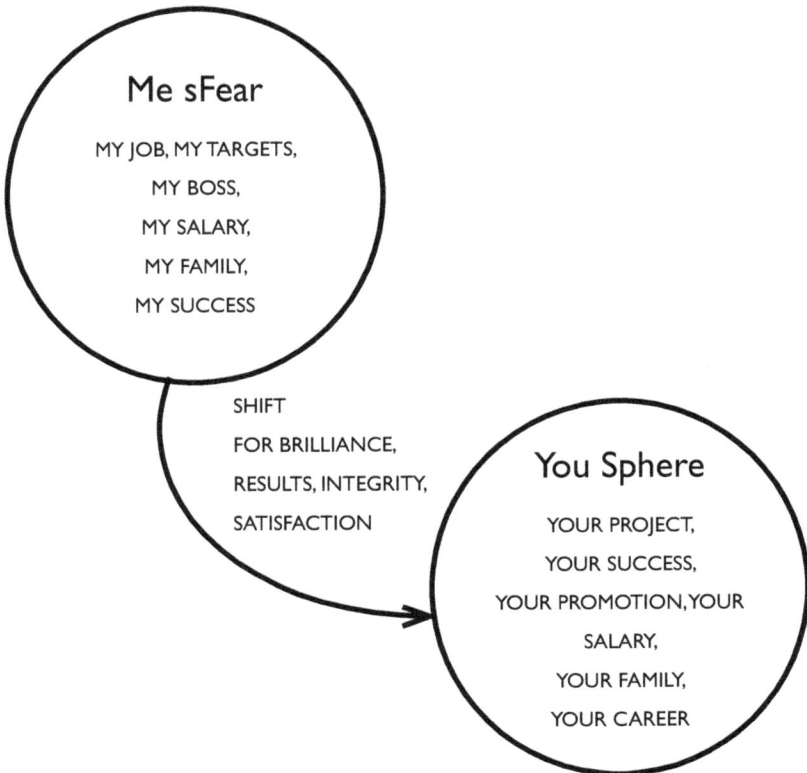

Me sFear

MY JOB, MY TARGETS,
MY BOSS,
MY SALARY,
MY FAMILY,
MY SUCCESS

SHIFT
FOR BRILLIANCE,
RESULTS, INTEGRITY,
SATISFACTION

You Sphere

YOUR PROJECT,
YOUR SUCCESS,
YOUR PROMOTION, YOUR
SALARY,
YOUR FAMILY,
YOUR CAREER

Observe conversations, meetings, or presentations in your work and how others around you are handling those communications. And just think which sphere are they in. You will be shocked. 95% of the time, and I am being kind to them with the 5%, they speak from the *Me Sphere*. Not because they intend anything bad, it's just the way our minds have become configured. But it is a mind in expectation. Frankly, we are begging. *Would you please give me this or that?* We should be in the *giving* mode of serving their value, which exists in abundance in every situation.

In the second conversation, whose sphere does Andy move into? Of course, it's the *You Sphere*, i.e., George's sphere. Now the conversation is turning around George's value of beating the sales forecast by 12%, and even a promotion for George. As a result, George is prepared to sign the project. His sphere is getting fulfilled, thanks to you addressing his value. And as a result, the project is being signed up, resulting in your success and your sphere becoming more abundant. It's a no-brainer.

But it's that mind which clouds the brain.

Just hear yourself speaking and thinking. Listen to yourself. In all scenarios, is my mind in the *Me sFear*, thinking about me, what I want, my expectations? Or am I obsessively in the *You Sphere*, thinking your value, how can it be served?

It's simple, and it's much easier than you think. Try it out in your next interactive situation that you come across today.

Another tip - sitting in meetings as a participant and observer, look at what someone else is saying, how they are saying it, and their thought pattern and direction. Are they speaking from *Me sFear*, or *You Sphere*?

I'm not asking you to judge them and definitely not to have any expectations of them. Just observe them for your own personal learning and shift. The more you imbibe this point by observation, the more you can shift your own thought patterns, and before you know it, it will become a reflex and a part of your natural make-up. You will rarely go wrong.

Don't Chase Profit

I spoke in Dubai on a program for top leaders entitled *Strategic Direction and People Leadership*. Discussing a similar point, I said, 'Don't chase profit.'

One CEO put his hand up. 'Sanjeev, why are you saying *don't make a profit?* That's my measure of performance and expectation of the Board.'

I said, 'Stop. Who said don't *make* a profit? Look at the title of this program? We are here to make you grow, expand, become wealthier, generate EBITDA, market share, etc.. Who said *don't make a profit?*'

Another participant put up her hand and said, 'I think Sanjeev said don't *chase* profit.'

And therein lies the difference. Don't chase profit, and you'll make a lot more.

So, what should we chase is the question? The answer is an unmitigated, absolute and obsessive understanding of and delivery of value to your customers. Of course, by customers here, we mean not only external customers but everyone to whom we bring value.

Just think in reverse, from whom would you prefer to buy? Someone in their own *Me sFear*, desperate to sell to you, win the contract, make the sale? Or the one who is obsessively interested in your value, in your success, i.e., in your SPHERE?

Remember my chug-chug van builder man (see 1.35)? And who would you negotiate harder with on price? The *Me sFear* person or *You Sphere* person? Who will make more profit?

And here is the rub. Not only will you make more money, but you will be doing it for a much higher purpose. This lack of desperation and expectation will definitely make you less fearful, less desperate, less expectant and far more confident, trusted by others and valued by yourself.

So, my friends, ultimately, integrity which is what I am talking about here. Integrity is not just profoundly and lastingly satisfying and the only way to be, but, as a by-product, makes you wealthy and far more successful.

Don't chase profit; make it.

What Do We Mean By Working With Integrity Here?

When you genuinely listen to the values of whomever you are serving – then, and only then match your talents and capabilities to bring excellent responses to these values - we can say you are working with integrity.

So genuinely listening means exploring *You Sphere,* with no craving after self-gain, i.e., the *Me sFear.* The latter would not be integrity. You would be in the receiving rather than the giving mode, begging for something. Its soul destroying brings down your confidence, devalues your skills and talents.

Play Without Fear

Now, suppose Frank Lampard plays with the abandonment of me. In that case, his destructive expectations and fears of not scoring will fall away. His acquired and established brilliance will undoubtedly result in goals.

Iceland Vs. England

In the world-famous Euro 2016 football championships, tiny Iceland knocked out the mighty England team. Its population is a mere 5% of England's. And a lot of Iceland's footballers are not even professional.

How did this happen?

Because the winning team played with a nothing to lose attitude, fearlessness and the losing team were over-conscious in their own *sFear* about their own reputation. What will the world think of us if we lose to Iceland? This worry, concern, fear and expectation made them play initially with over confidence and then after the first goal with nervousness – it effected their game. They themselves were the architects of their failure. And this is not about football. It's about human emotions, decisions and resulting actions.

Play without fear, my friends. Play without fear. Focus on value and the joy of the game.

Toyota Is Obsessed

An example in industry is Toyota. Living in the customer's sphere they are obsessed with the value they bring. Result? They can afford to be fearless.

When other car manufacturers build their cars to last seven years so customers replace them with new vehicles, Toyota goes the other way and make their cars last and last. Also, they build them not to break down, while the other manufacturers are less concerned on this so they can sell expensive replacement parts. Of course, the latter is a good revenue stream, but Toyota has the highest revenues and profits and doesn't need to look for desperate ways or even devious to make more money when serving value makes you richer in any case. Winning at the cost of your customer's value-impact is short-lived and the antithesis of valuepreneurship.

Who is more successful? – One who lives in the *Me sFear*, or the valuepreneur who lives in the *You Sphere?*

Confidence is a result not an action. Confidence is not something you should tell yourself to have. The more you try and tell yourself to have it, the more you will perpetuate the lack of confidence as you will be over-conscious about it. Confidence is a result. The more you shift from the *Me sFear* to the *You Sphere,* and from the receiving mode to the giving mode, confidence is guaranteed, nervousness will be reduced, even eliminated.

3.5

Spell it as SPHERE not SFEAR

Now, how do you spell sphere? SPHERE, right? So, I will succeed more by moving to the *You Sphere* away from me. Then why is it, my friends, that every day of our lives without us even recognising it and realising, we are constantly in our own, *Me sFear*?

Our mind says, *I hope it works, I hope I get the contract, I hope they listen to me, I hope they don't object, I hope competitors aren't there already, I hope they have the budgets...*

This is where our mind lives.

And the moment that you're in the I hope, it is driven by fear. You're in the *Me sFear*. How much confidence will the other person have in you? Don't you, as a customer, have much more trust, faith, confidence when a salesperson is focused on your value, whether he sells you anything or not, as opposed to the person who is in their *Me Sphere* trying to get you to buy? You shut them down. You push them hard on negotiation. You lose your patience and become comfortable to move away.

Don't be the latter. Be the former. In all your conversations, projects, presentations, negotiations, selling, all aspects of work and indeed life itself, remain in the *You Sphere*. You don't need to worry about the *Me Sphere* - that will be the result in any case.

Let's be completely clear on this - I am saying to you to care about others and not yourself? Not at all. I am saying that by caring for their value, the result will be a tremendous success for them and far more success for you than you ever allowed yourself.

In conclusion, in every situation, every action, in everything you do, every communication, every conversation, you will cut expectations and get the most by royally moving into the *You Sphere* spelled, of course, S-P-H-E-R-E. Then why is it that we constantly and painfully find ourselves in our own S-F-E-A-R?

3.6

Let's Talk About Fear

What is fear, where does it come from, what does it do, and what should we do to remove it? We've covered most of these points above. But let's reiterate.

From the moment we are born, we strive for self-preservation, physical protection, social acceptance, comfort, wealth and every step of our life is riddled with moments of gaining something and not losing something. And then the ultimate fear of all, the mother of all fears – Death.

But what the heck. It's going to happen in any case. By all means, delay matters. But not without reason. Delay it so that you may experience something, bring value, grow in yourself. And give the ultimate far less importance than you do. A powerful way of looking at things is by asking, *What's the worst that can happen in any situation?*

What's The Worst That Can Happen?

A senior leader was holding back on a significant decision for the company, despite knowing it was the right one. Because it carried a lot of risk for him personally if things went wrong, he was disturbed, and it was evident. He was losing the trust of the people around him.

And as the uncertainty grew, he had virtually decided not to take that decision. My approach with him was simple.

'What's the worst that can happen? You have a CV, you've been successful, even if you were to lose your job, how does that end the world?' Notice I am not telling him that he will lose his job.

On the contrary, the only way to keep his job is by taking that decision, but the mind clutches on through fear. The reason I said *What's the worst that can happen* to him was only to dilute the fear, and as the fear started to disintegrate, his confidence came further up, and he delivered his decision with strength and caring assertion.

People were destabilised with the decision but relieved as they could see a path forward. So, in the end, courage won over fear.

It's a great question to ask. *What's the worst that can happen?* It's liberating and shows us just to what an extreme extent we hang on to false realities, made up by our expectant misperceiving, misguided fearful mind.

Remember fear stands for:

F - False

E- Existence of the

A - Appearance of

R - Reality

I love it. Let's explain it using the example of the workload optimisation report we spoke of above (see 3.2).

The IT team had made a FALSE conclusion, through their misperceptions that this was a reprimand from the client that they were not working hard enough. It was false because this was not the case at all.

On the contrary, the client was trying to identify capacity to give them even more business. This false notion played around in the mind of the manager and the team. It started to amplify as a problem, and it began to APPEAR as a complaint from the client, but who made it EXIST? It never existed as a complaint or a reprimand from the client at all. As it came to live more and more in their minds, it turned into a belief, and it started to APPEAR as a REALITY.

We are constantly falsely bringing about the Existence of the worst scenarios in situations. And before we can take stock and realise, they start to Appear to us as Realities. But that's just the beginning of it. As we start believing in these False Realities as Existing, we start shifting our decisions and actions and, before we know it, do damage and harm to ourselves, just like that IT manager and his team. They lost the contract.

The same is true of our friend Sonia (see 3.2). The agitations of her mind made her believe that the reality was the girl was a thief and eventually the calmness of her mind, having found the earring, concluded that she was an angel.

So, fear is not real. It is a false appearance of reality.

Every external reality be it the earring, the maid, the workload optimisation report, etc.., becomes the object of the projections of our unstill minds; unstilled and agitated by our expectations and wants. We start believing that those stimuli, even though they are external, are causing the fear. They are not. They are mere objects. Our own agitations and desires and the worry of not fulfilling them are the real sources of our fears. That is why they are not real. They only appear as real. If you can see this, we start realising just how misguided our mind's expectations have left us. I'm requesting you to please leave the object - *Still the mind.*

Still The Mind

Here we are sitting by the river Thames. We can see the sky and the clouds in it. An hour ago, the tide was high, and the water was rough. A boat passed by it created waves. The reflection of the cloud in the water seemed to be broken into many, many pieces. Right now, the tide is down, the water is calm, and it's almost like a mirror. You can see the cloud in its entirety on the river's surface. The water here represents our mind. The cloud is the object. When the water is rough and agitated, that same object appears different, broken in pieces. And when the water is calm, we see the object, closer to its reality. So, everything we see is a reflection of the reality on our agitated mind and not the reality itself.

Still your mind, and you will see reality for reality sake. If it's agitated through your expectations, wants, fears, then every reality will appear as the object of that agitation. It is not. IT JUST IS. You are the one who needs to still yourself. The water needs to still itself. Not the cloud.

Please understand this as an illustrative image to grasp the workings of the mind. So again, referring to our example of the workload optimisation report, the reality was the report and had we seen its real purpose, we would have gained more business. Our agitated mind, like the water, disturbed that reality, and it started to take a different shape. Even a negative form perceived by our fearful mind and the same reality became the object of our fear. And we began to fear the report and the client, which was all false. It was our own agitation that was the source of that fear.

Free yourselves and simply observe reality, aside from your subjective and agitated mind. It will provide you with an incredible availability of the mind. That availability is suppressed by these false, self-manufactured fears. An available mind is free, unstressed and performant.

A fearful mind tends to materialise or make real what it fears most. In fear, the mind is agitated, and subconsciously, it will try to reduce or even remove agitations. But when what we fear actually happens, there is almost a feeling of saying to ourselves, I told you so. There is a perverse satisfaction and settling of the agitation in this state.

The Golf Shot

For example, you are a golfer about to take a long shot. You see the flag 200 yards away. This is your target. But in between you and the flag, there is a small lake.

As you prepare for the shot, your mind subconsciously says, *I hope it doesn't go in the lake; I hope it clears the lake.* With this in mind, where will the ball go?

So, you feared that the ball shouldn't go in the lake, but subconsciously your hands make that happen, and again subconsciously, the mind says, *See, I knew it would go in the lake,* and that is the perverse reassurance and satisfaction. In other words, we have a tendency to make what we fear actually transpire. Consciously, you will execute and take action from the path your subconscious mind has set you upon, good or bad.

The subconscious mind dictates the direction, and the conscious mind executes it. The subconscious is all-powerful. We will examine this later in the section under the title *Man is an Iceberg*.

So, if you are presenting a project and the chattering mind is fearing it might not get signed up;what if it doesn't get signed up, you will make yourself weak, nervous, unconfident, and it is pretty likely the project is rejected. And then you say, *I knew it wouldn't.*

So, my friends, there is only one thing to fear and one thing alone. And that is fear itself.

3.7

The Mind Will Always Reason
To Protect Itself

The mind is all-powerful. It is complex and most intelligent, but it's often in the wrong direction. In the wrong direction, it is uncomfortable, and to find comfort, it will look for reasons and justifications to everything and even assign blame.

In the project presentation example above, the mind will reason by saying, I told you so. This is a strange way of pushing back responsibility or even reaching a wrong conclusion like, I need to improve the content I was presenting, but missing the point that it wasn't the content at fault in this case. It was the lack of confidence brought on by the fear of not getting the project signed up in the first place. It's a circular argument and one to be explored in another text, but just understand the point in summary: the mind is essentially illogical and fired by emotion. When it gets things wrong, and it often does, it will desperately try to assign logic to the failure but often miss the reality. Still the mind and balance the emotion with intellect. We will talk more about this when we use the *Iceberg Model*.

When we can give ourselves an affirmation, for example, *I knew it would go wrong*, it's a feeling of absolving ourselves, raising ourselves in our eyes. Rather than saying, *I messed up*, it seems more of a consolation to say *I knew*. It's a let-off, a justification, a subtle misplaced vindication and takes the focus and sting away from the actual problem and I feel better.

For example, being beaten by a weaker team – rather than saying, *We were bad*, I tend towards, *I knew they would push very hard in their desperation to win.*

It's comforting to feel that we didn't lose because *we played poorly* but that *they worked hard*. Our focus needs to be more on us than others. This can only happen when we move out of the self-protection mode and move into self-understanding and courageously corrective mode. It's a transition from the subjective to the objective.

3.8

The Engine of The Mind – The EGO

EGO - Destructive If Mis-Directed; Amplifies Us If Channelled

Ego is simply the consciousness of the self – It's natural to us all. If well-directed it will fire excellence, fulfilment and serve. Mis-directed through our negative emotions and it will miss the target and even destruct – often through no conscious bad intention.

Ego, in the mis-directed sense, is our natural emotional make up for being over conscious of the self. It's me in my *sFear* – wanting something, needing something, being someone and the need to express that to others.

This excessive focus on the *me* makes us vulnerable. I fear not getting, not being, not recognised. The result is self-protection and the more I do this the more I shut out the world and reality. I create my own false realities. I'm isolated and lonely in my own fears, expectations, concerns and worries. I no longer take objective actions but engage in subjective reactions driven by emotions like fear, concern, anger, jealousy, hatred etc.. It's a dark veil which separates me from reality and the opportunities in it, which I miss. The more I miss the more I find the need to assert the me which further pushes me into subjectivity. Stress, burn out, pain are all outcomes of this expression of the ego.

No wonder most so-called leaders – be they corporate, political, organisational – fall prey to this ego. The more we have the more we can lose, the greater our need to protect it. We build walls, alienate people, take decisions and actions motivated by self-protection rather than bringing genuine value.

The one who can detach from this me and move into the you will at the same time save themselves from this veil and see the world and opportunities with clarity. They serve with care. Be fulfilled, stronger, confident yet operate with humility and integrity. This is the valuepreneur in all of us. And although I began by saying the ego, in the negative sense, is our natural emotional make up – our real natural state is a giving nature. We just need to simplify things and, in this book, I'm not teaching you anything but removing the misconceptions we have acquired through our emotional make up. I'm just setting the record straight to set free your true capacities.

Ego is natural to all of us but turning it from the negative emotional, wanting state to a giving, caring and value bringing state will give us the real consciousness of ourselves (good ego), our capabilities and efforts to bring value-impact. We are through, we are valuepreneurs.

With the three conditions of the mind, and an understanding of the ego, it's abundantly clear we put up significant barriers to our own success – be it professional, business, communication or life as a whole. So, let's discuss these barriers, which we will call our three constraining natures and then the lifting of those barriers, which we will call our enabling natures.

3.9

The Three Big Barriers to Success: Our Three Constraining Natures

These are self-imposed blockages, barriers, constraints. They are barriers to communication, barriers to our work and everything we do and indeed barriers to life itself, and I want to emphasise that they are self-imposed; no one needs to do it for us.

Understand and recognise these self-imposed obstacles. Confront them. Then remove them with the three enabling natures, which are the gateways to success.

The three barriers are:

1. The presumptive nature of our prejudice – Biases, Prejudices

2. Our closed nature – Opposition

3. Our defensive nature – Justification

3.10

Barrier 1: Constraining Nature – Our Presumptive Nature Or Our Prejudices

This is our natural human tendency to make judgements, assumptions, hypotheses, conclusions before and often without proper objective analysis. This prejudice could be about us, about someone else, the environment, objects, etc.. Let's take some examples.

1.1 Prejudice About Me

Let's say two weeks ago you were presenting to your senior management. And let's just say it didn't go too well. This afternoon, you have to do a similar presentation to a similar audience. What is now turning over in your mind? *I hope it goes better than last time, I hope they like it, I hope they don't ask too many awkward questions...* and so on.

With this state of mind, do you think you will be weaker or stronger in delivering the value in that meeting? The answer is clear - You will be weaker. You will be distracted. You will be subjective, thinking about *me, my presentation I hope, I hope,*

I hope... and that I makes it about you. You're subjective. You're actually in the *Me sFear*—what a prejudice!

Why should today's meeting go as badly as the last one? You're presuming, assuming, prejudging. Look at the word *pre - judice*, in other words, judging before something - before a proper objective analysis. It is your worry, your fear, your mind which is pushing you into this subjective frame. You've distanced yourself from reality and therefore, from your success. We come in the way of our own success. 95% of what happens to us is our own responsibility. Therefore, our fearful, presumptive nature pushed us into making conclusions which had no objective or logical basis.

Remember Sonia? It was the same thing. Or Andy? And this prejudicial, presumptive nature hits us several times in a day without us even recognising and realising it.

So, what is the antidote? The answer is understanding objectively.

Ask yourself, *In that presentation, two weeks ago, what was I doing when things were going well? Ah yes, my content was well prepared. I had excellent presentation slides. It was well structured. And I had the technical knowledge* and so on. So, which was the part that didn't go well? *Ah yes, when the audience started to make objections and asked difficult questions.*

So, having identified your strengths to leverage and the vulnerabilities to address, you can go to the right place and find a solution, help or training to strengthen your handling of questions and objections in presentations. Where is the worry? Where is the concern? The job is done.

By objective instead of subjective, we mean analysing without emotionally entangled worry, concerns or fears. That's what spoils everything. We end up listening to these concerns and worries. As I have made it about me, it is subjective.

In this state, how can we possibly listen objectively and understand the reality of the situation? We have listened to our subconscious mind telling us it will go wrong again; I will fail again. And we have ignored the simple reality that if I strengthen my handling of objections and questions, my skill and talent and the knowledge from which I am presenting can really bring value and therefore be worthwhile.

I'm a leader in that sense, but I have turned myself into a worrying weakling, reduced my significance and, consequently, the value of what I can *bring*.

This presumptive nature and the prejudices that it constantly generates needs to be carefully observed and consciously destroyed. Assume nothing. Understand everything, independent of my perceptions, misperceptions.

I'm sure you all know the famous acronym for *assume*, which is to make an *ass* out of *you* and *me* because that is what prejudice does. It harms whom I am interacting with and to me, myself. It is the very nature of doubt, which is another way of saying the same thing.

Doubt is to be crushed and despised. But our reactionary, concerned, agitated mind finds it easier and faster to jump to a conclusion through that emotion. It often makes wrong conclusions, rather than intelligently and objectively taking the time and care to understand. For this to happen, the removal of worry is essential. This anxiety only serves to perpetuate false conclusions and understanding, wrong decisions and actions and later regret and more anxiety.

So, in summary, my friends worry only about worry itself. Have the simple courage to understand things in their raw, unadulterated, non-prejudicial, straightforward, factual form, and you will find solid answers and solutions and achieve great things.

1.2 Prejudice About Others

Again, we jump to conclusions about others. *He is like this…
she is like that… David is nasty, horrible, obstructive, negative…*
If this is what my mind is saying and I am running a meeting,
the door opens, and David comes in, where will my mind focus be?
On David, correct?

And my mind will be saying, *Any minute, any minute now.
How will he obstruct, what he will say,* and again in this state,
I'm distracted. Will I be stronger or weaker in making that meeting
successful? The answer is clear.

So, once again, we've messed up.

How can we get it right? Well, think about this. People are not
difficult because they want to be difficult, a least, let's say 95%
of the time. Aren't you difficult from time to time? Don't you
get angry, upset, frustrated? Of course you do. But in that state,
which of these two statements are truer for you?

1. That you are attacking the other person.

2. You're upset that your work is not getting done, or you're looking
   for a particular value.

I am sure that you've answered that second statement is the truer
one, as everyone does when I ask this question. If that is the case,
you don't attack anyone. It is just an expression of your value
not being served. So, in reverse, why do you have a prejudice
about someone else? *He is like this; she is like that* – They are not
attacking you. They are just looking for something, some value.
They are just expressing it with frustration. It's that value, which
is objective and the straightforward reality. However, through
your presumptive nature and prejudging the situation through
your own emotions, you concluded it was an attack or difficulty
for you, and it becomes subjective.

So, once again, we are missing objectivity and rushing to subjectivity, and again it is all subconscious. The trouble is it shifts your behaviour, and you start reacting to that person as if they were attacking you, generating unnecessary conflicts and unpleasant disagreements. I see relationships breaking down for no reason, and people losing out on genuine collaboration, cooperation and rarely seeing eye-to-eye.

In summary, instead of concluding, *he is good, she is bad, he is nasty, she is obstructive...* just understand what are they looking for. Move from the subjective to the objective.

You see, there is only one simple reality – that every human being, assuming they were born of a mother on this planet, has their own personal Value Onion. Just understand that value and where you, your work, your talents, and capabilities can bring Response Onions to that Value Onion. Then make it your simple duty and dedication to do just that. And in return, your own purpose will certainly be achieved. You don't even have to try, so long as you serve genuine value. So, don't conclude, include.

1.3 Prejudice About The Environment

Remember Anita's story (1.10)? She'd made wrong conclusions, again through her subjectivity, driven by fears and emotions that her business was about to fold. And the conclusion was *I'm going to fail, the economic downturn is going to sink my business.* It was prejudice from a presumptive nature. The moment she had turned on the light of objective understanding, in other words seeing the situation in its raw reality, and not a reflection on her agitated mind, she saw tremendous opportunity. The same downturn suddenly turned into a Godsend. Her business – which she had come to that programme to close down and desperately seek something else to do – became the very source of her success. What a prejudice!

Every object, every situation in life is met through our agitated minds. Misread and misperceived subjectively – Ending up in wrong conclusions, wrong decisions, wrong actions.

Take the situation of the workload optimisation report at the beginning of this chapter. The client was trying to see how much capacity we have to give us more business. It was in our interest to show there was capacity, but our prejudicial nature concluded that they were checking up on us; the client thinks we don't work hard enough. This prejudice drove us to wrong actions. We showed that we were overcapacity – what a prejudice! And we missed out.

Although I've been showing the problem and the antidote simultaneously, the first enabler below will give more answers.

3.11

Barrier 2: The Second Constraining Nature - Our Closed Nature Or Opposition

Opposition is our natural human tendency to say my point is the right one, and I don't consider yours. I want to clarify; I am not saying don't oppose. I spend a lot of time training people to say no and still get motivation and collaboration. Opposition is when we oppose without considering the others' view or perception.

16 Or 61?

You and I are sitting across a table, facing each other. I write the number 19 and ask what number do you see? You'll say 19 but I say 61. Then you say 19, and I say 61... and we can go on for the whole day.

And this is not a problem, because problems have solutions. This is a conflict. One of us needs the courage to get up and move to the other side, look over the shoulder of the other and say, Ah, I can see you're seeing a 19... and not only the fact that you see the 19 but the context in which you see the 19.

Now we can find the real problem and, therefore, a solution.

Having seen your 19, the problem is no longer your 19 or my 61 because that is a conflict.

The real problem is 42, i.e., the difference between 61 and 19 or the gap between us. Now think about this, in this story, to whom does the 19 belong? You, right? To whom does the 61 belong? Me.

But to whom does the 42 belong? It's both of us.

And that, my friends, is what we call *commun-/-ication*. Something in common on which we can both work. This is not the etymology or the origin of this word; I am using artistic licence, but you get the point.

When we are standing on common ground, we both recognise, realise and indeed own that starting point to build something together. We can construct a solution which is in our common interest, and we are mutually engaged.

The Medical Sales Reps

You'll recall the story about a massive medical device company in France (1.3 and 2.36), make clever machines in electrocardiography, a vital treatment for heart patients. But the marketing director, Antoine, and the finance director, Charles, had an enormous disagreement.

Antoine said, 'I want to recruit an extra twenty-five maintenance engineers.'

Charles said, 'No way!'

Why? What do twenty-five additional maintenance engineers represent to Antoine, the marketing director in this story? Faster response times, better customer service, stronger brand, more sales, market share, something great, right? What does it represent to the finance director? Cost, expense, i.e., something horrible.

Now, look at this. One simple reality, which is twenty-five maintenance engineers, one sees as something beautiful and positive, and the other's perception is of something horrible. And the disagreement continues. So, what's the answer?

When I give you the answer, it will seem obvious and intellectually speaking, it certainly is. But immersed in that situation, we don't see it with that objective clarity. We complicate it with a cloud of emotion. So, the answer was I asked Antoine why? That simple three-lettered question which deludes us, just like we had said in the Excel/SQL scenario (1.22).

I asked Antoine,'Why twenty-five additional maintenance engineers?' And this is how the conversation went:

Antoine (A): So that we can give a better service and grow the business.

ME (S): What do you mean by a better service?

A: We could halve the time to repair a machine when it breaks down in a hospital or clinic.

S: How long does it take now?

A: Nine hours.

S: Do you mean you can repair machines in 4.5 hours?

A: That is guaranteed, and mostly within three hours.

S: Wow! How important is that for your market and to whom?

A: It has no impact on State hospitals in Germany because of the way devices are funded - you can keep a spare one. However, for private cardiology clinics in France, it is critical.

S: OK, and what are your competitors doing?

A: Nine hours.

S: So, it is a significant point of differentiation with your customers.

And if you said to the private cardiology clinics in France that we can repair in three to four hours, what would happen?

Out came his laptop, and he named six clinics, Nantes, Paris, Lille, Toulouse, Marseilles and Rennes and said:

A: For these six, fast repair is the main point of value, and if I can solve that, I can close the deal tomorrow.

Wow, at €1.2 million each, that's €7.2 straight away and a lot more behind it. And just with these six customers, a €2.5 million profit against twenty-five salaries just in the first three months and maybe €10 million over the year.

And you turn to the finance director and ask, 'Would you like that?' Suddenly we're all on the same side. And no longer in opposition.

So, let's analyse the Antoine's 19, the marketing director; and the 61 of Charles, the finance man?

Antoine's perspective was, I'm an expert in customer service, generating sales, differentiating our brand, etc.. Charles's perspective was that I've learned all about control, handling the finances to secure the business etc.. Neither was wrong. They were both right in their own way and context, but they were in opposition.

So, what was that 42? The difference? And what was the common ground for communication?

It was indeed the Value Onion of the French cardiology clinics who would benefit from having the machines constantly operational. At that point, there was zero argument. After all the customer and their Value Onion is common to both Antoine and Charles. If one of them, let us say, Charles, had the courage to leave his perspective, his knowledge just for five minutes and move across to the other side and understand it from Antoine's point of view, we would find the answer.

None of this happens through any bad intention. We don't oppose because we want to. We oppose because we find ourselves secure and comfortable in what we know and therefore lack the courage to step outside of that comfort, perspective, context, knowledge, experience and see it from the other's point of view.

Notice my use of the word *courage* here.

What drives us to remain stuck in our comfort zone comes from that famous fear of losing something, losing control and then we push our point, and push it hard, and we miss opportunities. Hence our closed nature, which forces us into opposition, will definitely hold us back and prevent us from the proper delivery of value.

The answer is don't oppose, propose! But to propose, you need to move out of yourself and see things from other perspectives. Move from the subjective to the objective from a closed nature to an open nature.

3.12

Barrier 3: The Third Constraining Nature - Our Defensive Nature – Justification

This is our natural human tendency to say, it wasn't me. It's like that song from Shaggy where the constant refrain was *it wasn't me*. To everything that happens, he says, *It wasn't me.* The song is a little rude but worth listening to.

The Understanding Waiter

Let's say you go to a restaurant with a friend. Your food comes first, and you are waiting a long time for your friends' food to arrive. Annoyed, you call the waiter and ask him what's going on. Defensively he says, it wasn't me Sir. You see, the kitchen is very busy today. Hearing this, as a customer, what does your mind say? It says do I care about your kitchen or you? And then, having lost respect for him, you speak even more sternly. And the tip is gone. You see these situations constantly.

So, what should have been the waiter's best response? Try this.

Waiter: I'm sorry Sir, may I understand your concern?

You: What do you mean, my concern? Only my food has arrived, and we'd like to eat together. We've come here for a good evening…

Waiter: I understand, Sir, my sincere apologies. Our mistake. Let me just take your plate and see what's happening in the kitchen, and I'll bring you fresh plates served together.

In other words, he cares to understand the problem and then solve that particular problem. And then he adds:

Waiter: It may just take fifteen minutes extra, my apologies for that, it's a busy kitchen tonight, but in the meanwhile may I offer you a drink?…

Now, not only does this become acceptable, but there is a much higher chance that you will have respect for him, be tolerant of the delay and yes, leave a tip.

It's as easy as that.

Why do we find it necessary to protect ourselves and be defensive, with an attitude that it wasn't me? We are trying to show that we are usually better than this, don't think badly of me etc.. The stark reality is that the other person really doesn't care about you. They care about their value, their evening with their friend - wouldn't you as the customer? That people are concerned about you is prejudice in itself. You end up doing wrong actions by justifying and not bringing a viable solution. Let's wake up, folks. Justification will bring us a loss of credibility; respect is lost, and so is dialogue. We lose out. And this happens to us daily, and several times a day without even realising or recognising it.

It happens subconsciously.

You might be running a meeting. And someone challenges you on a statement you have just made. Instantly, you become defensive and start over-explaining why you are making that point.

Your prejudicial misconception is *they don't like what I'm saying*, and worse, *they don't like me*. You quickly conclude this will cause me a problem, and with that futile emotion in your subconscious, you proceed to defend yourself and say *it wasn't me*. Reality is obscured - You don't bother to understand their real concern and the result they are seeking.

The chances of making rational decisions and doing proper actions or providing the best solution are meagre - What a complication!

Simplify life, engage and understand the issue, then offer a solution, albeit not perfect in their eyes, but regain their respect as the waiter did in the second round.

The Difference Between Explanations And Justifications

By all means, give explanations - you would expect that of others. So, what's the difference between an *explanation* and a *justification*? *Explanations* are desirable, and *justifications* aren't - here is the difference.

Justification is done for ME, *don't think badly of me, I'm usually better than this*. It's done to protect and defend myself.

An *explanation*, however, is done for YOU, the person with who I am communicating, to bring you facts, respect and a solution, as the waiter did the second time.

It's not fact or lies that's the issue here. In other words, I am not saying that *justifications* are lies and *explanations* are true. For the waiter in both cases, the kitchen *was* too busy.

So, it was a simple fact, but what turns it from *explanation* to *justification* or vice versa is my motivation behind it.

In other words, if my motivation is to protect myself, it will always sound bad, defensive and result in my loss of credibility.

But if the motivation is your value and despite the problem or the mistake, I want to solve it for you and bring you the best possible result in the circumstances, then it's an explanation.

In the second round, the waiter did give the reason, i.e., the kitchen is busy, but he gave it after he took responsibility and gave a solution and not upfront in a save my skin, desperate, way.

Explanation Vs. Justification

Summarising the sequence:

- In *justifications*, we tend to state the problem upfront — the kitchen is busy. As it begins with the problem, it's an excuse — it wasn't me.
- In *explanations*, the problem is still stated, but at the end.

In *explanations*, the right way, the sequence is:

- **Understand the problem**
- **Apologise** - *My sincere apologies for this.* It's not simple politeness, but an active taking of responsibility and ownership, strengthening and building credibility and respect. People often ask, *Why should I apologise if it wasn't my mistake?* If it wasn't your mistake, what the apology is actually saying is — *I'm sorry this happened to you,* with sincerity and care for the other person.
- **Offer a solution** — that can only happen if you understand the problem. Value Onions pre-cede Response Onions — *I'll bring fresh plates together.*
- **State the problem** — The *kitchen is busy - it may take fifteen minutes extra.*
- **Goodwill offer** — only if relevant — *May I offer you a drink while you wait?*

So here are the other main differences between *explanation* and *justification.*

- **In explanations** we take ownership, just like the waiter who said *I am sorry, we've made a mistake*. This instantly builds respect, and anxieties come down.
- **In justifications**, we push responsibility away, *Don't think badly of me*. In most situations, especially where there is a lot at stake, we react with justification and protect ourselves most of the time. Not taking ownership, responsibility and then dealing with it with our best efforts possible.

But who would you respect?

All of this happens to us every day. In a project, in a meeting, the moment someone challenges us with *that's wrong, how can you say that, etc.*, we don't seek to understand, and where we have made a mistake, we don't take responsibility and ownership. We are defensive.

It all happens with such subtlety in the depth of our subconscious mind that we are rarely aware we are justifying. It just happens.

But my friends, even though it happens in our subconscious mind, it subconsciously and therefore most powerfully negatively impacts our confidence, demeanour, and strength. Without even realising, it brings us down. It's not worth it.

The point is a simple one.

In all situations, remain objective, understand the problem, take it on your shoulders squarely and solve their problem. It's a position of absolute integrity. What have you got to lose?

Please don't make it about yourself. Keep perspective of the value they are seeking. This will strengthen you.

Defensiveness will only weaken you.

3.13

The 3 Big Enablers of Our Communication, Work, Success And Life – Our Three Enabling Natures

They are also the antidote to our *Three Constraining Natures,* explored above.

Having closed down our *Three Constraining Natures,* the self-imposed barriers in everything we do, let's open the flood gates to our *Three Enabling Natures.* Together they will bring us great success and also act as an antidote to the *Three Constraining Natures.*

In some ways, we have already talked about these in the previous discussion. But let's look at them specifically. The first of these is:

- Understand
- Committed decisions
- Action

3.14

The First Enabling Nature – Understand

In life, we go through the vast majority of situations without understanding. Most of them are misunderstandings which are driven by the state of our minds. They are misperceptions, at the source of which reside our fears, concerns, worries, egos. Reality is constantly filtered through these complexities of the mind and forms patterns of behaviour and reactions which are alien to the raw, objective reality. A reality which definitely deludes us.

We can even say, the first three enabling natures are understand, understand, understand. Don't move in work or indeed life without understanding.

So, the question is, *understand what?*

Let's go back to all the examples in the constraining natures.

When you messed up the presentation two weeks ago, instead of reacting with worry and concern that you will mess up this afternoon as well, understand. Understand what was I doing when it was going well?

You might say, 'Ah, I was strong in content, I had practised the presentation, my slides were well prepared. These were all the things in my favour which I would be mindful of and leverage to bring me success.'

So, which part didn't go well? 'Ah yes. When the audience started asking me questions and making objections.'

Now, my friends, the whole thing has become simpler. I leverage my strengths, and without any worry, concern or emotional entanglement, I simply look for ways to help me handle questions and objections in presentations a lot better, such as getting trained or coached on it.

Remember the workload optimisation report? Understand why. Rather than be prejudiced they are checking up on you, understand why, and you will discover the opportunity. Look how we easily miss things.

Understand everything before moving forward.

- Understand, in Anita's story, the architect's priorities.
- Understand why the other person is seeing a 19 when I saw a 61.
- Understand why twenty-five extra maintenance engineers.
- Understand what the customer in the restaurant wanted and how to bring a solution.
- And so on.

So, you see, with all of these examples, what was royally and absolutely missing was understanding. We rarely understand. In this section, we will continue on ways to enhance our understanding in every situation.

3.15

The Second Enabling Nature – Committed Decisions

Making decisions is all about a determined, structured, sustainable plan or path to letting my understanding turn into valuable, practical, sustainable actions.

It is a critical step. Typically, having understood, we instantly jump to the third enabler: Action, as you will see below. And we miss this second step. This is dangerous. At best, our understandings turn into actions which are flukes and often short-lived.

Stop Smoking

A friend of mine smoked a lot. Like forty cigarettes a day. One day he saw a huge roadside anti-smoking advert as we were driving along – a graphic, gruesome advert, where the cigarette was an artery, and the tobacco represented the clogs in it. His first enabler was turned on; in other words; he understood, got the message loud and clear. Instantly he picked up his packet of cigarettes and threw it in the bin, and said to me, *That's it, never again.* There was no action here, it was a reaction. How long do you think it took him to start smoking again? Did I hear you say two hours? You're absolutely right.

The problem with reaction is it doesn't come from the intellect. It comes from our emotions and therefore, it is unstable and even rampant.

Two things must happen for sustainable action, rather than a momentary reaction: firstly, the understanding itself must be complete. It's not enough to understand that smoking is bad for you. You also need to understand that smoking is good. It's relaxing, it's distressing, it tastes good, what's bad about this? And it's only in this completeness of understanding that we can make informed, committed decisions through a plan.

Knowing that I can't just give it up instantly. I may first need to bring it down to 20 a day, then only smoke after meals. Or you may use patches or an electronic cigarette.

Whatever this plan, it's a means to make your changes with total personal commitment - A sustainable and permanent change.

So once again, we will not be just reacting in life, but taking decisive, committed, sustainable actions and bringing immense success.

3.16

Third Enabling Nature – Action (Not Reaction)

Actions are about making it happen, implementing and moving forward, constructively and solidly, taking the proper steps and actually, we've said it all in the previous paragraphs. When understanding is complete, when you have given your commitment and planned the way forward, you can afford to just go for it and do it. Nothing more to say.

Enablers 1 and 2 will lay down the essential conditions, and you will find joy in taking action. But action you must take.

I often see that people get it; they are committed but then fall short of actually going for it. It may happen due to a combination of reasons, the biggest of which is fear – the fear of failure – therefore, an innate risk aversion. Don't hold back. If Enablers 1 and 2 have been lit up, then you can afford to implement and take action with complete confidence.

3.17

Distorted Images Which Hold Us Back

Everything we see, hear or come across is a distorted version of reality. We miss the truth and quickly conclude that the distortion is the reality. We then act on it, and at best, we miss opportunities and, at worst, create a mess. These distortions prevent us from listening to others to ourselves to the world, and listening genuinely is the key to success. Let us explore what prevents genuine listening and therefore getting a correct interpretation of everything.

If understanding is the first enabler, this clarity comes from our power to listen and correctly interpret everything, everyone and ourselves. We hear a lot but listen to very little. We form prejudices, misperceptions - and we miss out. There are ways to listen, but first, let's understand what prevents us from listening in the first place. This is not just about listening; it is about an overall state of mind, which is misplaced and actually quite dangerous.

Our Prism – Distortion Of Reality

As a descriptive image the prism has been often used. Here is my version to understand this point about listening.

Black Is...?

Recently, while coaching a group of managers, I asked them to write down the first important thought that came into their minds when I said the word *black*. Their answers were unsurprisingly varied – night, dark, Africa, Obama, Porsche, death, hole, galaxy, Mandela, serenity, Armani, peace, etc..

Now, look at this. There is a straightforward reality, which is black. But the image of that reality, in the mind of every individual, is something completely different. Someone sees it as beauty; another sees it as death or hope, and so on.

To understand this, look at the diagram below. When light enters a prism, what happens? It diffracts into its many colours and forms very different images onto a screen, and that screen is us. Each of us sees a different image, i.e., a different colour, of the same simple reality. This image is being processed through our own personal individual prism to form the image and, therefore, perception of that reality in each of us. What makes this colour, this image, so different for each of us? What is inside our personal prism that causes the image to be so different?

THE PRISM - DISTORTION OF REALITY

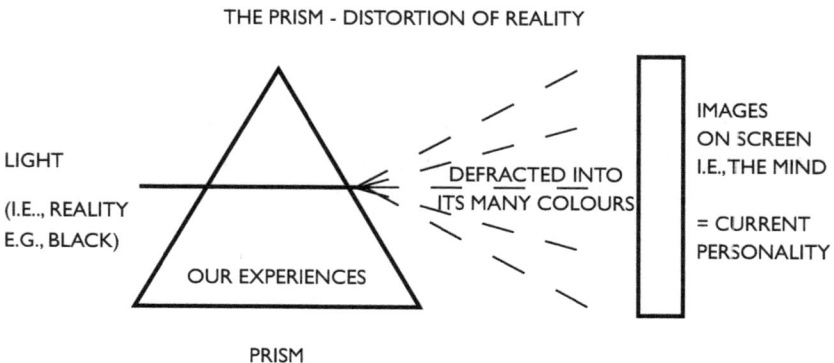

LIGHT

(I.E., REALITY
E.G., BLACK)

OUR EXPERIENCES

DEFRACTED INTO
ITS MANY COLOURS

IMAGES
ON SCREEN
I.E., THE MIND

= CURRENT
PERSONALITY

PRISM

It is the sum of all our experiences during our life so far. What kind of experiences? Our culture, country, religion, the school we went to, our teachers, our parents, in other words, every situation, every experience shapes these images. It could be the news this morning. For example, if on tenth of September 2001 I had said to you *aeroplane*, which is a simple reality, it may project the image of a holiday. But if I say the same word, *aeroplane*, two days later, the image you see is devastation, terrorism, war. An aeroplane is an aeroplane; it's a simple reality, but your reaction to it depends on your perceptions. In other words, the image that aeroplane forms in your mind could be completely different from one day to the next.

So, these are associations, which in summary, we can call our own prism. The prism then represents the sum of all our experiences, our personalities. I am not a geneticist, and I don't think that even geneticists can answer this question - is your personality a function of nature or nurture?Are we born with it, or does it shape along the way? But one thing I can say with absolute conviction - having had the great opportunity to coach thousands of people in the last 35 years, is that our reactions are significantly and almost entirely determined by our experiences shaping our minds. Those experiences have interacted with our egos to form patterns of behaviour through our emotions. Therefore, every reaction of ours is a result of the state of this interpretative and, should I say, over-interpretative mind.

 How can we possible listen?

3.18

Experiences To Behaviour Flow

Summarising this Flow from Experiences to Behaviours:

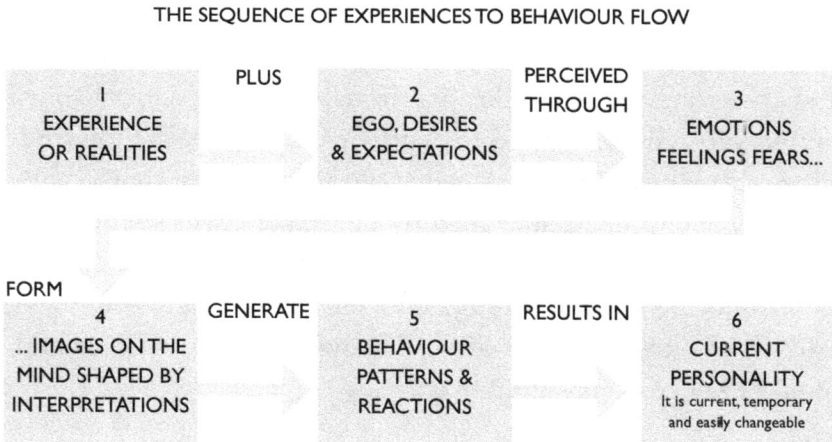

THE SEQUENCE OF EXPERIENCES TO BEHAVIOUR FLOW

	PLUS		PERCEIVED THROUGH	
1 EXPERIENCE OR REALITIES		**2** EGO, DESIRES & EXPECTATIONS		**3** EMOTIONS FEELINGS FEARS...

FORM		GENERATE		RESULTS IN	
4 ... IMAGES ON THE MIND SHAPED BY INTERPRETATIONS		**5** BEHAVIOUR PATTERNS & REACTIONS		**6** CURRENT PERSONALITY It is current, temporary and easily changeable

Notice I call the result our current personality. It's not necessarily in our genes, but our behaviours due to the current state of our minds. As this has been triggered by factors external to us, i.e., experiences, then reversing it is also in our capability, hands and power.

How? Simplify the mind, redirect our emotions by observing, shaping and even negating the ego.

Genuine listening means listening without assigning values and filtered interpretations. It means looking at every situation and everything in its essential raw form without judgment. Only then can we act upon it and react to it objectively and therefore productively by taking up opportunities and achieving great results.

3.19

The Prism
And The Mirror Of Communication

Let's build on the *Prism of Distortion* by looking at the *Mirror of Communication*.

THE MIRROR OF COMMUNICATION

ANGER

What we
Put into
The mirror
is determined
by the
images on
our mind

Clean your
images and the
mirror will
reflect good
things

ANGER

ME

YOU

At a social, personal, individual level, while the different images we all have, give us individuality and can be desirable in life, they can really get in the way of everything we do.

For example, when you are communicating with someone, there is what we can call a *mirror of communication*. What you put in this mirror will be reflected back. For example, if you show anger at someone, you will probably get anger back instead of calmness. The mirror is at work.

But the problem is that everything you put into this mirror of communication is determined by the image formed in your mind of every reality being processed through your own prism. It can be dangerous and often is. It could hurt, or you may miss opportunities.

The CFO Presentation

I recently coached a CFO (Chief Finance Officer) of a large corporation in London. He called me and said, 'I need your help to make my presentation successful. This Thursday, I am presenting to the board to open up the Far East market, and the project requires a USD$30m investment.'

I went in on Tuesday to practice his presentation, and strangely I found a lack of confidence in him, doubt, hesitation, discomfort. It was surprising as he is a brilliant finance director, communicator and presenter. The conclusion was clear. There was something in his prism which was causing the disturbance.

And guess what I discovered? That morning, he received an SMS from his private bank, saying... *Your account is over the limit, please bring it back into credit.*

He usually is very well organised; it may just have been a slip of the mind that he hadn't replenished the account. The experience, i.e., SMS, which was fresh in his prism, processed through the emotion meant that anything to do with money and asking for money was being processed and distorted. It was generating a very negative image in his mind.

And the worst of it was he was not even aware of the distortion. It was in his subconscious mind (see *Iceberg*), which is far more powerful than our conscious mind. So now, this simple reality, money, was being distorted as it was diffracted through the prism of experience, projecting a negative image.

Subconsciously, it influenced what he was putting into the mirror of communication in his presentation and shaping his behaviour. His voice and body language showed hesitation, doubt, low confidence and so on. If he puts doubt and lack of conviction into the mirror of communication with the Board, do you really think the reflection back will be positive? No chance! They would have low confidence in the project and reject the $30m investment.

Subconsciously, and with perfectly good intention, he is, or should I say his mind is the sole architect of the failure – quite unnecessary!

He is not listening; he doesn't see reality in its raw form, it's massively distorted, and it has hindered his success.

Where is the link? There is absolutely no link between the SMS from his bank and asking for the $30m to invest in the Far East. With this prism and everything that happens inside it, we constantly link one event with another as human beings. Objectivity is lost, and so are opportunities.

So, what was the answer with Anthony?

Having understood this sequence and cycle working in him, I conversed with him as follows:

Me: Imagine if you get these $30m signed off on Thursday, what would it do for the company?

Anthony (A): It would be great, and we would generate significantly higher income, profitability, brand value and share value growth.

Me: Wow, and what would that do for you?

A: Well, I think I would get the big job, CEO Far East, with an excellent ex-pat package, healthy bonus, ….

Me: And what would that do to your bank account?

Do you get the picture? We don't see reality, and by listening to everything and everyone without evaluating it, prejudging it, in fact misjudging it, we constantly miss out.

An additional thought - the mirror of communication also applies to communication with ourselves. Whatever you are worried about gets reflected back at you, and you make it seem like a reality. It's not reality, but you act on it as if it was.

If you look in a mirror concerned that your skin is wrinkled, you will see more wrinkles. Then the conclusion that you are getting old will shape your behaviour, and you may start behaving like you are old. I see this happening.

You've heard the saying, *You are as old as you feel!*

Please listen! So now the question is, how do we listen?

3.20

Listeners Win

Listen, really listen. Understand the depth, the vastness and the implications of the point we are making here. Listen is no ordinary word. It can be life debilitating or life-elevating.

We rarely listen. We listen through the filter of our wants, desires, fears and expectations. These reside in that prism we talked about above, i.e., our current personality. And I do mean our current personality because our permanent personality is void of the distortions we've discussed. In our essential natures, we are magnificent.

Practically speaking, when we are listening to others, there are three levels of listening.

Level 1 – Passive Listening

Showing signs of interest. It's the nodding of the head, verbal cues like *hmm, ah, I see*, plus eye contact. It's good, but it's one-way traffic. The engagement will be limited, as will your comprehension.

In Level 2, you listen far more actively.

Level 2 – Active Listening

How do you listen *actively*? By using these seven open questions: *Who, what, where, when, how, why, which?* These are the seven friends and the only words you need to listen to others effectively. You could be conversing with a brain surgeon at dinner, use their words, adding a *who, what, where, when, how, why, which* before it. The conversation would flow beautifully all evening. For example... *so you know when you said that at the point of incision, we have to protect all the brain cells and not damage them, how do you manage that? And to locate the exact position of the growth, what is critical to finding it,* and so on.

The result is that you will engage the person a lot more.

They will open up to you. It will be a great conversation, you will understand a lot, and at the end of the evening, they may even say, 'Seriously, in which institution did you learn your brain surgery?'

These seven friends are a practical, magical tool in generating dialogue and gathering genuine understanding and reducing the chances of misinterpretations. Apply this in your work, meetings and social life and your understanding of people, their Value Onions (the First Enabling Nature), dialogue and engagement will be significantly enhanced.

Now, let's go deeper in our listening, and that is *Double Active Listening,* which we can call *reformulation.*

Level 3 – Reformulation

Reformulation or paraphrasing is taking their idea and rephrasing it to validate your understanding. For example, *If I understand you correctly, what you mean is... Am I right?*

Reformulations confirm and validate your understanding, not through your interpretations and often misinterpretations but from their perspective. You are likely to be aligned and not in opposition.

Another important point here is to use constructive reformulation as opposed to negative phrases. For example, if they say, *the competition is killing us...*then your constructive reformulation could be, *So, if I understand you correctly, you would like to find ways to gain greater market share.* It's saying the same thing, but it is the subtle yet impactful difference between opening people up and closing them down.

It's human nature. People will be more closed in a negative thought pattern but open up more and provide more information when they see a way forward and opportunity. This is not tricking people but genuinely and with integrity allowing them to express their value. Reformulation brings four significant benefits. By validating what they are really saying:

- Firstly, *I really do understand,* which is the first Enabling Nature and helps us listen beyond distortions, thoroughly.

- Secondly, *they understand that I understand.* In other words, they *feel* understood. In life, in communication, there is nothing more powerful than *feeling* understood. It builds confidence, dialogue and trust.
  And never be scared of receiving a no on this question, i.e., *If I understand you correctly, what you are saying is...*
  If the answer is *yes,* great, we can move forward. But if the answer is *no,* then without the distortions of my emotional state, worry or concern, I can simply say, *'OK, so I'd like to understand more. What have I missed?'*
  In building relationships, this is powerful, and you are well on your way to being an ace listener and most successful.

- Thirdly, *a commitment, which is critical to achieving.* Because if you say, *If I understand you correctly, the point you are making is...* and they say, *Yes that is correct,* then they can never go back and say, *No, that's not what I meant.* And this happens so often.

Validating your understanding means you will constantly move forward in your dialogue and, therefore, in the relationship. It's worthwhile.

- Finally, *it gives you time to think*, especially in tricky situations. How often do you react and then later feel bad that I jumped too soon? I should have given it more thought before reacting; it went wrong. But with reformulation, those three or four precious seconds provide you with time to get your intellectual thoughts together, enough to overcome the emotion, and you bring more studied answers with a balanced mind. This lag between the emotion and the intellect we will further explore in the *Iceberg* later.

Listening is above all *wanting* to listen.

Reformulation then, is indeed powerful. But despite these three levels of listening, which are worth using, there is one overarching point in listening: *genuinely wanting to listen.* Wanting to listen to others, to ourselves, situations, environment, etc.., means dropping our filters, clearing the prism and perceiving reality as it stands. *Black* is simply black. Yes, having understood, if you were then to use black to achieve different outcomes like fashion, style, design, that's a separate matter and a powerful way to go. The point I am making is don't let *black* represent a false reality automatically in your mind, which then shapes your decisions and actions of which you are not in charge.

What prevents us wanting to listen is our fear we may hear things unfavourable to us or which will make more work for us.

Remember the workload optimisation report example?

Although natural, this is a delusion. By avoiding listening, the issue, problem or value don't disappear, they still remain. Avoiding it will at best make you miss opportunities. At worst it will hamper your progress.

So, listen to whatever the reality is detached from our fears and concerns.

Not only will this strengthen the relationship and the respect from others for you but also give you the necessary information to bring solutions and progression for them and you.

Wanting to listen means having the courage in all situations to be aware of any prism which may be affecting your listening, your understanding, as I did with Anthony. And the moment he was prepared to drop or, let's say, clean out his prism so that light can pass undistorted, he started seeing the $30 million as a brilliant investment as opposed to the negativity around money because of the SMS from the bank.

He went on to present with great confidence, and yes, the investment was approved.

While I've given you some practical tips on listening to others in this section, the principle applies widely. It will help you be clear-headed, clear-minded, seeing everything, hearing everything, listening to it, perceiving it in its absolute factual form. Only then will you be able to utilise it to bring you the best results.

Listening is, above all *wanting to listen.*

3.21

Balancing The Mind And The Intellect, The EQ And The IQ
Perfect Balance For Perfect Outcomes

Let's utilise a metaphor, an image, to describe this difference between the mind and the intellect, first introduced by the great Sigmund Freud. Here we take this metaphor to understand the simple but highly influential dynamics in utilising everything we have to release our true potential.

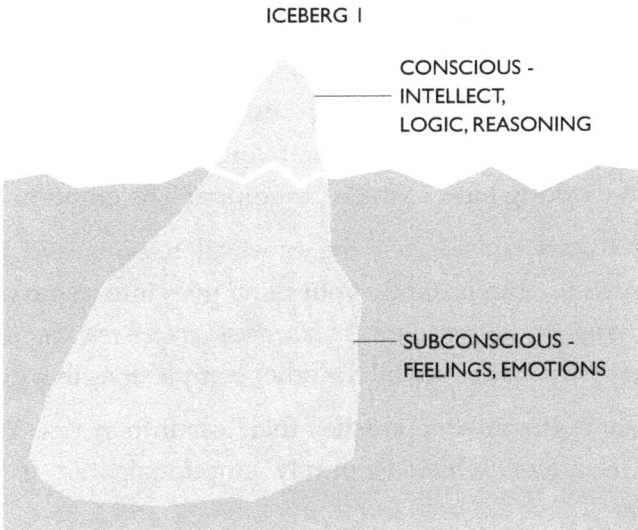

ICEBERG I

CONSCIOUS -
INTELLECT,
LOGIC, REASONING

SUBCONSCIOUS -
FEELINGS, EMOTIONS

Let's just say that man is like an iceberg, and I use the word *man* generically, in other words, every human being is like an iceberg. So, think of the iceberg's structure? Only the tip – a tiny part is emerged – and the great mass is submerged underwater.

In the diagram above, the emerged part represents our *conscious* mind; submerged represents the *subconscious*. The emerged part is our IQ and the submerged area, the EQ; and the two need to be balanced.

The conscious, which is easily seen, contains our logic, intellect, reasoning. Therefore, what is submerged represents emotions and feelings. Which is bigger? And it is the same for every single human being. We are a tiny bit of logic and a mass of emotions. And don't let any deluded human being come to you and say, *I am a very logical person.* There is no such thing. It doesn't exist. Yes, they might be, but then all they are saying is my logic kicks in fast enough to prevent my emotions from running wild and causing damage in any situation.

This simple understanding is critical in being sensitive to others' emotions, managing our own emotions, and getting the best out of our intellect and emotions. Let's face it, in any situation we come across, what kicks in first, your intellect or the emotion?

Your boss says, *Sorry, but we can't go ahead with your project.* Do you reason with it instantly and understand the situation or feel sad and upset as you've had your heart set on this project and been working hard to make it happen? The emotion kicks in.

You don't start considering the practical reasons and financial constraints, etc.., but instantly your mind goes into a spin of... *what this will mean for me, what are the repercussions for me, and how I will get the next promotion?* And all the other complexities that go with it.

It's the same if someone crashes their car into yours. Your first reaction is anger, which is purely emotional, and it kicks in instantly.

Later, you call up the logic that the road was wet, and a cyclist has just dashed out in front of him, and as a result, as he had to swerve, he hit your rear and so on. In every single situation, our emotion engages much before the intellect does.

Looking at Iceberg 1, you can see the emotion engages first, then there is a lag, and it's only when the emotion has started to calm down, abate, that logic starts to awaken.

If you are upset with someone and write them a strong email, don't send it. Leave it in your draft, and I guarantee you will completely reword it when you come back to send it. Isn't that right?

So what is happening? As represented by the submerged part of the iceberg, we are so significantly made up of emotion, it prevails. And often, we're not even aware of it, as it resides in the subconscious. These things just happen to us without consulting as an involuntary reaction well before voluntary action can happen. There is a lag and as the emotion starts to reduce and diminish the intellect has half a chance to be utilised. Putting it differently, we can also say the intellect is weaker than the emotion in us. The more we strengthen our intellect, the better we will manage the emotion. It applies vice-versa too.

Now think about this. Two icebergs are floating around in the water, and they collide (see Iceberg 2). Where does the collision take place? Where do they meet?

The *depth* of the iceberg meets the *depth* of the other iceberg. It's the same when two human beings interact. In other words, human beings meet emotion to emotion, subconscious to subconscious, long before the intellect has a chance to engage. On the contrary, if the ice at the bottom is so massive in both cases, it may be that logic never meets logic. You see this every day.

ICEBERG 2

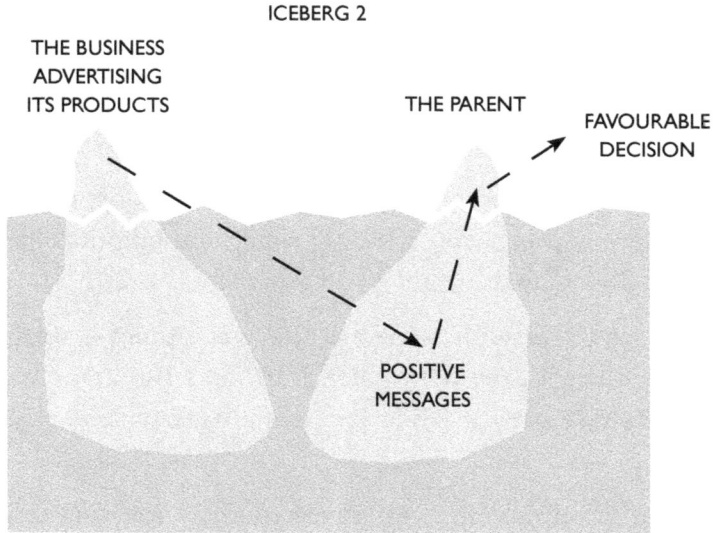

As a human being, it doesn't matter how professional you are, logic rarely meets logic. It's a little bit like a company advertising its products or services. In the diagram, the left iceberg is the business, and the one on the right represents the customer. Consciously, the advertiser or the company sends nice positive messages into the depth of the iceberg of the customer.

Yoghurt

For example, I saw an advert for a famous yoghurt company. It showed a mother and her young son, he was running around playing football, and they even ended up showing an x-ray of his bones, suggesting lots of yoghurt means lots of calcium, healthy bones, healthy child.

The left iceberg is the yoghurt company. The right-side iceberg is the mum or dad. Where in the parents' iceberg is the desire created to see your child healthy and happy? Absolutely. It is in the subconscious, the emotion.

Then where does the mum or dad take the decision when they go to the supermarket to pick up that brand of yoghurt and put it in the basket? Yes, that decision is taken in the conscious. And this is the most efficient route to communication.

We don't communicate to communicate. We communicate because there will be an outcome, a result, a decision. Then in professional life or indeed in our private lives, why do you we often go directly from logic to logic? It will not work for you as well as if you go via the subconscious. The emotion is evoked in the depth of the iceberg, and the decision is taken from the top – logic.

I want to make one point absolutely clear. I am definitely *not* saying manipulate people. After all, what is manipulation?

An interpretation of manipulation is when I use this understanding to get decisions made in my favour without concern that it may or may not benefit or even harm the other person. Definitely not. We are talking about simple human to human understanding and evoking in them their own personal value and then serving that value which in the main resides in the emotion, in the subconscious, to bring them genuine success.

So actually, I am talking about a position of the highest integrity and saying to you just don't miss the human being. Someone deluded enough to go logic to logic is first doing a disservice to whom they are serving by missing their actual and highest value as it sits in the emotion. And secondly, a disservice to themselves as they will miss out on getting the best decisions made for both parties.

Andy, His Boss And Marrakesh

Remember Andy trying to get his boss to invest $90,000 for a conference in Marrakesh (1.13)? In the first instance, he was using logic by saying, *this is an important conference, in Marrakesh, for two hundred people, and we need to find the budgets.*

It was all only logic, and the decision from the Andy's boss didn't go in Andy's favour, nor indeed, in the boss's favour either, because the boss would gain a vast amount from the operation. Still, Andy had missed the boss's emotion and his mind was focused on logic.

The second time around and doing it much better, he evoked the emotion and addressed the emotional value of the boss. He had touched the emotional nerve of outer most layer of the Value Onion when he said,I have a way to beat our sales forecast by 12% and gain market share to be more successful as a business unit.

Then the boss asks *How*, because it was bringing him value in the depth of his iceberg. Andy now confidently spoke about the conference and the cost, etc.. In other words, logic served as means to satisfy values that reside truly in the emotion.

Every human being long before being a professional, a boss, a scientist, an engineer is a human being, principally made up of emotions and a little bit of logic and intellect, which only when utilised correctly in this way takes on high importance.

Let's say you are in Alaska, flying around in a helicopter and below you is an iceberg. Let's say the water is crystal clear so you can see the iceberg fully. If I asked you to draw what you see, wouldn't the diagram look something like this?

ICEBERG 3: PLAN VIEW - VIEW FROM ABOVE

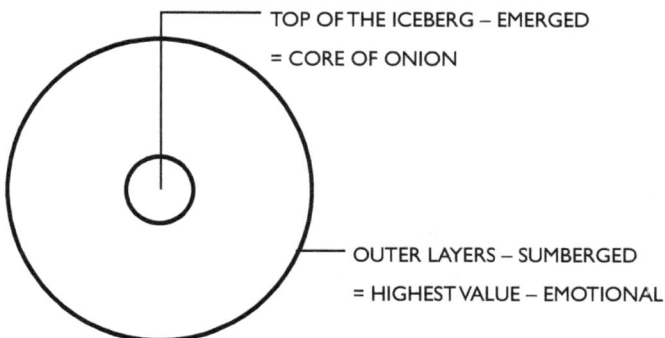

TOP OF THE ICEBERG – EMERGED
= CORE OF ONION

OUTER LAYERS – SUMBERGED
= HIGHEST VALUE – EMOTIONAL

What does this remind you of? Yes, you got it! It is the Value Onion, where the core is the logic, the nuts and bolts, the product itself. It's in the centre, and it's the smallest part of the onion, and the value for the other person from that product or service resides outside the core, and as you go further and further out in the Value Onion, the value them is increasing.

Further, thinking about the Value Onion, as you go outwards and the circles become larger, the emotional factor rises - would you agree? So, value and emotion are directly linked and proportionate. We can even say they are synonymous. The larger the circle or layer of the onion, the greater the value, the bigger the emotion.

Relating that back to the iceberg, you can see that the value to the individual is the highest at the bottom of the iceberg where the circumference of the ice is the largest, in other words it's the outer layers of their Value Onion. An interesting correlation?

Let's just call it the consistency of human understanding.

So again, for Andy's boss, the core of the onion, in other words, the logic in the iceberg was the conference, the number of attendees, the cost, the organisation, the location. But in the depth in the iceberg, the lowest and the widest part, the most emotional part, was the boss's personal success and results well beyond the forecast and potentially even a promotion.

Do you get it?

These metaphors are not points of theory but illustrations of essential human understanding to make the right decisions and pathways to our success.

3.22

Good Emotions And Bad Emotions –
A Helpful Distinction

Let's take the image of the iceberg to another level. Look at the diagram below and imagine if you can split the emotion in two –see the diagonal line cutting through the sub-conscious. The left half of the sub-conscious represents good emotions, and the right side is bad emotions.

ICEBERG 4

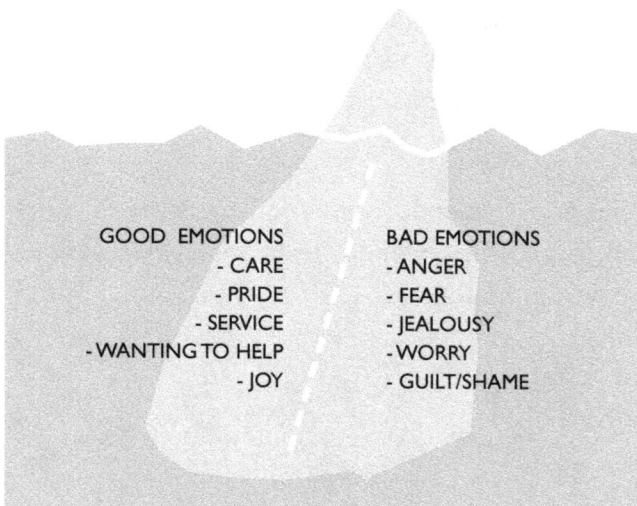

GOOD EMOTIONS	BAD EMOTIONS
- CARE	- ANGER
- PRIDE	- FEAR
- SERVICE	- JEALOUSY
- WANTING TO HELP	- WORRY
- JOY	- GUILT/SHAME

- **What is bad emotion?** Fear, anger, worry, jealousy, doubt, regret and so on.

- **What is good emotion?** Care, pride, satisfaction, certainty, joy, love etc..

The supreme negative emotion and the root cause of all other destructive emotions is FEAR - because it is deep-rooted in the *Me Sphere* - or as we spelt it earlier, *Me sFear* – what will happen to me!

The most powerful positive emotion is CARE – care for others and their value being satisfied – this is the pre-occupation of a Valuepreneur. It is also the root cause of other good emotions, because it is rooted in the *You Sphere* – we feel most joy and satisfaction when we can bring value. But I hear you say, *I get the most joy when 'I' get value.* Sure, and there's nothing wrong with it, but that is more pleasure than satisfaction. The former is short-lived, and the latter is dominant and long-lasting in propelling us and our endeavours.

Again, I'm not speaking against your own value being satisfied – on the contrary, ultimately, that's what it's all about and the reason you are reading this book. However, your own value will be an assured result and much better achieved when you become a purveyor of others' value.

Just as you have your good and bad emotions – the person you are dealing with has their good and bad emotions (see Iceberg 5).

ICEBERG 5

INTELLECT MEETS INTELLECT FIRED
ONLY BY GOOD EMOTIONS

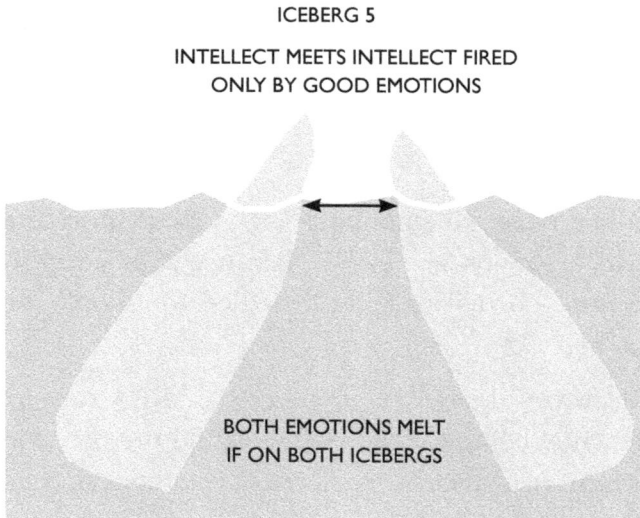

BOTH EMOTIONS MELT
IF ON BOTH ICEBERGS

Now, imagine if your bad emotion i.e., the right-hand side of your subconscious was to disappear, be wiped out. This is not a theoretical concept - how can you actually do it? The first thing is don't focus on your negative emotion or try to fight it – it could end up strengthened.

The way to melt it is to replace it with good emotion, i.e., care. The more obsessive you become about bringing value and caring for the advancement of others – be they customers, bosses, team members, colleagues or family and friends – the stronger you will become emotionally. You will be more confident and accomplished, less fearful, nervous, stressed or vulnerable. Your talent, knowledge and capabilities will be better applied, your productivity raised - and you owe this to yourself. You will transition into a stronger Valuepreneur. The deep fulfilment (a good emotion) will simply replace the destructive emotion. There will be less and less room for it and then eventually no space for it at all.

The answer for removing bad emotions is to replace them with good ones.

There is no fear in giving and caring but a lot of fear in wanting and expecting. Again, we are moving from the *Me sFear* to the *You Sphere.*

Now, looking at the other person's iceberg, their bad emotions are represented on the left and good emotions on the right. A bi-product of erasing our bad emotions and replacing them with care for their value will be to remove their bad emotions, like frustration and fear, in this transaction or communication. In other words, the more people feel cared for, i.e., that someone (you) is trying to help them and bring them value, their own fears and frustrations will melt.

In Andy's case – Andy's bad emotion was fear – *What if my boss doesn't accept the project? What if he feels I'm asking for too much, i.e.,$90K, what will that mean for me... ?*

His boss's negative emotion is, *What if I don't make my targets, how will I ask senior management for a $90K project when my sales are down? What will it mean for me… ?*

Now, suppose Andy replaces this FEAR with good emotion (CARE), which is the value I can bring to the company and my boss with this project, i.e., beating the forecast by 12% and opening up new markets. In that case, his own fears and hesitations will melt, and as a biproduct, his boss's fears and frustrations of budget constraints etc.., will melt.

Looking at the diagram Iceberg 5, how do the icebergs look as both sets of bad emotions have melted? As the icebergs meet, look where the meeting point is – yes, it is the logic. Logic will now meet with logic, and that is a desirable state. It will generate dialogue from intellect to intellect, and in the emotional engine underneath is the good emotion of care, achievement and joy. The result is success for Andy, his boss, their company, and the customer, not to mention the team members.

3.23

The Conclusion
Be Sensitive To Others' Emotions
And Manage Our Own

Being Sensitive To Other's Emotions

Understand their entire iceberg by genuinely listening and revealing their whole Value Onion. Remember that listening and understanding, as explored earlier, are the top priority on your way to valuepreneurship and success.

It means asking to grasp their priority and highest values, with intelligent questions from the *You Sphere*, not from the *Me sFear* - e.g., Andy needed to be sensitive to his boss's Value Onion.

You will remember the camera in the phone example (1.30) where the questions were being asked logically, from the top of the iceberg, such as, do you want a camera in your phone. The reaction of the customer was indifference.

The camera in the phone is a mere tool, a means to serving the more considerable emotional value of the son getting a first-class degree. However, addressing the customer's emotions, in the depth of the iceberg, when they asked questions around the outer layer of their Value Onion, they understood the camera in the phone is not the real issue but the means to serve the much bigger emotional value. Now they will be much better prepared to develop responses to perfectly match and serve that value, un-obscured by the frailties of negative emotions and doubts – I hope they like my camera and go for it.

Managing Your Own Emotions

Means replacing bad ones with good, fear with care, *Me* with *You*. This is where listening to ourselves and questioning our own emotions is critical.

In any situation, ask yourself, *In which sphere am I as I deal with this situation – the Me sFear or the You Sphere? What value am I bringing?*

It's a critical observation and one which we rarely do. What prevents us is the negative state of our fearful mind full of wants and expectations, which comes in the way of clarity and obscures intellect.

3.24

The Intellect Emotion Grid

The ultimate aim and a balanced state is to have a strong intellect and strong emotion. An imbalance can make us less able to explore and fully utilise our potential.

Look at this grid on the facing page. Here *High Intellect* means having the intellectual reasoning capability and using it well. And *High Emotion* means good emotion and strong emotional management. *Low Emotion* means destructive emotion and poor management.

This grid doesn't necessarily describe any individual entirely – instead, we can find ourselves in any of these boxes at different times in life or other contexts or circumstances. There is a dominant profile, however, which we have grown into over the years. We can loosely call this a part of our personality.

I'm not a geneticist, and frankly, even geneticists cannot answer fully if this profile is down to our DNA or experiences. However, with the privilege of coaching thousands of people, I can confidently conclude that this personality profile expresses how our emotions, fired by the ego, have interacted with every situation we have experienced – including our background, education, religion, parentage etc..

THE INTELLECT EMOTION GRID

INTELLECT
High

DANGEROUS COCKTAIL	TRUE VALUEPRENEUR A LEADER
Intellectual energy, easily hi-jacked by brittle emotion and mis-channelled. High stress, extremely fearful. Aggressive and protectionist behaviour. Easily alienates others who may be fearful of this person. Potential for nervous breakdown. Approach – reason on outcomes and intellectualise behaviour of negativity with them. No emotional retaliation or defensiveness	Comfortable, satisfied, productive, creative, innovative, fearless. A bringer of value. Visionary – sees the major outcomes and works towards them. Approach – Take their advice. Drive conversations from value to customers/recipients. Put them in situations of innovation and growth.
SAFE / MUNDANE	OVER SENSITIVE
Often recluse, plays safe. Despondent and easily disappointed. Good in fixed tasks and working on their own area. Need to be directed. Approach – bring out their best – train, develop in a skill and build their confidence from it. Allow application and chance to prove.	Caring but often for wrong reasons – mainly through fear and over-consciousness of others. Sensitive - often without reason. Likes others and likes to be liked. Tends to see themselves through others' eyes. Soft and loving nature. Good in social professions and care. Approach – encourage, be considerate, sensitive to their feelings. Praise when genuine achievement. Use constructive rather than negative language.

Low   High   EMOTION

So, if our profile is primarily a function of how external factors have influenced us, it also makes sense that we can reverse this if we really wish. We may be what we eat, but we are really what we think. The answer – become a Valuepreneur.

Shifting from the *Me sFear* to the *You Sphere* will shift the emotional emphasis from being a net taker – expecting, wishing, hoping – all of which engender a state of fear, to bringing value, giving – which brings confidence, emotional strength and awakens the logic, the intellect.

3.25

Handling Difficult People For Excellent Outcomes – Four Steps

Observing The Mind, De-Stressing And Achieving Equilibrium

This part examines how to handle challenging people – situations, attitudes, anger, aggression, closed-mindedness, etc.. We will first understand the issues through a situational case. Then we will go through the Four Steps.

But first, three vital points:

- The case we will look at is a situation with an angry boss, we are just borrowing that scenario as an example to give you the method. The technique, principles and method apply in ALL situations, personal or professional with difficult attitudes of others towards us.

- This case and indeed this chapter is a comprehensive summary of the entire book. You will find almost all elements here – value and Response Onions; constraining and enabling natures; mind management; collaboration; co-operation; communication and unity.

- Please use this example and chapter for your own scenarios – take your situations and using the models replace the data with your own for practical, real outcomes.

In many situations in life, we come across people who behave strangely in that scenario. Maybe at work, when someone is not willing to listen to you or becoming confrontational, angry, upset or in your private life, it could be your partner or indeed someone whose car you bump into accidentally, and they react angrily. How do you feel in these situations, how do you react, how efficiently are you able to deal with it?

The keyword here is *react*. *How do we react?*

There is a vast difference between reacting and taking action. Reactions come from our emotion which is most powerful, energised, volatile and even explosive. It's driven by our subjective rather than objective nature (explored in the Iceberg model). Actions, however, come from the intellect, which is logic-based. It is objective, balanced, driven by understanding rather than prejudices and fearful conclusions.

Let me present to you a situation that really transpired and see how you would respond.

An Angry Boss

It is Thursday at 1pm, and on Monday your boss had requested a special report from you which he was expecting today at noon. The report isn't ready, and you are already one hour late. Further, it will take another five hours to complete. Oh, and another thing, it isn't your fault as a colleague who was to give you vital information for this report didn't turn up to work yesterday as she was unwell. As a result, you were working late last night and have tried your best to get it done.

It's quite a regular ordinary occurrence, and all situations like it. In coaching people at all levels, I have used this exact case. We simulate it, where I play the role of the boss, and rather immodestly, it is an Oscar-winning performance which piles on the pressure on the protagonist who was supposed to give me the report, let's just call him Ben. I'll describe how Ben, or everyone reacts in such a situation, and then you will find the answer fascinating.

The Boss Goes Wild With Anger.

The boss, calls Ben into his office and explodes with anger, shouting:

'*Where is the report?* I was expecting it at 12. You are one hour late. Why isn't it here? The meeting is at 5! Crucial stakeholders will be there – and my boss! I will be in deep trouble. You are irresponsible and have let me down. Why isn't it ready and when will I get it?'

It's loud, unpleasant and intimidating and piles the pressure onto Ben, who reacts by saying, 'Well, I've been trying my very best, but Lisa didn't turn up to work yesterday. I'm constructing the information myself, but I promise, I'm working on it and will get to you as quickly as I can.'

It's a balanced and well-intentioned response.

The boss explodes further. '*What?! You're blaming it on someone else?* I entrusted you with this vital task. In the 5pm meeting today, key stakeholders will be there – and my boss – and you're standing here making excuses? I want to know when will be ready?'

Under pressure, Ben says, 'Well, it will take another five hours, but I promise you I'll try my best.'

'*Try? Five hours?* That's 6pm? Have you even listened to anything I'm saying? The meeting is at 5pm. I may not make it to 6pm! It will be like the lion's den in there. There are tough issues to resolve! We need answers! And you are saying *it will be ready at 6pm?*'

Ben nervously and anxiously says, 'OK, I'll try my best, prioritise the key parts and aim to get it done by 5pm.'

'It's too late, Ben. I need to discuss the issues with my boss for an hour before the meeting.'

'OK, I'll try for 4pm...' knowing full well it will take five hours.

It's a miserable situation. How would you react if you were in Ben's place? When I ask this question, people give me a range of responses:

- **I'd do what Ben did**, tell him *I'll try my best* and then get on with it. Well, yes, he does seem to be trying to sort it out, find a solution, prioritising and is and remaining professional and committed, but is it getting him anywhere? Also, through fear and just wanting the situation to go away. Ben has given a false commitment for 4pm, which is in three hours, and we've already said it will take five hours. When Ben comes at 4pm and says, *Sorry boss, I could only get 60% done,* he has created a much bigger problem for himself and his boss.

- **I'd get very upset.** The boss has no right to speak to me like that. I would ask the boss to calm down... and then I can help him.

  Really? So, you are taking it personally, and also, try telling him to calm down! It will be like pouring petrol directly into the fire. Your objective should never be to calm someone down or change their demeanour. It will not work, you will further anger or agitate them, and you will certainly not solve the real problem. Let's face it, in a similar situation, if you were upset and angry and the other person tried to calm you down, you would get more upset and feel who are you to change my mood and behaviour. So, what should your objective be? We will discover this below.

- **I'd make sure he understands that it wasn't my fault and explain to him what happened.** Well, it's an honest approach, but is he really concerned about why it isn't here? Also, by defending yourself, will you find a solution? You will be in your third constraining nature of *Justification*.

Your credibility with him will go down and it will damage the interaction and, indeed the relationship. Although he is shouting, why isn't it here? Is this his real concern at this time? We say things through emotions and anger but need something completely different. If you start giving reasons, the emphasis will be on the reasons rather than the solution, and you will lose credibility and respect.

There are many other responses in addition to these three main ones. Unfortunately, none of them result in good outcomes.

What's the answer? The answer is straightforward, and it deludes us. There is an elephant in the room, trumpeting crazily, and you don't see it. No one sees it. I have simulated this exact case with people over 1,500 times, and I have never seen anyone pick up the simple, real issue and deal with it. Intriguing, isn't it? You will kick yourself when I give you the answer in all its simplicity.

The Elephant In The Room

So here is a different approach to this conversation. I now reverse the roles, so you are the boss, and I am you. It's exactly the same case. I will first outline the conversation, and then I'll give you the *Four Steps Of Dealing With Difficult People* and practical tips to make it happen.

Angry Boss: Take 2

Same as before, the boss goes wild with anger and explodes with rage, shouting, 'Where is the report? I was expecting it at 12. You are one hour late, why is it not here? In the 5pm meeting, I'll have a massive problem as key stakeholders will be there – *and my boss* – and I will be in deep, deep trouble. You are irresponsible and have let me down. Why is it not ready and when will I get it?'

It can be as loud and unpleasant as you want, and in these simulations, people really go for it to see if Sanjeev can solve it. The decibels are high, the tone intimidating. It gets personal and nasty – no problem.

My reaction in Ben's role is as follows. It is very easy and tempting to react emotionally, defensively or offensively as we had mentioned above, but I remain attentive, respectful and patient: *how?*

I say the following:

'Firstly, I'm sorry this has happened.' (Step 1 below)

Boss *(angrily)*, 'I don't care whether you are sorry; why isn't it here?'

I remain unhassled, respectful and focused. On what? (It's coming in Step 2.)

Now I hear you saying, *Why should I say I'm sorry if it wasn't my fault? It was Lisa, not me…* Well, if it *was* your fault, then an apology shows the taking of responsibility squarely on your shoulders with courage, this may not stop the anger, which is fine, but inside them, it builds respect and relationships. However, if it *isn't* your fault, as is the case here, you are *still* saying sorry, but not sorry because you messed up – sorry because *this* has gone wrong for him – there is empathy and care. It's compelling, humbling and their respect for you will undoubtedly go up.

Now I say the following: 'Boss, there are reasons why this happened, and I promise you I'll do a complete root cause analysis for you tomorrow. I'll also show you what I am doing to prevent this from happening again. But today, my concern is with your 5pm meeting, the key stakeholders, their priorities which you need to present and the success of the meeting.'

Now notice:

- I haven't justified by saying it wasn't me; it was my colleague, pushing away the responsibility and losing credibility and respect, and;

- I remained objective and focused on the *real issue*, which was the success of the 5pm meeting, key stakeholders, their priorities and making that meeting go well, i.e., *his* Value Onion.

This 5pm meeting and what the boss needs to achieve from it, was the elephant in the room. It was sitting there waving its colossal trunk and trumpeting loud and clear, as he was shouting – 5pm meeting, key stakeholders, we will be crucified etc..

I have done this case thousands of times, and would you believe no one to date has picked up on it and time and time again, I see people miss it in their actual situations.

Be honest, did you pick it up as you were reading the text above? If unusually you did, then bravo, but here you are not actually in that situation and therefore not emotionally entangled; you are objective. If this were your own situation, it's almost guaranteed you would not see the elephant in the room. You would be subjective, take it personally and miss the real issue.

He may be obstinate and say something like, 'What's the point in asking me all of this now? You should have just delivered as promised.'

But you will notice his voice will have softened, maybe only just a little bit, but it will, and it will be subconscious for him because in the depth of his iceberg, i.e., in his emotion, your concern for his value will have had an impact and given him hope of success at 5pm.

Now remaining as objective as I can, unhassled and respectful, I don't engage with his comment, and I say, 'Sure boss, but if you can help me understand the priorities for the 5pm meeting and the stakeholders, I can really work on helping to make it go well.'

The boss will almost invariably and a little more calmly say, 'Alright, so what do you want to know?

After all it's in *his* interest. And that is all that matters to him right now. I say. 'If you can help me identify who the main stakeholders are for you and your boss, in that meeting, *and* their key priorities you need to deliver on, I can get 40% done by 3pm and another 20% done at 4pm (these 60% are outer layers of his Value Onion). I can provide the other 40% in summary format and complete it tomorrow.' (These are the inner layers of his Value Onion – important but lower priority).

You are providing a solution, but it is an excellent one, and what makes it brilliant is that it responds perfectly to his Value Onion which you have cared to understand.

The simple truth is that given this situation, you can only get 60% done, don't get stuck because your fearful and emotionally entangled mind makes you think of the whole report, but if it is 60%, then so be it. The real question is which 60%. And you can only answer this question if you know his Value Onion, then the matching Response Onion is that 60%.

Again and again, I say to you, when you are holding their Value Onion, i.e., you understand it and have a response to it, you needn't worry or be concerned. Yet, we offer to prioritise without understanding his value. And he, as a result, can never feel confident that you are genuinely trying to serve him. Instead, he sees your solution as a self-protection exercise, which, frankly, it is.

With the above response, you will see his attitude change, the decibels come down, and you are in dialogue. He will say something like:

'OK, let's sit down. This new project is significantly delayed, and all stakeholders are anxious, which puts my boss and me in a difficult position. The CEO is going to be there and, she is looking for the market share growth analysis. The HR head is concerned about the aggressive speed of recruitment. The Ops head wants to see that all processes are in place. The Finance director urgently needs the ROI numbers as the deadline for the board meeting to approve the project is next week. Of these, my highest priorities are the FD and CEO…'

I see this happen every single time.

The person just seems to become more comfortable, less difficult and angry, more in dialogue. It makes sense as in your approach, you didn't get emotionally de-railed, justify and protect yourself. Instead, you remained obsessively but respectfully focused on his value. You didn't make it about you and how it affected you but his value and the 5pm meeting. He will react positively, and it's as simple as that. After all, if he is born of a mother on this planet, and that's a reasonable assumption to make, then there is only one truth – that he has a Value Onion. If you obsessively attach to his value, seek to understand it and build a response to it as close as possible given the circumstances and constraints, he will respond favourably.

The issue has shifted from the report, the delay, the reasons and you – to his value, i.e., the 5pm meeting, his stakeholders and their expectations, saving his neck and making a success of the meeting. After all, this is what crucially matters. Think about this as you tend to pick the wrong straw.

The Issue Behind The Issue

You see, this meeting was never about the report, the delay and the reasons. That was merely the issue in front which we saw and engaged with. We needed to look beyond and find the real issues - *The Issue Behind The Issue.*

It was the 5pm meeting, the considerable difficulty he and his boss was going to face at 5pm, their reputation etc..

It was the real issue. But we, through our own needs, worries, concerns and fears, don't see it. Even though he was shouting at the top of his voice – *I'll be crucified at 5pm, key stakeholders will be expecting answers from us,* and so on – we didn't listen. We hear a lot and listen to very little.

We mostly listen to our own selves, our prejudices and our concerns, so we miss the real issue even though it's being shouted at in our face. To what extent is our mind distracted by our emotions, we live in subjectivity, but success will come from moving into objectivity.

Your Response Onion

Having understood his stakeholders and their priorities, I respond as follows:

'Thanks for sharing that with me boss, now that I understand, this is what I propose. Let me quickly get the ROI slides for the FD done, and I can get these to you by 2pm. Simultaneously, could you lend me Joan from your team, and I can ask her to do the market share growth figures as she has great experience in that area? Then I'll get the recruitment numbers and the processes for the Ops head. I'll do it in summary format and detail it tomorrow. Also, I'll give you an update each hour. Also, would it help you if I kept myself free during the meeting if you need to reach out to get any additional information?

The boss says, 'This looks like a good plan, and yes, it would work well.'

He may even say, 'I'm sorry I got upset. It wasn't at you. It's just that a lot is riding on this meeting.'

But this shouldn't be your expectation.

The Two Extremes Of Their Behaviour
And Everything In-Between

We have been speaking about a highly vocal, loud, shouting reaction to generate the most incredible stress within us. Thankfully, this extreme and rude behaviour rarely happens in today's day and age, and it is considered outside the social norms. I have illustrated it as it will de-rail us the most, but if we can deal with this kind of behaviour, then using the same approach, less harsh and more frequent day to day reactions of people to us will become effortless to handle.

However, someone else in the same situation may react differently, with silence and intensity rather than shouting, and a whole range of reactions in between. Don't be fooled; the pain, frustration and fear in them in the depth of their iceberg will be precisely the same. Therefore, your own reaction needs to be exactly the same, and the four steps given below will be the same. Don't be deluded into thinking, *Phew, thank God he didn't get too angry* – underneath it is the same feeling. It just didn't manifest in the same way. Instead of aggression, it manifested with intensity.

In fact, it's better with the aggressive person because you can really see what's in their mind and what their iceberg is experiencing. When it is hidden, it's more difficult for us to deal with, and therefore we could become less efficient at finding a solution. So, I emphasise this point - understand their value, regardless of their reaction and behaviour and follow the four steps outlined below. Shouting or silent – it's the same thing.

There Is No Such Thing As A Difficult Person

While we call this discussion the *Four Steps of Handling Difficult People*, I want to clarify that this is only for convenience - calling it what our mind sees.

But the title itself is wrong. There is no such thing as a *difficult* person. It is only someone requiring their value to be fulfilled.

As we said in discussing the *Three Constraining Natures* earlier, this is a prejudice. After all, don't you get sometimes get frustrated or angry? Of course, we all do. So are you a difficult person? Let's say you are mad with me about something – maybe I didn't do something you were expecting. Which of these two statements is truer:

- You are attacking me.
- You are frustrated that your work isn't getting done, i.e., that you have a value to be fulfilled.

Yes, indeed, it is the second. Well, if it is the second one for you, why isn't it the same for someone else? They were born of a mother on this planet, the same as all of us. But the problem is that our engaged and prejudiced mind labels people as difficult, nasty, evil etc.. It's a *prejudice* my friends - our First Constraining Nature.

It's so simple and frankly liberating. You will never see a problematic person again. You will only see value. You will not disturb yourself or stress yourself out. You will listen to understand the value and, where possible, become a response to it.

In our discussion, we will continue to refer to them as difficult people for convenience. The more accurate term is people with a tough attitude. There is no such thing as a *difficult* person.

3.26

The Four Steps to Handling Difficult People Situations And Tough Attitudes

Now let's unravel this case and clearly identify the practical steps and methods to handle such, and frankly any situations where the other person is being difficult, angry, upset. If we can handle a situation of such intensity and get a great result, then the day to day more minor issues will become a cinch.

Before I give you the four steps, let's establish a critical point with this thought. When the other person is getting angry and upset, there are two possibilities.

1. I *have* done something wrong; or

2. I *haven't* done something wrong

I am going at this step by step, logically and arithmetically. Follow it with me; it will become extremely clear and easy.

If I *have* done something wrong, as in 1 above, this is the simplest of all situations to handle. There is nothing more powerful and winning of respect than putting your hands up, taking responsibility and ownership and saying, *My sincere apologies, I've made a mistake and messed up. Here is a solution for it; I'll get right on to it.*

This broad-shouldered approach will always win respect. Even if they continue to be angry, deeper in their iceberg, they will have respect for you. In the end, what are people concerned more about, who messed up and why; or their own value? Certainly, the latter. Yes, if we don't engage with their value and try to defend ourselves, the focus will be on who messed up and why. I will end up making it about me, I have put myself into the *Me sFear*, and as discussed, this is actually what happens most, if not all, of the time. By going into the *You Sphere*, in other words, obsessing with their value, the focus shifts from me to you, which is the best way to achieve exceptional outcomes.

However, if I *haven't* done something wrong and they are getting angry and upset, then think about this - is the problem with them or me? Of course, it's with them. My iceberg, subconscious, and unhinged emotion betray me and make me believe the problem is with me. But that's a prejudice which leads me in the wrong direction. I want to be very clear on this and leave no doubt – think about this. In this situation, have they chosen me as the only person on earth to vent their angst on, or would they behave like this with a hundred other people or, frankly, anyone else who was in my position?

Of course, I hear you say, *They would be like this with anyone in this situation where they feel let down and upset.* So again I ask the question, *is the problem with them or with me?* Yes, it's with them – we have just proven that logically and conclusively. Then, I ask, *Why, oh why, do we make it about me? It's not about me.*

Now, in this situation, my heart normally says one of two things:

- *How dare you say that to me!* i.e.,Don't speak to me like that. I feel disrespected, hurt and angry. Even if you don't say this out aloud, you are thinking it.

- *Oh no, this will give me a problem.* i.e. how will it affect my position in the company, my review, my promotion, and many other concerns for me.

Even on the way to the meeting, I'm in fear, in my own *sfear,* thinking – *what will this mean for me?*

Agitatedly I oscillate between these two thoughts. Now in these two thoughts, *how dare you say that to me* and *Oh no, this will give me a problem,* what is the one common word causing the entire problem? Yes, indeed ME. It's the *me* that derails everything, and I have proven to you arithmetically that it's not about me. It's about them and their value.

Isn't it fascinating and crazy that we are constantly derailing ourselves by our own thinking and emotion? I am always picking the wrong straw. I am the architect of almost everything that happens to me and around me. It can be a scary thought, but it will be a relief and uplifting to know that you have the key to solving anything and everything if you truly understand it. Yet we are deluded enough to think it's the other person who must change or behave like this or that. This false and dangerous expectation will mess me up.

By the way, I want to clarify that whether you have done something wrong or not, the four steps below and the approach will be exactly the same. I made the distinction above to highlight two points:

1. Take ownership. It builds respect.

2. To prove to you that you make it about yourself, the 'me' that betrays us, and it's not about me, it's about them.

With this in mind, here are the four steps to handling difficult people and challenging situations

3.27

Four Steps To Handling Difficult People And Challenging Situations

The four steps to handling difficult people and challenging situations are:

1. Disengage

2. Understand

3. How can I help? or Here is a solution

4. Get Well Soon

Let's unpack each step.

3.28

Step 1 – DISENGAGE

Disengage from what? Last week, I asked a group this question, and someone said, *Disengage from the situation!*

No, no! We have to *engage* with the situation. The answer is to disengage from your emotion, your worry, fears, concerns. This emotion and feeling make me make it about me and gives me anxiety and anger in return. But in this state, I'm not objective, I am subjective. Objective is intellect, reason and understanding; Subjective is emotion and feeling. I lose the sense of reality and make wrong and dangerous conclusions like – *it will hurt my career, I'll be out of favour with my boss,* and so on. You are royally in the *Constraining Nature of Prejudice.* These futile, harmful thoughts will perpetuate and cause more and more problems for me. In fact, only when you disengage from your emotion can you really engage with the situation. I know you are thinking – *It's easy for you to tell us to disengage, but that's very difficult,* and *how do you do it?* Frankly, it's as easy and as difficult as your mind makes it, and here is how:

They are being angry, even shouting and being aggressive:

Tip 1 – Mantra 1 – It's Not About Me; It's About Your Value

With a blink of an eye, say to yourself, *It's not about me, it's about your value.* It's nothing short of a mantra. It should be easy to understand and accept due to our logical, arithmetical analysis above of showing you it's not about me at all, but I choose the wrong straw and *make it about me.*

Taking the same example, as you go to the meeting, keep the mantra in your mind – *It's not about me, it's about your value.* It really is as simple as that. Of course, couple this with the technique of mind centricity for a meditative, balanced available mind which is readily available.

This simple mantra technique is what you need, and it will automatically take you from the *Me sFear* to the *You Sphere.* You will start listening, which is the key to understanding their value objectively and intelligently and not reacting subjectively and emotionally. It's worth meditating on this point to see how simple it is if you are dedicated to making it happen.

I hear you asking, *But why should I think of his value when he behaves so nastily to me?*

I understand you and am wholly sympathetic with your thoughts. Still, again and again, I say to you that we have proven definitively, arithmetically and absolutely that his anger is not an attack on you or disrespect of you. It is nothing to do with you. It's an expression of his frustration for his value. Please get this point, and you will never be disturbed by anyone ever again. You will see objective reality and handle situations without stress and with much better results and outcomes. Don't be proud and self-important, don't be precious, however tempting it is, this will keep your ego fired and agitated, prevent you from being great and keep you small. You are much bigger than that.

It's only with this dis-engagement that you will see the elephant in the room sitting there waving its trunk and trumpeting loud and clear – my 5pm meeting, key stakeholders, my neck is on the line etc.. You hear it but don't listen to it because you are engaged emotionally, and your emotion is telling you all the rubbish like *what this will mean for me* or *how dare you speak to me like that*, etc.. It's not worth it.

Let's change it, shape our relationships, the respect people have for us and get the job done by genuinely applying my talents efficiently and productively.

So once again, faced with this attitude from someone, just blink your eye and say to yourself, It's not about me, it's about your value. The blink is just a physical trigger for you. They won't realise you have explicitly blinked, but it's a hard reminder of the mantra for you.

Tip 2 – Mantra 2 – I Am Just The Screen; The Screen Doesn't Burn

The Towering Inferno (1974), was box office film in its day with a superstar cast. It's a disaster movie about a New York skyscraper on fire. For two hours, you will see a lot of fire on the screen, but here's my question, when the movie ends – and every movie must end – *does the screen burn?* No, the screen is neutral. The film is just being projected onto it, so, no, the screen doesn't burn.

Further, every movie needs a screen, so, no screen, no movie.

In the same way, someone shouting at you, angry at you or displaying any negative attitude to you is just their unhappiness being projected onto you, and you have become the *screen for this movie.* You are the screen on which the frustration of their value not being served is being projected. However, you are just a screen. You are neutral. You won't burn, so long as you understand that you are the screen and neutral. If you have the clarity to understand it's not about you but their value, you will be impartial and remain the screen.

However, you *will* burn if you think you are the building itself instead of the screen.

Practically this means that if you think you are the object of the angst, in other words, if you make about the *me – he is attacking me; what will it mean for me,* then you no longer understand that you are just the screen. You now see yourself as the building, the object of this fire, this shouting. You have made it about yourself, even though we have proven conclusively in the above section that it's not about me.

As a result, you will defend and protect yourself, justify, not take ownership, push responsibility away, get upset and even offended. Is your resulting action going to help solve the problem, win their respect, and even calm them down (even though calming them down should never be your objective)? Not at all. You will lose dialogue, respect and confidence from him and will impact the relationship. He may not trust you with important projects, and it may even impair your position in the organisation – so you have burned. You didn't understand you were the screen but thought you were the building. The sad thing is that your intentions were good, but as the saying goes, the road to hell was built on good intentions. It's just that you didn't see the issue in the right way, you saw the issue and made it about you, but the real issue was his value – *The issue behind the issue.*

Do you ever cry in movies? I do regularly.

Have you ever thought about why we cry in movies? It's because we associate with the character who is going through sadness - as if we are that character. We make about me. We become the object of the sadness – we are no longer the audience; we are the burning building. The only difference is that in a sad movie, we pay to feel sad and even cry. If we didn't, our entertainment value wouldn't be satisfied, and we would feel cheated. In dealing with difficult attitudes, we pay for our misguided association by inserting myself in the story, making it about me.

It's a false, misguided prejudice that can cost me dearly. We end up disturbing ourselves and harming our-self with stress, concern, fears and not wishing to work with that person. It's fine in a movie, you're being entertained. But in life remain disengaged.

If you use this mantra well and make it a natural reflex, there will come a time when not only does your mind in such a situation say, *I'm just the screen, the screen doesn't burn*, but it will say, *I'm just the screen, the screen doesn't burn, and thank God I was there – worse it could have happened to a colleague of mine, and they don't know they are the screen, they would burn.*

Wow, at this level, you are unstoppable, unphased, appreciated and at your full potential.

Even in being the screen and taking this onslaught, you are a response to the angry person's value. One of his values is to be able to vent his fears, anxieties, concerns. So never again see an angry person on that chair; see a big fat Value Onion. In fact, the greater the angst, the better it is because there is more value to serve. When your thinking has evolved to this level you have reached – you are realised. A lot of experience has shown me this is not theory but a practical reality as I see many people along my journey who have got there (see Rob's example).

It is well established with research that one of the top reasons why people quit their jobs… is their boss. However, the stark reality is that you will encounter such people or attitudes in many places, situations, and guises. How far will you run? You are only running from yourself.

Still the mind, contemplate everything we have discussed above, and you will find the answer lies here and now within you. The more you understand that it's not about you but their value, the more you will solve it immediately and not carry the problem with you. The problem is within you, and so is the answer. If you grasp it and follow it, nothing and no one ever again in your life can disturb you. You will be clear-headed, objective, successful and frankly your magnificent self.

One point of clarity here is that we have taken the example of an angry boss because his value wasn't being met. Of course, you could have a situation where you don't have a solution or are required to have a solution. For example, an awkward person like a bad-tempered waiter or a driver with road rage, and so on. You don't have to bring a solution, but the point remains the same, their frustration is not with you, but something is bothering them. It's still their value. Remain disengaged, but we tend to misread it as an attack on us. Just walk away, with the awareness in the mind that *it's about them* and *I am just the screen.*

Keep these two mantras close to you and always in your head. At the moment, they feel like tools you have to apply consciously, but the more you use them, they will become subconscious reactions, of which you will not even be aware.

It's like using a crutch if you break a leg. What is the purpose of a crutch? That you can take its' support for a while. You have to, or else you will fall. But the idea, assuming that it's not permanent damage, is to let go of the crutch and walk yourself.

These mantras serve the same purpose as with any of the tips, tools and techniques I am giving you in this book. Use them consciously and soon they will become an automatic, subconscious reflex. But that is only if you use them as I am showing you.

Rob's Tough Client

Two years ago, I was doing a program for senior partners of a prominent law firm – let's call them Law. One of the partners– let's call him Rob – who was on the program, was going through hell with his client, a major UK retailer.

The CFO (Chief Finance Officer) was very unhappy with Law, and he would shout and be very unpleasant. That account was in danger of being lost. Rob was nearly at a nervous breakdown. He said to me, 'Every time I come out of a coaching session with you, I feel stronger and feel now I can handle it. However, the next day the client is shouting and unpleasantness starts, and I forget everything you have taught me... *and I just want to quit.*'

He was not getting much support from his seniors at Law either. It was a miserable situation. Here's what we did.

I got one of my admin staff to send Rob a text message every day at 8.30am on his way to work. It was sent every single weekday at 8.30am for six weeks. The text read:

It's not about me; it's about your value.

I'm just the screen; the screen doesn't burn.

It was a trigger, and the result was incredible. Two weeks later, Rob said, 'Sanjeev, the decibels have come down at the client massively.'

Another week later, he said, 'We seem to be in dialogue...' and so it went. That account was saved and grew. Rob is still at the firm and is one of the most successful senior equity partners.

As a concluding remark to the discussion on this Step 1, *Disengage,* think about this: *Your style belongs to you, but your value belongs to me.* It's another powerful thought as a trigger to remind yourself and get it right.

What I mean is your style is your prerogative. If you are an angry type of person, please go ahead and be angry. It's fine with me. Or a calm person, that's fine too. Your style and attitude is your asset. Enjoy it, it's nothing to do with me, and it is not my place to tell you how you should behave in the same way I wouldn't like anyone to tell me how to behave. If I said to you, *Don't be an angry person,* would that change you? No, you would tell me where to go. So don't have any expectations of how someone should behave and their style. I can't and shouldn't do anything about your style, which is why I say your style belongs to you.

However, regarding your value – I can help you with this. Of course, your value belongs to you, and I am using artistic licence when I say it belongs to me. I am saying that I can do something about your value, understand it, and bring a response to serve it. It is powerful and liberating.

Let me ask you, in a challenging situation, or frankly in most situations of interaction with someone, for example, if they get angry or shout etc.., what do you instantly react to, their style or their value?

Yes, indeed, their style, their behaviour, their attitude. Such is the nature of our mind, our emotion, the depth of our iceberg, our sub-conscious nature. But this prejudiced, discriminatory, deluded, filtered way of seeing the situation betrays us, and we react with badly altered actions, defensively, negatively and even confrontationally. It gets us nowhere.

Keeping this central thought that *your style belongs to you, but your value belongs to me* will drive you to objectivity and the real issue. You will listen and understand correctly, intellectually and not emotionally, objectively not subjectively. You will build the best solution and response, favourably alter the other person's attitude, develop better relationships of trust and get the job done every time.

Have No Expectations Of Others' Behaviours

Changing their behaviours must never be your objective – you will only disturb yourself. The first point to make is to have no expectations in life. Expectation, as we have said already, is the killer of man. It takes away from your resolve your effort and ties you down with the weight of dependence on something or someone else. It will slow you down and make you less open for success. Applying this to difficult people or someone who is being disrespectful, our sense of social propriety arises, and we start applying norms of behaviour. For example, *she shouldn't have said that; he should be more considerate; he must control his behaviour; she shouldn't be rude to me.* These kinds of statements are futile and will disturb you in life and not achieve any change in the other.

It's a false expectation within the context of a so-called norm, and you have missed that they have their own context under which this behaviour has arisen. I am not asking you to condone it. But I am asking you to accept it, understand it and the context, i.e., their value behind it. Help if you can, move away if you can't. Don't judge or expect. Why trouble yourself? The freer you are of these futile projections and missed realities, the more productive and fulfilled you will be.

Two Angry Clients

A life coach was trying to resolve a conflict between two furious colleagues to get them to cooperate. 'I've been telling them that you need to listen to each other, and that this behaviour is unprofessional and unacceptable; you should communicate, respect each other and behave with decorum.'

I asked her if it had worked.

She said, 'I am working on it…' in other words, *No.*

Poor deluded soul, she is working on the wrong thing. There is a pathetic expectation of how people should behave. If you were angry, upset, frustrated, and I came to you with this kind of crass advice and forced expected norms on you, would you accept it blindly as if someone has turned on a great light for you, there is a revelation for you, and as a result, you change your behaviour?

Let's wake up from this delusion and dream.

I am not saying that it is not desirable that everyone gets to a stage where they interact with mutual respect, care and kindness; in fact, this is in every human being's nature. But I am saying that when you place this as a condition and expectation, as did this coach and the millions of so-called communication experts in the world, you will generate more agitation for yourself and miss the actual point.

It's much more straightforward and, in its simplicity, much higher than this naïve expectation of social norms. I am speaking about humbling down, putting aside your ego, understanding that this is not an attack on you but an expression of their value not being served. Then you will not disturb yourself, listen, serve value where you can, step back where you can't but remain untarnished or unaffected in life. Life is more remarkable than ordinary expectations of others' behaviours. Live it; don't be distracted by wrong things.

When you approach harsh attitudes and behaviours with the method I have described, you will achieve much more. And one of the bi-products will be that their behaviour, style, attitudes will change and become a lot more respectful and collaborative as it did with the boss in our case above. Yet this was never our objective. Do you get this point?

Never Ever Ask Them To Calm Down – In The Situation Of Someone Expressing Anger And Agitation

Never make it your objective to get someone to calm down or change their behaviour or attitude, and yet by our Four Steps approach, this change will be one of the outcomes – it's still not my objective.

I know I am repeating the same point several times and in different ways, and you may be thinking, *OK, Sanjeev, I get it. But I make no excuses for this my friends, and it's done on purpose.*

It is not enough that you get it – it needs to become a reflex, a part of your nature. Actually, I am teaching you nothing. Have you noticed? I am removing the unnecessary complications you put on yourself. It's a process of simplification to your beautiful natural state and nature. It's a revelation, not development.

As for solving conflict and getting greater collaboration, we will discuss this later and speak more about operating from the *Point Of Zero Conflict* in Section 5. We will also discuss one of the most significant dysfunctions of any organisation – the lack of UNITY and how to UNIFY people, teams….

Having discussed Step 1, Disengage - Steps 2, 3 and 4 have now become much easier. Let us work on these.

3.29

Step 2 – I'd Like To UNDERSTAND

Returning to the case of the angry boss with the delayed report, do you remember I reassured him with... *My concern is with your 5pm meeting, the key stakeholders, their priorities that you want to address, and the success of the meeting. If you can help me with this understanding, I can work on helping with the 5pm meeting to go well.*

The boss will almost invariably and a little more calmly say: *Alright, so what do you want to know?*

Now I turn on my first Enabling Nature which is *Understand*, and I say, 'If you can help me identify who the main stakeholders are for you and your boss in that meeting and their key priorities you need to deliver on, I can get 40% done by 3pm and another 20% done by 4pm. I can provide the other 40% in summary format and complete it tomorrow.'

It was a powerful step where I was genuinely concerned with and obsessively attached to his value i.e., the success of the 5pm meeting, his and his boss's reputation and satisfying the key stakeholders the CEO, Finance Director, Ops Head and HR head. But in your conversation with the boss, this vital information, the real issue, the *issue behind the issue*, remained unrevealed. Why? Because you were not disengaged.

You were engaged with your own emotion of what will this anger mean for me in your own *sFear*.

The Boss's Value Onion –
Reminder of EV BV PV (Section1)

NOTE: The methods, principles and models we are using in this book are universally applicable across all sections and subjects we are discussing. There is a consistency and totality of usage be it in the value culture, strategy, planning, conversing, the mind etc..

Here we examine the boss's priorities and our understanding of them using the conversational version of the Value Onion – EV BV PV In the case of the delayed report:

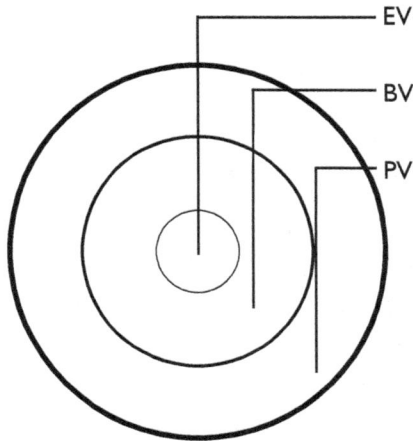

EV – Essential Value. The core of the Value Onion.

- The report
- Its structure
- The sections
- Content

- Time lines
- Presentation software e.g., PowerPoint, PDF.

These are the essential and critical features of the report but in themselves represent lowest value to the boss. It's the core of the onion. Greater than EV is BV – going outwards in the Value Onion and the layers or circles of value are bigger, representing greater value to the boss.

BV – Business Value. Which business priorities will the report help to serve

- An excellent meeting at 5pm.
- Good business decisions made.
- All stakeholders on board and satisfied.
- Increased sales and margins.
- Business expansion.

Our mind focus, and therefore discussion should be driven from BV. It's powerful and engages the boss. We genuinely understand true value and are able to serve its for great outcomes.

As we go even further to the outermost layers of the Value Onion, we get into the biggest values of all – PV, personal value. This is the pinnacle of achievement and ultimately it motivates all decisions –private or professional.

PV – Personal Value Of The Boss

- Respect from his boss, colleagues and other senior stakeholders.
- Not be pressured and pulled apart in the meeting.

- Deal with all topics in the meeting with personal confidence and conviction.

- No stress.

- Promotion to board level.

- Bigger bonus from company's results.

- Support and co-operation from his team.

Some people find it difficult to accept saying we should keep professional and personal motivations separate – let's wake up. Think about your own decisions, which of these lists motivate and drive you the most. It's the third one for me. The trick is to align all three EV, BV and PV and in this example and all the examples in this book that's exactly what a valuepreneur does.

Returning to Step 2 – I'd Like to Understand

As I remained disengaged and interested in him and his value in the *You Sphere,* his anger fell away, his attitude changed, we were in dialogue, he calmed down. It was a bi-product, and as we have discussed above, it was not my objective.

So *Understanding* is the second step in dealing with so-called *difficult* people and tough attitudes.

BUT I can only really understand if I have DIS-ENGAGED. It is sequential, and Step 2 can only happen after a well-done Step 1.

3.30

Step 3 – How Can I HELP?
Or Here Is The SOLUTION

Having understood his stakeholders and their priorities, I responded as follows:

'Thanks for sharing that with me boss, now that I understand the issues and priorities, here's what I propose: Let me quickly get the ROI slides for the FD done. I can get these to you by 2pm, simultaneously could you give me Joan and I can ask her to do the market share growth figures as she has good experience in that area. Then I'll get the recruitment numbers and the processes for the Ops head. I'll do the lower priority points in summary format and detail them tomorrow. Also, I'll give you an update each hour and then would it help you if I kept myself free during the meeting if you need to reach out to get any additional information?'

The boss says, 'This looks like a good plan, and yes, it would work well.'

He may even say, 'I'm sorry I got upset. It wasn't at you; it's just that a lot is riding on this meeting.'

But this shouldn't be an expectation from you.

Can you see how powerful this is? Suddenly, the anger has gone. We are in dialogue and achieving results. Our Response Onion is to Serve The Boss's Value Onion.

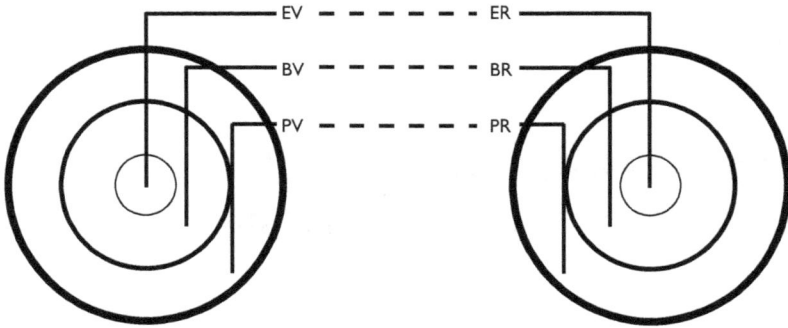

Examples of Response Onions:

ER – Essential Response

- The Report completed in stages.
- Time lines – by 2pm I'll give you x; By 4 pm I'll give you y etc..
- Prepare the slides in PowerPoint with an additional document in Word.
- Etc..

BR – Business Response

A lot of ER will also give BRs but here are some more specifically:

- High priority for the Finance Director with ROI calculations completed
- Market share growth figures – with Joan's help.
- Recruitment numbers analysed as the Ops Head likes.
- Etc..

PR – Personal Response

A lot of BR will also give PRs but here are some more specifically:

- Keeping him updated every 60 minutes – reassuring and destressing.
- By prioritising the information for the CEO, FD, HR and Ops heads and preparing slides and information to their taste – the boss will be respected and admired.
- Remaining at hand during the meeting to answer queries – will prevent the boss from getting into sticky situations.

So, can you see the responses are perfectly matched to values. It's fail safe, rewarding for all and full of integrity. However, I can only offer response solutions when, and only when I have understood the problem in Step 2. We get this wrong and start offering solutions before understanding the value, the real issue. Remember, in the first conversation (our usual way), we were saying, *I will prioritise and try my best.* Yes, it was an attempt at a solution, but on what basis will you prioritise? Have you even understood his priorities, his Value Onion? Trying your best is valiant, but it has come from fear without understanding and serving value but protecting yourself. It's not the way of a Valuepreneur.

Here is a simple arithmetical formula:

Responding – Understanding = Justification

Most of the time, we are not really responding but justifying, i.e., our actions are often to protect ourselves rather than serving value. No wonder we are not as efficient as we can be or indeed as satisfied as we can be. Protecting ourselves will generate more expectations, fears and engagement of the ego. Serving value will bring deep satisfaction and elevate us.

Let's get to where we deserve to be.

3.31

Step 4 – Get Well Soon

If and only if you have done Steps 1, 2 and 3 as we have described above, then in 95% of the situations, you will get success – job done. But I stress that it will only succeed if you have done 1, 2, and 3 well; and in sequence.

However, there is a slight chance; let's say 5%, where despite doing Steps 1, 2 and 3 perfectly, the anger and angst still continues, and you haven't got to a satisfactory solution. Then, and only then will you need to invoke Step 4.

Step 4 will be needed only as an exception in exceptional circumstances, and this step involves you gently stepping back and saying, *Get Well Soon*. (By the way, you *don't* actually say *Get Well Soon!* Can you imagine if you said that to your angry boss or anyone in that state of mind?) The principle is *Get Well Soon* but what you say and do is as follows:

You remind them of their value, gently step back and reassure them of your help. It goes like this - despite their continuing anger, start stepping back gently saying: 'Boss, I can certainly help make the 5pm meeting with those key stakeholders go well for you and prioritise, but I will need your help. I'll be at my desk. Please give me a shout.'

Then you gently walk away. Maintain respect at all times. If you make them lose face, for example by saying, *Boss I'm trying to understand and help you, but you are continuing to be angry.* Or worse, *If you stop shouting, I can help...* then you have taken a path from which getting back is near impossible as you will have made them lose face. There will be a wall of pride in that relationship which is tough to break. The relationship will be impacted trust will be impaired.

Can you see yourself – hear yourself – taking the approach I have given above?

It's constructive and straightforward and leaves all doors open, and you remain a bringer of value. This is true leadership, and profoundly satisfying. It brings results and builds relationships. You will always be appreciated, advocated and even advertised. You are still not doing it for that, it's one of the outcomes.

Even in this situation, I have seen whenever Step 4 is needed to be invoked, ten minutes later, half an hour later, two hours later. They will come to you, *knock-knock* and say, *Right, you were saying you can help. How?* That's it, the job is done.

Why wouldn't they? You didn't take it personally or defend yourself, you remained objective, focused on their value and success, you were in the giving mode in the *You Sphere*. You didn't let them lose face, disrespect them, judge them or had any expectations.

Next time you are the person who will be trusted, promoted, propelled and successful and still, you are not doing it for that but simply to use your skills and talents to serve value. Such integrity, clarity and strength – you are an invincible, formidable valuepreneur.

This Case Summarises The Whole Book

This case is all-encompassing and more than just handling difficult people and harsh attitudes efficiently. And, it is a summary of the whole book. It includes:

- VORO

- EV BV PV

- Managing yourself and your mind and emotions, expectations, mindfulness.

- Listening understanding *Spirit of Enquiry*.

- Our *Three Constraining* and *Three Enabling Natures*.

- *Me sFear — You Sphere*.

- Building collaboration.

- Purpose and deep satisfaction.

- Route to personal success – a result.

- Leadership – *bringer of value*.

Section 4

The Character And Leadership
Of A Valuepreneur

4.1

The New Age Leader Defined

Leadership is not isolated to this Section. This entire book and all five sections are about leadership and creating a legacy of value. Sections 4 and 5 delve into practical application and conversations in leadership. These conversations are the result of a dedication to serving value. In this section we are exploring some critical aspects of becoming a true value leader – bringing immense achievement to others and through it accomplishment and distinction for ourselves.

Let's begin by defining an exceptional leader for the new age and then exploring what leadership really is. I will then give you practical tools and techniques to grow into this leader. It's worth noting at this stage the sequel to this book, will carry an in-depth framework of leadership excellence and cover many situations and scenarios and further practical tools.

4.2

How Do You Define An Ace Leader?

Please prepare to be shocked at the simplicity of the answer and its practical, immediate applicability. When I ask the question to people, what is the definition of an *ace leader*, they list many qualities and say: a leader is determined, transparent, charismatic, trustworthy, honest, full of integrity, a visionary, well planned, respectful... and the list goes on and on. While I agree these are great virtues for a leader to have or to adopt, they are mere enabling qualities and don't in themselves define an ace leader.

The One And Only Habit Of An Extraordinary Leader

I'm sure you've read all the good works, but going forward in the new age, there aren't seven habits or fifty habits that define an exceptional leader. These are desirable virtues and practices of reasonably good leaders but are inadequate and insufficient to define the extraordinary leader or leadership. To put yourself in the ninth-gear, as a distinguished leader, indisputable and respected, you only need ONE habit and ONE attitude.

This is critical to understand.

Are you ready for the answer?

Before I give you the answer, consider this. Wouldn't you agree the best possible leader is someone you would follow naturally, voluntarily, happily and committedly of your own volition? Not someone you have to follow due to hierarchy, age or because your salary, promotion and career depend on them. Most so-called leaders fall into this latter category – you don't have a choice and involuntarily have to follow them.

In the new era, hierarchy on its own is a poor form of leadership. To such a leader, in the daytime and in front of them, you respond with *Yes Sir/Yes Ma'am* and in the evening at home saying, *What an idiot.*

So going back to our point – an ace leader is someone I would naturally, voluntarily, happily and committedly follow. Before the definition, we now need to ask what is that one single thing they need to be doing, such as the one single habit they need to have to make me voluntarily be committed to them and follow them.

The answer, of course, is making *Me* successful, in other words, helping *my values* to be fulfilled, looking after my Value Onion.

Can there be any other habit? So here is a complete and the only definition you need for an exceptionally distinguished leader:

A fearless, selfless, bringer of value to others – i.e., the valuepreneur.

That's it. Simple, isn't it? The valuepreneur takes it – they are the ultimate leader. You may know such a person, but you will be hard pushed to find one. Some people in varying degrees may be en-route to becoming one, and I have come across some, but they are few and far between. Most so-called leaders are actually looking out for themselves – they say they are bringing value but inadvertently are in the process of achieving only their own gains. They may bring about some or even a lot of value to others, but as their motive and motivation are self-gain, they fall short. So, who fits this bill?

There is no point taking the names of famous leaders – they are transient, and whether they bring value or not is subjective – it depends on who you are and if those leaders' work happens to correspond to your values.

Become the leader by whom you yourself would like to be led. Thinking about it in this way will strengthen the understanding of a true leader for you.

Two insights on true leadership:

- **Leadership is not just a role or position in the organisation.** It is an attitude, a demeanour, disposition, state of mind, actions and a spirit of understanding and serving value. A valuepreneur.

- **Leadership is not about getting people to do things.** It's about getting them to realise the value their talent and capabilities can serve then supporting them to deliver that value. In this, their own value is also served – satisfaction and of course growth, promotion, remuneration are certain.

If I ask you to describe the leader you would most enjoy working under, feel inspired by, be most productive under and realise the best of yourself and your potential, you would certainly say the person who truly cares for my success and makes a pathway for my talent to flow to achieve my dreams, and my value.

All I can say is: become the leader by whom you would like to be led.

A leader who asks and understands – *what inspires you? Which of your talents are being underutilised here? What would you like to strengthen most to achieve the best? How can I help you direct your career?* - and genuinely means it, is the kind of person I am describing. And they are aware of these things even in crises. Many people ask these questions in good times, and sadly mostly behind those questions is self-motive.

Let's just briefly examine the keywords I've used in the definition:

Selfless

This means a constant pursuit and almost obsessive nature of making my talents and capabilities respond to the value of the people I am serving. We can pick up any of the stories I have cited and see this principle working.

Let's take Anita's story. (1.10) If her emphasis and mind shift from *How can I win this contract* or *I hope I can make more money from this customer* to *How can I help the architects build their business or make the end customer happy...* she will be a bringer of value and therefore be in leadership. Those architects will choose her and even follow her if she becomes an obsessive bringer of value, to the exclusion of her competitors.

Yes, selfless really does mean a passionate pursuit of value of whom I am serving to the exclusion of my own gain and requirements.

Now I hear you becoming uncomfortable and saying, *But what about my value?* Let's be absolutely clear, I am not saying don't become successful, wealthy, expand, or whatever success means to you. After all, building your own success is the very reason you are reading this book. As long as we are born of a mother on this planet, each of us is looking for personal success, and there is nothing wrong with that. It would be strange if it weren't the case. So why am I saying be selfless in bringing value? Because that is the best way of achieving your own success.

Who would you rather buy from – someone trying to sell their products to you with an attitude and mind of getting business from you and making money from you?

Or someone unconcerned whether or not they get the contract but obsessively understanding your value, your end gain and helping you achieve it? Who would become wealthier and more successful in any case?

In other words, don't make *your* value the motivation or driver in your work. Make the value of whoever you are serving your mission, objective, reason, inspiration and even motivation – how can your success not happen? If you do what I am asking you to do, you cannot escape success, and that, too, well beyond your own plans expectations. While I am taking a business/ sales example, the principle is the same in leading and managing people. We will see the true multi-dimensional nature of leadership with the diagram below defining leadership.

Fearless

As discussed in the section on *Fear* (3.6), whenever we want something, we are living in expectation or the *Me sFear*, motivated principally by our own gain, the fear of not getting it or losing it is ever-present. Then you are in the *receiving* mode and the antithesis of leadership and, therefore, the opposite of valuepreneurship.

When you shift into the *bringing* or *giving* mode, i.e., the *You Sphere* and become a *fearless bringer of value* with low and ideally no expectation for your own gain, you move into true leadership.

Where there is no expectation driven by our wanting egos, there is nothing to lose. If you have nothing to lose, you cannot be in fear. The football team, who are last years' champions of England (3.4), have already been beaten twice early in the season by teams at the bottom of the league. Why? It's because these teams play with a nothing to lose attitude. *We are playing the champions, so if we lose, it's no shame on us, so let's go for it.* Consequently, they play fearlessly.

Whereas the champions have a leadership position and reputation to protect, they have moved into the *Me Sphere* and are playing with an expectation and, therefore, fear. The mind is saying, *I hope we don't lose to this lower team; we are the champions after all.* Their leadership is at risk.

A valuepreneurial attitude would be: *How can I apply my skills and talent, without an ego, to give my best to this game and serve the value of the fans, my club?* In this *giving* mode, every kick of the ball is joyful, not fearful.

In the same way, leaders are vulnerable. The higher you reach, the greater the potential to fall, the more there is to protect. We are in the *Me sFear.*

Leaders in this position are pushed further into self-protection. They will behave to exert and display authority, keep control in their own hands, not allow talent to flow and even suppress it, and be aggressive in extreme cases. How can such leaders enable the flow of innovative ideas and creativity, facilitate the implementation, and bring valuable outcomes for and from people? That confidence by shifting from the *receiving* mode to the *giving* mode is the essence of the best leader, the valuepreneur.

Value

The value leader lives in the *You Sphere* and not the *Me sFear.* They have an obsession and get joy from seeing people succeed rather than chasing their own success, which would leave them vulnerable and exposed and therefore fearful. Such leaders are unclouded by *getting;* and achieve exceptional results and greatness. They achieve it but don't chase it. They pursue value for others.

Your success as a leader is of extreme importance, but don't obsess about it. The more you are obsessively focused on serving the values of others, your own outcomes will be much superior than ever imagined.

Your success is a result; the driver is others' success.

4.3

What Then Is Value Leadership?

Before answering this question, let's examine what it is not, why is it needed, and what is it replacing.

Old Hierarchical Leadership Is Dying

Unfortunately, when we speak about leadership in organisations, we usually only refer to the hierarchical position and the people who work under us. We are the leaders, and they are the led. We exert authority and control, instruct and direct. It's outdated, passé, naïve at best. It's debilitating, suppresses talent, capabilities, inspiration, potential and is soul-destroying. It is also old fashioned and out of touch with the priorities and values of people of the new world. Let's face it, the only reason people very often respond to or listen to such a leader is that they are scared to lose their job or miss out on a promotion or salary increase.

Let's take the Gen Zs and early millennials (people in their twenties), and in the modern context and environment, there is millennialism in all of us. These people are becoming less and less sub-ordinate in their nature and behaviour. Why? Because they feel less dependent on others and more self-reliant.

They are not looking to build long careers in one or two organisations and move up the hierarchical ladder step-by-step. As a result, they are less reliant on their bosses than the generations before them. Yet, they are heavily impacted by their managers, and it is well researched that the most common reason people leave their work is how they were managed. The converse applies, and the more they are allowed to utilise and express their talent, knowledge, opinions, etc.., the more they are inspired and make that environment their own, take responsibility, and enjoy working hard.

They are looking for a life full of great experiences, and when they don't get it, they are happy to quit and move. It is their most significant value from work. Thanks to the online world, they are much more conscious of their capabilities and aware of the vast opportunities. As a result, they are much more interested in learning and using their talents and capabilities to make a difference, bringing value and growing themselves. If they find themselves in a situation not conducive to this growth or which blocks the learning and prevents them from expressing their abilities to create and innovate, they will leave.

When I speak to organisations today, they cite talent retention as one of their greatest difficulties and constraints. Well, they need to put a mirror up to themselves, and I regularly do. By the way, just to emphasise the point, I'm not speaking only about people in their twenties – this is a universally applicable phenomenon due to the tremendous change in the environment today. The exposure to and availability of possibilities or opportunities is limitless to all of us.

So, leadership is dead. Long live value leadership.

As we have said, it is no longer about hierarchy; that's not leadership, that's management, operational and ordinary, all be it essential in its context.

A leader is a true bringer of value. It means a leader in a situation can be working several rungs below you.

Thinking back to Andy's case (1.13), the moment he shifted his focus from emphasising the conference in Marrakesh to beating targets by 12% above forecast, he was bringing value. His boss was compelled to listen and not just accept but even request him to do the conference in Marrakesh. Who was giving and who was taking, who is the leader and who is the led?

The arrogance of old-style leadership can be shown the door.

Value Hierarchies In India

Recently my cousin and her husband came to visit us in London from India. They have both retired from the Indian Administrative Service (IAS), which means they are top-notch, powerful civil servants and VIP official leaders in the highest echelons of the fabric of Indian society. IAS officers are the crème de la crème and from around 600,000 applicants about nine hundred are selected.

You then work your way up to top ranks, and it is the perfect display of dated hierarchical leadership.

Having tea in the evening and conversing about my work, my brother-in-law said to me, 'You know Sanjeev, you can carry on with this value stuff in the West, but it won't work in India.'

Intrigued, I asked him why.

'You see, India is a made of levels of leadership. I give instructions to the person below me who then instructs his subordinate and he the next and so on, the lower guy takes orders from his boss, who takes orders from his boss etc.. and eventually from me. What value and value leadership are you speaking about?'

Notice the conversation is in the masculine gender! I listened respectfully.

Later that evening, at dinner and with the previous conversation long forgotten, I painted a scenario for him.

'Imagine you are being driven in your shining black government car by your smartly uniformed driver. And as your car pulls into your palatial Delhi office and the stones on the ground crinkle luxuriously, the security guard comes and opens your door, clicks his heels and gives you a firm salute. As you are getting out, he respectfully and humbly says, '*Sir, in case you have two minutes, with your permission, I'd like to present you an idea of how we could improve the security and reduce the bill by 20%.* What would you do?'

He instantly replied in his most officious tone, 'What would I do? I'd go to my office and then send for him.'

I looked at him in the eye and said, 'Now who is *receiving* and who is *giving*? Who's value is that guard serving? Who is suddenly interested and listening? Who is the leader, and who is the led? And you tell me don't talk about value in India?'

To be fair to him, he put his hands up and said, 'I get your point.' And look, there was no compromise with respect from the security guard for his boss several levels above him. He said it with a lot of respect and humbleness and even asked his permission. Of course, this story has to be culturally adapted.

In such relationships, we often confuse being respectful to our seniors and bringing value. There is no conflict – it exists in our twisted minds. Keep the tone respectful, but the content should be value. You will have confidence and actually show even greater respect, apart from achieving the objective as it was with the security guard above.

Often ideas, especially in a strong hierarchical set-up, are held back because subconsciously, we feel we may disturb the leader or tread on their patch, as we are led by those leaders and subtly fear for our own position. It is very subtle and sits in the subconscious, and therefore we are not even aware of it.

In working with organisations and leaders across the globe and all industries, I am abundantly exposed to the sad reality of just how much so-called leaders come in the way of people's success and indeed through prevention of expression of other's talent block their own success all because it becomes about ME, my position, my status which we live to protect rather than genuinely serve value. Am I being too harsh? Well, it's only by facing the reality that we can progress to elevating ourselves to being a true value leader, for which I'll give you practical tools later in this chapter.

Leadership Beats LADDERSHIP

The story above is not about India's IAS, I have chosen it as we are dealing in extremes of hierarchy, and if we can make *value leadership* happen in that context, we can do it in any. The same principle applies to lesser or greater degrees across the globe. In reality, there is very little leadership in the world. What we mostly do is LADDERSHIP. Our deluded sense of leadership is often no more than exerting influence on those on the rungs of the ladder below us. The higher we get, the more deluded we are and the greater the power and inadvertent suppression we impose. The potential fall would be so much more painful, so we are in greater fear and hang on tighter. I say *inadvertent suppression* because, most often, our intentions are not bad. It's just a human behavioural state to which we are all susceptible.

Leadership is not just a role or position in the organisation – it is an attitude, a demeanour, disposition, state of mind, actions and a spirit of understanding and serving value. A valuepreneur.

The Big Five Points Of This Chapter

1. An ace leader is someone I would naturally, voluntarily and committedly follow. So it's not about hierarchy.

2. The one and only habit of a true leader, a value leader, is someone who brings me success, serves value to me, i.e. *A fearless, selfless, bringer of value to others* – the valuepreneur.

3. The value leader lives in the *You Sphere* and not the *Me sFear*. They have an obsession and derive joy from seeing people succeed rather than chasing their own success, which would leave them vulnerable and exposed and therefore fearful. Such leaders unclouded by getting, getting, getting, attain the greatest outcomes for others and themselves. They achieve it but don't chase it. They pursue value for others.

4. Old hierarchical leadership is dying. Often, people respond to this kind of leader because they are scared to lose their job or miss out on a promotion or salary increase. True leadership beats *Laddership* – i.e. exerting influence on those who are on the rungs of the ladder below us. The higher we get, the more deluded we are and the greater the power and inadvertent suppression we impose. It's time to wake up.

5. People today feel less dependent on others and more self-reliant. They are more conscious of their capabilities and aware, thanks in part to the online world, of the vast opportunities. As a result, they are much more interested in learning and using their talents and capabilities to make a difference, bringing value and growing themselves.

4.4

Value Leadership
And Our Total People Environment

Let me ask you, in your working life, who is an important professional contact for you? In other words, who are you interacting with and dealing with daily? Of course, you will answer with this list:

- My boss/management/hierarchy.

- Shareholders, financiers.

- My team – people who report to me.

- Customers/clients, suppliers and other external bodies.

- Colleagues, peers.

Yet there is one vital professional contact missing:

- ME myself

Ultimate leadership, i.e. *Value Leadership,* is about bringing value to and enabling productivity and success of the *Total People Environment* around me and, as a result, and only as a result, value to myself.

Serving Value Onions of and bringing value to the total people environment.

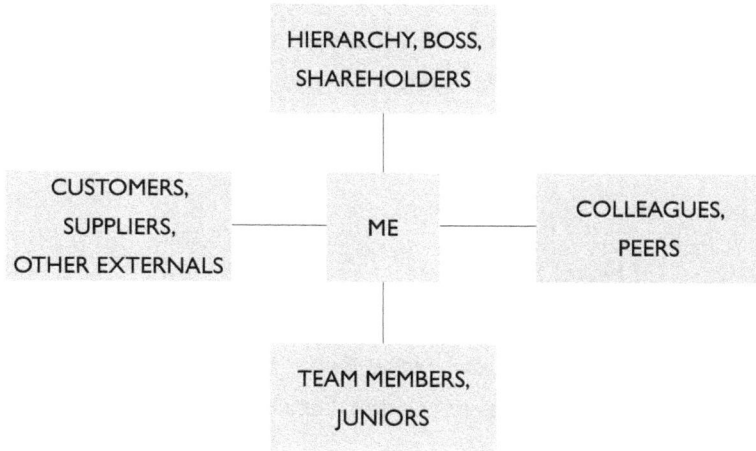

```
                    ┌──────────────────┐
                    │ HIERARCHY, BOSS, │
                    │  SHAREHOLDERS    │
                    └────────┬─────────┘
                             │
┌──────────────────┐   ┌─────────┐   ┌──────────────┐
│   CUSTOMERS,     │   │         │   │ COLLEAGUES,  │
│   SUPPLIERS,     ├───┤   ME    ├───┤   PEERS      │
│ OTHER EXTERNALS  │   │         │   │              │
└──────────────────┘   └────┬────┘   └──────────────┘
                            │
                    ┌───────────────┐
                    │ TEAM MEMBERS, │
                    │   JUNIORS     │
                    └───────────────┘
```

In this diagram, I have described the *total people environment* from a corporate perspective, but please interpret it within your own organisation or people context, work or private. It fully applies also in a private context as value to parents, friends, siblings, children or in a social welfare and care environment like charities you may work or volunteer for etc..

Value Leadership Example - In A Situation Of Change

Leading Your Total People Environment

Let's take a real practical example from a recent situation at one of my client organisations and examine *Value Leadership* from a *total people perspective* and the approach and technique in undertaking that leadership. I'll take an example from the hotel industry for ease of understanding by all.

Note – this case may appear to be a simple case of good customer service. It's not. It is about taking full value leadership of your total people environment. Please transport the principles and method to your own situations of leadership.

Further, a customer is anyone to whom we bring value with our skills, talents, capabilities. So although we are referring in this case to a classic external customer, the same principle applies to your team members, colleagues, seniors, other externals and anyone who's value we serve.

The Case Of Hotel Serve Ltd

The organisation – a company specialising in plumbing and electrics serving large hotels, let's call Hotel Serve Ltd (HSL). Their client is a prominent five-star hotel in London. Let's call it Sterling Grand.

HSL has been doing a huge overhaul project for Sterling to significantly increase the water pressure in the showers and taps in all the rooms as the existing systems are ageing and water pressures in London have been reduced. HSL has fitted eighteen new state of the art pumping systems.

It's Thursday morning, and there is a leak in two rooms from burst pipes on the floor, where HSL fitted the last six systems, that has forced Sterling's maintenance department to shut off the water resulting in no water to one hundred and twenty rooms, of which seventy-five are occupied.

As panic sets in, the head of maintenance at Sterling, Justin, who was also responsible for contracting HSL as a supplier, calls Alex, the project director at HSL and furiously summons him for an urgent meeting and immediate action.

Angrily, Justin tells Alex that an emergency meeting with the whole management team – including his General Manager Geraldine – has been called at 4pm where urgent answers and solutions are needed. Geraldine has instructed that all 120 rooms must have high-pressure water working by 6pm on Sunday – *or else!*

The cause of the problem? Justin's team didn't inform Alex that the pipes on this floor were older and too narrow for the new pressure levels. So in large part, it was the customer's fault. Alex's team were also at fault as they assumed the pipes would be the same and therefore as good as the other floors and didn't run complete checks.

Now we will examine Alex's leadership in this challenging situation through a summary of his conversations with different people in the total people environment and then how he progressed to Value Leadership. In each case, I'll label these as *before* (i.e., leadership) and *after* (i.e., value leadership).

Before: Meeting with Justin

Justin is furious, and as his anger raises the decibels. Alex is pushed into the *Me sFear*; he knows there is a lot to lose as HSL are about to sign a five-year contract for all plumbing and electrics at Sterling. He worries how his boss, Carlos, the owner of HSL, will react. In this worry and the need to protect himself, Alex reacts by telling Justin how it's not HSL's fault and that Sterling's maintenance did not tell them about the old and narrow pipes on that floor.

Do you recognise this response? – yes, indeed, he is in his *Third Constraining Nature* - defensively *Justifying*. (3.12)

Predictably, Justin reacts badly to this justification and sees Alex as trying to protect himself rather than solve his problem, i.e. addressing his value. In *Justification*, you will remember, there is a loss of credibility and, therefore, trust.

Justin loses his patience, and he threatens Alex with giving the five-year contract to HSL's competitor. In this position of fear, Alex accepts the demand of having all one hundred and twenty rooms... with high pressure... operational... by Sunday 6pm. He knows this is impossible, even with his team working flat out all weekend.

Getting the team to work at the weekend is another battle he will have to face, and he is subsequently, also worried about that.

You might say Alex seems to have taken leadership and responsibility as he is responsive to the customer by promising to deliver by Sunday 6pm. But in reality, he has created a bigger problem for himself because when he doesn't fully deliver on time, there will be hell to play. This is what fear does - it forces us into wrong actions and false commitments without thinking of the later consequences.

And it's not *value leadership*.

Responsiveness Vs. Responding

There is a massive distinction between *responsiveness* and *responding*. *Responsiveness* is when the customer says, *jump, we jump,* as in this case.

Responding is when we first fully engage with and understand the customer and their entire Value Onion in the situation and then and only then work out the perfect Response Onion to bring them an outcome and true value. We are deluded into thinking this is good customer service through leadership. It is not. It's driven from the *Me sFear* and has little notion of serving true value.

After

A much better value leadership approach would be as follows.

Alex to Justin

'I appreciate that the loss of water in one hundred and twenty rooms is a massive problem Justin, and rest assured we'll bust a gut to get it sorted ASAP.' This is reassuring and taking on the responsibility to solve the problem with confidence.

'Why it's happened won't help right now, and on Monday, I'll give you a full report and a plan so this never happens again. My main concern right now is to get this sorted with zero or minimum disturbance to your guests.'

This brings the focus onto the main issue at this time – which is how can we get the rooms operational and no guest disturbance and not the reasons it occurred. Even though the customer asks why it happened, it's not his main concern right now.

'To sort the problem, may I understand what's the occupancy over the next five days and if there are any special events or priorities which we need to take into account.'

It is a *spirit of enquiry* to first understand the real end problem and, therefore, the values of the customer and the hotel the guests. There can be no argument with this as Justin subtly appreciates Alex's approach to solving his real fears and values.

Still, with anger in his voice, although less than before, Justin says, 'I don't have the exact number, but we are less busy at the weekend. The big issue is that the major pharmaceutical conference starting on Tuesday at the hotel is vital for us, so everyone is panicking after today's fiasco. The press conferences will begin on Monday for this event, and the hotel's reputation is at stake...'

When you *dare to care* and are prepared to listen from the *You Sphere* genuinely, people will tell you their values because they feel you are willing to sort their problem. This value must be revealed so you can genuinely build responses to it.

'Ah, I see. Is this why Geraldine is pushing for all rooms to be operational with high pressure by Sunday?' says Alex.

'Yes and hence the meeting at 4pm and it's going to be uncomfortable – so I need answers, Alex.' says Justin. The tone is much more collaborative now. Why wouldn't it be? As in Justin's *iceberg* he gets the feeling Alex will help him out.

'OK, thanks for sharing this with me, Justin – my first priority is to ensure the conference goes super smoothly from the room's point of view and that there are no complaints or impacts from the guests. If we can provide this, would Geraldine be satisfied? Yes. So, here's what I propose.

'Firstly, let me share with you if we try and open all rooms by Sunday 6pm it would be a rush job, and we'd have to cut corners, and I want the job to be done once and for all to perfection. We will have sixty rooms done by Saturday and eighty by Sunday, especially to accommodate the press conferences and the rest by Monday evening ready for Tuesday's conference.

'So let me understand the rooming list for the weekend and make a plan for doing one section at a time so that all occupied rooms are dealt with at the weekend. We will need to request twenty-weekend guests to shift rooms on Saturday, but reservations can upgrade them for this as the fourth floor is working perfectly.'

'With this solution, Justin, there would be no disturbance to guests, the press conference or the pharma conference. Does this work out for you?' Alex pauses.

Well, yes, it makes perfect sense so long as you can commit to it – but I still need to convince the management team this afternoon and deal with their concerns.'

'Sure, who are you most concerned about and what are their priorities? Alex keeps focused, obsessively on Justin's and Sterling's values.'

Justin reflects. 'The head of Finance, Sally, will be concerned about any additional cost and loss of revenue, and Geraldine will be concerned about protecting our reputation with the pharma client.' These are more Value Onion points from Justin discovered by Alex who as can bring better solutions with this understanding. Alex is listening – he is in leadership.

Alex's Response Onion – 'OK, would it help if, after I meet with reservations, we created a couple of slides showing there would be no impact on revenue with the current occupancy and our planned repairs a section at a time. Also, re costs – the old pipes would have had to be changed in any case, so no costs are added, but we will take half the labour cost off as our investment.

'Secondly, I propose a pre-presentation at 3pm, which you and I can do together for Geraldine so she goes into the meeting satisfied. Does that work?'

Justin is happy. 'Yes, thank you, Alex. Despite the problem, you have helped me out. Let's do it.'

Problems and situations arise, everyone knows that. Even in these challenging scenarios, when we genuinely understand their values and build responses to those values, people gain confidence in us and trust us. This is the nature of a Value Leader. People will attack you and lose faith in you if you are in the *Me sFear* protecting and caring only for yourself. Every individual has values – it's ours to serve it. Then we are in the *giving* rather than *receiving* mode. We are more confident, not nervous, respected and even advocated by others.

In serving value we are infallible and in leadership.

When your mind is single-pointedly focused on the value of people you are serving and strive to find solutions to serve that value, you are infallible, powerful, confident, respected and trusted. You are in true leadership, value leadership. It's irrefutable, so simple and yet not done.

Shift your mind away from futile concerns, fears, and self-preservation, i.e., negative emotional responses, and see how chilled out and productive you become. In this state, how can you ever be innovative and creative in bringing solutions? That only happens when you see value beyond fears.

Look how Alex was able to build robust, creative solutions, and it was well beyond plumbing when he is working with the reservations department, making presentations for the FD etc..

It all sounds too easy, *I hear you say*. Well, actually it is.

And having had the joy of coaching thousands of people, I have seen how people change their approach and how easy it actually is with commitment. The trick is being able to see yourself at a distance. This is where meditation and mind control will help you.

Referring this back to our circles of value from 1.20 and 1.39:

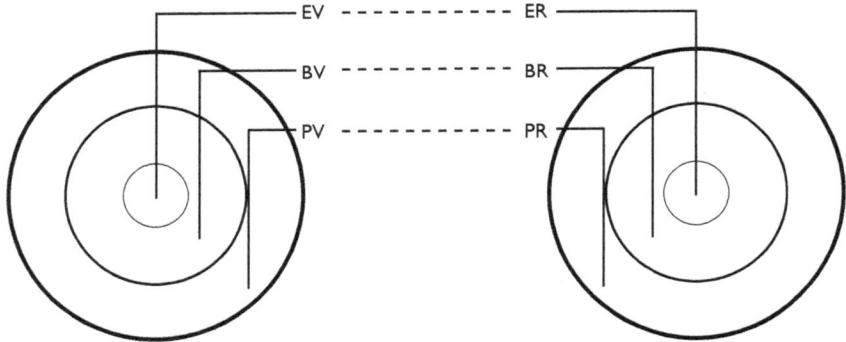

First understand the *Circles of Value (COVs)*(see 1.39):

- EV – Essential Value
- BV – Business Value (bigger than EV)
- PV – Personal Value (biggest value)

Then build matching Responses:

- ER – Essential Response
- BR – Business Response
- PR – Personal Response

Let's see that with key points distributed across *Circles of Value* and *Circles of Response.*

Circles of Value (COV)	Circles of Response (COR)
EV – Essential Value	**ER – Essential Response**
• 120 rooms • Sunday 6pm • All pumps fixed • Leaks repaired	• 60 rooms by Saturday, • 80 by Sunday, • 140 by Monday night • Limited crew at the weekend and whole team on Monday
BV – Business Value	**BR – Business Response**
• No loss of revenue • Smooth pharma conference • Strategic account of pharma company secured • Reputation on Sterling protected	• Working with reservations to work out a staggered repair plan • Shifting guests to rotate the repairs with a limited weekend crew • Hiring temporary staff to complement the crew at the weekend...
PV – Personal Value	**PR – Personal Response**
• How will the 4pm meeting go for me (Justin) • My colleagues' image of me • My future and position (Geraldine) • How will I convince the Finance Director...	• Presentation for Finance Director • Supporting Justin by meeting Geraldine before the management meeting • Reassuring Justin with a plan...

Summary Of The Value Leadership Approach With The End Beneficiary Of Value (Justin The Customer) Step-By-Step:

1. Show understanding of the problem. If you don't understand, then first ask and reassure him that you are focused on working the best solution for him. No justification.

2. Style: taking responsibility, ownership of their value, confident.

3. Ask questions (see Spirit of Enquiry 5.13 for the technique to understand their total value (EV, BV, and PV).

4. Style: In the *You Sphere* and not *Me sFear*. Disengaged from their anger (if any). Listening and caring for their value.

5. Propose a solution for all main points of value ER, BR, PR. Keep it directly correlating to their actual values.

6. Style: Clear, unambiguous, specific plan, resources, time lines.

7. Keep listening without clouding it with your own fears as their points of value may continue coming. It's because they feel more comfortable with you.

Application - Make It Real – Make It Yours

Identify an actual situation you need to handle with your customer/client – it could be external or internal – i.e., the end beneficiary of your work.

1. Please make a note of how you would have approached it before.

2. Using the description of the conversation above and the summary – make notes on how you will approach it

3. Use the question framework described in the Spirit of Enquiry (Section 5) and make notes on how you will understand their values – then do it in the meeting.

4. Write down the end values you are serving and the responses to those values (use the COVs/CORs template in the table above).

5. Write feedback notes to yourself, i.e., what went well and why then what could have been better.

6. Next time be aware and focus on correcting things to improve.

Before: Meeting with Carlos

Having achieved an excellent meeting with Justin, it's time for our value leader Alex to talk to his boss, Carlos.

Normally, and in ordinary leadership, this meeting is a fearful one asking for extra resources, save my skin mind-set. In this state, Alex would not tell the whole story as it is. He would continue blaming the customer's for not providing the complete information. Alex is justifying, protecting himself. This would give Carlos an even bigger problem to worry about: *how will he retain Sterling as a customer and not lose respect from them?* In fact, in this scenario, Alex wouldn't even have discovered the customer's true BV and PV, and frankly, he wouldn't have moved beyond EV.

At best, he would have given ordinary solutions and asked Carlos to speak to Justin and explain why we can't have all the rooms completed. At worst, he would complain to Carlos that Justin is being too harsh, especially since it was their fault and ask Carlos to take over. Fears fuel this self-protection behaviour and justifications.

We don't bring value and find ourselves in the *Me sFear*. There is no ownership; instead, we push the problem to someone else, in this case the boss, Carlos. Unfortunately, this is a vicious circle as sub-consciously it pre-prepares us for the same reaction next time.

It's not an unusual scenario – to a lesser or greater degree, this is where we remain a lot of the time. Our capabilities and real potential are suppressed and, inadvertently, sub-consciously, our productivity is reduced.

After

Approaching the conversation with Carlos from the value leader mindset goes like this: (Assume Carlos knows about the problem already).

Alex to Carlos: 'I've just been in a meeting with Justin, and I have a solid solution with which he is comfortable.'

This automatically puts Carlos' troubled *iceberg* at ease, and he feels relieved in his subconscious that we'll get through it. He is also opened to listening. Alex moves into the *giving* mode, and Carlos is *receiving*; who is the leader?

He says, 'Let me first share with you what's critical for Sterling.'

Alex continues and lists Sterling and their key player's Value Onion i.e.,

- The pharma conference and its success.
- Winning the pharma account as a strategic business.
- No loss of revenue, no additional costs.
- Convincing Sally, Geraldine and Sterling's other managers.
- Sterling's reputation.

He then gives the Response Onion to Carlos. 'Here is the solution I propose.' He is absolutely in value leadership, in control, respected by Carlos, and with this confidence, he is creative and innovative. See the *Circles of Response* in the table above for the solution (p448).

Carlos says, 'Thanks, I like the plan. What do you need?'

With confidence, Alex asks Carlos for his help and for additional resources – i.e.

- To get help from another colleague's team for the weekend as only half of his staff will be able to work at short notice.
- Five additional plumbers subcontracted for the weekend from another company. Although it will be at a cost, this will be a small investment compared to what we have at stake and a tiny outlay to win the significant contract from Sterling.

It's a responsible entrepreneurial approach but even more a valuepreneurial one. Sadly, we tend to ask these questions from our begging nature, in the *receiving* mode - e.g., *Please let me have this or that.* Yet what you ask is equated to and valued by what you bring, i.e., a response to value. It's a big return on a small investment. With this valuepreneurial stance, you will speak with confidence. If there is hesitation or refusal from the boss, which will be a rarity, you can comfortably say, how in your opinion can we bring that outcome then? i.e., having clearly established the value to the customer and the gain for us, the onus is now on the boss to come up with an equally good solution with fewer resources. And by the way, if they do this successfully, be open enough to listen and adapt.

So far, with Alex's value leadership:

Justin has given his and Sterling's total Value Onion. Carlos is relieved and looking forward to more business with Sterling. So, his Value Onion is served.

The customer and his boss well respect Alex. He'll probably get promoted etc.. And most importantly, he will feel deeply satisfied at using his talents to bring so much value.

Summary Of The Value Leadership Approach With The Boss (Carlos) Step By Step:

1. The subject and reassurance – I've just met Justin and have a solid solution to the issue.

2. Style – Confident, constructive, respectful.

3. The context – framed as the Value Onion of the client and key stakeholders. (Pharma conference, Sterling's reputation, convincing Geraldine and Sally).

4. Style – Caring, clear, value obsessed for the client, fearless.

5. The solution. I propose (see *Circles of Response* p448).

6. Style – Taking responsibility and ownership, creative and even innovative. A true value leader.

7. I need your help to get this value to the customer.
    (Help from a colleague's team, sub-contracted plumbers.)

8. Style – respectful, return on investment approach, determined.

9. CAP – concrete action plan – who does what by when.

10. Thanks.

Application - Make It Real – Make It Yours

Identify an actual situation you need to handle with your manager / senior.

1. Please make a note of how you would have approached it before.

2. Using the description of the conversation above and the summary – make notes on how you will approach it.

3. Write down the end value (COVs) you are serving, firstly the clients, secondly the company's, thirdly the manager's – in that order.
   These also form the context in the summary above, Point 2.

4. Write the solutions (CORs).

5. Have the meeting and write feedback notes to yourself, i.e., what went well and why then what could have been better.

6. Next time be aware and focus on correcting things to improve.

Before Meeting With Team Members

Having achieved excellent meetings with Justin at Sterling and his boss Carlos, Alex now has to convince his team members, i.e., people he manages, to work at the weekend.

Ordinary or *so called* leaders approach this meeting again with fear, hesitation and concern of how their team members will react. *Will they collaborate or think badly of me?* Again, we find ourselves in the *Me sFear*, trying to persuade them, and as the team resist, Alex starts virtually begging them to work.

Other ordinary or *so called* leaders will take an unnecessarily authoritative stance and demand or virtually order the team to do it. The team may well agree, but it will be through fear of displeasing the boss or protecting their own positions – which again is short-lived, and people soon get demotivated and work for the wrong purpose rather than the joy of *bringing* value. How can they bring value if it isn't even evident to them?

Leadership is not about getting people to do things. It's about getting them to realise the value their talent and capabilities can serve then supporting them to deliver that value. In this, their own value is also served – satisfaction and of course growth, promotion, remuneration are certain. Value leadership will inspire team members to happily cooperate, collaborate and take responsibility:

There is only one point at which no two people in any organisation can disagree. It's that *Point Of Zero Conflict*, which, as you will remember, is the Value Onion of the person or people who we are ultimately serving - in this case, the customer Justin at Sterling Grand Hotel.

As a point aside, before having the meeting with the team, it is essential to meet with the team member responsible for the mistake one to one and sort out that corrective issue. The reason is that when we have the full team meeting, the focus must be on finding a collective solution and not derail that process by dwelling on the fault of individuals, which typically happens. How to handle this will be covered later under managing reprimands.

After

The conversation goes more like this:

'Team, I need your help to sort out a big issue at Sterling. Let me first fill you in on what's happening. They have a major pharma conference from Tuesday, which is critical to their business, and one hundred and twenty rooms are without high-pressure water, sixty of which have no water at all. It won't help to focus too much right now on why it's happened. They can do a detailed analysis next week and make improvements for the future. Right now, there is a lot at stake.

'Sterling has huge concerns about their reputation, business, revenue loss and cost. We can help them out on all these fronts.

'There is a lot at stake for us – we stand to win the electrical maintenance business for five years and the plumbing if we can get them out of this mess. Importantly, it will also mean good opportunities; and learning and growth for all of us as a team.'

Three sets of values have been expressed. Firstly, the customer's – this must be the first value we address. Also, by serving it, our own outcomes will be achieved.

Secondly, the company's (HCL); and then thirdly the team members. The team's value should be firmly stated – but at the end – otherwise, it can feel like manipulation. Also, it happens as a consequence of making the customer and HSL successful. Then people work for a *bringing* value and only as a result, *getting* value. This is working for a higher purpose and, therefore, more powerful, inspirational and motivational.

Alex continues:

'The GM Geraldine was demanding all one hundred and twenty rooms to be up and running with high pressure by Sunday evening, but by looking at their occupancy and guests this weekend, I've managed to get them a plan to do sixty by Saturday, another twenty by Sunday and the rest when we have a full crew on Monday.

'Now, the question is: *how in your opinion could we get this plan to work?*'

Now the team feels very respected. They're not just being told what to do but, importantly, *why* it needs to be done. Their opinion on *how* can it be done is also being sought.

The beauty is that people will be more engaged as they realise their inputs and skills would be applied visibly to bring value to Sterling the customer, HSL, and themselves. *Bringing value* is highly motivational and deeply satisfying.

The team will undoubtedly come up with creative suggestions, which is more likely than if they are simply ordered to do it in this way and to work at the weekend.

Also, when asked for their opinion, one of the solutions will have to be weekend working, but this is in the context of *bringing value* rather than the boss saying, *Save my skin.*

4.5

Six Steps For Getting Collaboration, Cooperation, Initiative And Responsibility

Let's summarise the structure of the Value Leadership approach with the team.

1. STATE THE CONTEXT – With Clarity And Completeness.

Frame the context, the issue. See the *After* conversation above (p456). *We have an issue to resolve for Sterling etc..* State what is at stake for Sterling, HSL and us as a team and individuals. In other words the *why*; the Value Onions of all three.

The Why – Pharma conference, Sterling's reputation, five-year contract for HSL, growth gain and opportunity for the team members ......

Sterling's Value Onion here is the *Point Of Zero Conflict*. There is no argument on it and the entire conversation is contextualised to it and the whole team is aligned though it. Collaboration is set up. Starting with the why is also very respectful to the team and it invokes the voluntary taking of responsibility.

I can't emphasise it enough.

Never ask them to do anything without bringing them into the *why*.

Style – inclusive and respectful.

2. STATE THE OBJECTIVE – With Clarity And Decisiveness.

'We need to have sixty done by Saturday; eighty by Sunday... That's our commitment to Justin at Sterling.'

Style – decisive, determined and clear. No ambiguity or doubt in the voice or body language.

3. HOW IN YOUR OPINION (HIYO) - How Shall We Do It?

In your opinion what's the best way to achieve it? Invite ideas and explore with open questions. Discuss together which ideas have the greatest *Depth of Impact* on the customer's Value Onion. Working at the weekend will certainly be discussed, but now it will be constructive.

Style – Listening, involving, respecting opinions and exploring answers – keeping focused on the objective. Style – seeking their advice, working together on a common goal – the customer's value. Use open neutral and open oriented questions (see 5.17).

4. CAP – Concrete Action Plan – Who Does What When.

5. CONFIRM AND VALIDATE

- Summarise all ideas and plans.
- Check resources and capabilities are in place – for any gaps provide solutions e.g., training; additional staff etc..
- Check if there is anything yet to be covered – all in the context of Stirling's Value Onion – close all gaps.

- Confirm agreement from all members, address any concerns – This will ensure their commitment.

6. THANKS

'I knew I could count on you.'

4.6

The Three Critical Conditions
Of Leading The Team In Any Situation
A Test Of Our Approach
And Taking Better People Decisions

In any situation of leadership check your approach and see if you fulfilled the following three critical conditions:

1. Be clear and complete on the CONTEXT – Look at Step 1 in the six steps structure above (p458).

2. Be clear and decisive on the OBJECTIVE – See Step 2 (p459).

3. Give them the full MEANS & SUPPORT to perform (p459).

If there was a shortage on any of these three points – the correction is needed in you, don't blame them if it goes wrong. No problem, correct it and move forward.

If, however all three conditions were done to perfection, as described, then you then you can expect the earth from the team. Any failures need to be handled by building them and reaching improvement.

At an extreme, if despite this good method, they don't respond well then you can safely remove them from the team. Interestingly, you will rarely reach this point if you use this approach. Sadly, in reality, we reach it too early in the innocence that the fault with their non-performance lay with me, their leader and not the team members. We then reach decisions of removing team members from the team all too soon. We lose talent unreasonably. We just didn't see the reality.

There is vast potential locked in our team and people around us. It's up to us to enable it and dynamize it.

Application - Make It Real – Make It Yours

Identify an actual situation you need to handle with your team members or colleagues.

1. Make a note of how you would have approached it before.

2. Using the description of the conversation above, the summary and six steps structure – make notes on how you will approach it.

3. Write down the end value you are serving, firstly the clients, secondly the company's, thirdly the team members – in that order (the *why* in the summary above).

4. Write the objective.

5. Have the meeting and write feedback notes to yourself, i.e., what went well and why then what could have been better? Next time, be aware and focus on correcting things to improve.

Importance Of The WHY – It Is Engaging, And It Motivates

US Leadership Program

I was doing a Leadership program in the US recently. I asked the eighteen managers/directors to write down a moment in their professional life when they felt the most engaged, creative, innovative, committed and enjoying their work.

Why don't you try it now before reading the next part?

As I went around the room hearing their answers, you may be surprised to know, and you probably see this in your own response - no one – and I mean no one, had written about the moment when they received a salary increase or a promotion. Very few people said, *when I won an award or praise from my seniors.* Everyone had written about an experience when their capability, talent, skills had visibly brought xyz value to the customer and the company. As you look back to the best times of your career, I am confident you will say the same.

Stop. We don't need any more research, this is the essential human condition, and I'm sure you recognise it. It's no great revelation. The problem is that it's in the subconscious, in the depth of our *iceberg*. We are deluded into thinking that we get engaged and motivated from salary increases and promotions. I'm not speaking against these, they are great and an endorsement of our performance, but they can be better classified as pleasure rather than satisfaction. They burn out fast.

Lasting growth and satisfaction come from serving value. But we can only be aware of the value we are serving if it is clarified and illuminated to us and our leaders are respectful to bring us into the *why,* i.e., the value.

Mostly, they just tell us what to do.

The truth is that often they don't know the *why*, the end gain, the value, but that doesn't mean saying it doesn't exist. If this is the case, make it your responsibility and duty to get to the *why* before doing the work

Is it making sense? Then it is all you need. You just need to put yourself in the reverse situation, i.e., the recipient of value as the customer, and you will not be able to argue against it. It's straightforward, and we complicate it by being in the *Me sFear*, our prejudices, expectations, defensiveness etc.. In developing and coaching thousands of people, I have seen this approach bring excellence and success.

I have a problem with people complicating the issue, researching human behaviour excessively. Most of the time, it is just about trying to justify theories and creating work for themselves. We are all human, look in reverse and see what would work for you, and you have the research.

Be a *bringer of value.*

Meeting with colleagues to win their support, cooperation and collaboration

This will simply follow the same pattern as the meeting with team members. Just understand their values and what this will bring them, and they will be more collaborative.

4.7

The Six Big Points Of Section 4

1. Value Leadership is about bringing value to and enabling the productivity and success of our *Total People Environment* around me and, as a result, and only as a result, value to myself. It's not just about people under me — that's just management.

2. A Value Leader genuinely understands the values of whom they are serving, EV, BV, PV and genuinely builds responses to those values ER, BR, PR.

3. It always starts with the end or ultimate beneficiary of who's value we are impacting. In HSL's case above, it was the customer — all other values result from and are contextualised to that value.

4. Listen to their values in their raw form — without clouding it with our own desires, expectations, fears, prejudices or points of view.

5. Impact value of people above us in the hierarchy. In HSL's case, the boss Carlos. This is partnering with your seniors. In the *giving* mode, you are the leader, and they are the led. But there is no compromise with respect for seniority.

6. Bring value to people below you or equal to you in the hierarchy — your team and colleagues. Involve them by telling them the WHY (which we miss), then the objective and then involve them by asking them *how*. It's respectful, and as they work for a higher purpose, they will be more engaged, creative, innovative, motivated, productive.

4.8

Is Tomorrow's True Leader An Individual?

So far, we've been discussing the virtues of value leadership as individuals who are bringers of value.

Amsterdam Business Graduates

I coached a group of twenty-five, mid-20 millennials in Amsterdam who have recently graduated and work for a major European corporation. I asked them to name me an organisation whose strategy they are impressed by; and why.

It's fascinating how the answers to this question have changed even in the last five years.

People used to name giant corporations, and they were impressed by their size, growth rate, how great their products are or how well known the brand is and so on. They used to name Samsung, GSK, Apple....

All that has changed. Whether they cite organisations like Google, Tesla, or even small or medium enterprises that I've never heard of, the reasoning is no longer size, profits, growth, or product. It is all about their principles, ethics, and ethos as bringers of value and positively impact the world. Until recently, they mentioned Facebook as an organisation with an impressive strategy, but last week no one spoke about Facebook after the controversy and evidence of data misuse.

Companies led by a value ethos are where people increasingly want to work, feel they can be most motivated and inspired, and work harder. So, it's not individuals who will be the leaders but the principles and ethos of the organisation. People will be easily replaced. They will come and go, but the guiding ethos of value will sustain an organisation and is much better poised to generate growth and success. After all, from whom will people buy more and pay them well? I am not saying you should have a value ethos to sell more and be wealthier, but I am saying that this will be one of the outcomes of value ethos. So, a value ethos brings great respect and is deeply satisfying and, as it happens, also make you wealthier.

Conversely, a fall in principles – like Facebook – will hit the organisation hard and even destroy it, think Lehman Brothers or Enron in the late 1990s.

Having established that it's not people who will be tomorrow's true leaders but the value ethos, this ethos is established, driven and sustained by people. So, although this principle of value will be hailed as leadership, much more than individuals – those individual leaders who imbibe these principles of impacting the value of others and then with integrity work and live by them – will be the most outstanding leaders of the future, appreciated, admired and followed.

Great leaders like Mandela, Lincoln and Mahatma Gandhi come to mind. But in the corporate world we saw this with Apple. Steve Jobs infectiously spread the principle of obsession with value. The more they innovated from value impact, the more the individuals saw success, and it became established as a culture. It has lasted several years after him, but now that ethos has gone and was not replaced fast enough, it hasn't been sustained. Apple has not been innovating. Their market leadership is riding on a great legacy of value leadership which is still carrying them. This legacy has built a formidable brand, but if they continue, they are vulnerable in the future.

The two questions are: *how do you establish the ethos of value as the centrepiece of the organisation's culture*; and secondly, *how can it be sustained despite the risk that people may not change?*

Establishing Value Culture

On the question of establishing the value culture, here is what I find in all the organisations I work with and reshape. When each individual recognises that putting value-impact at the centre of everything they do will bring them tremendous personal success, and the joy of not just what they are doing but what value they are bringing, then sustainable change happens. At that point, and as they taste the resultant success, the ethos spreads like wildfire and gets established as part of the organisation's DNA. After that, whether the leader leaves or stays, it is irreversible.

Now there is a large body of people who plan, function and transact with value-impact at the heart of all decisions and actions, and it colours new people who join automatically. The principle of value ethos has now become the new leader.

Digital Marketing Brussels

In a 2,000 people European arm of a US digital marketing company headed in Brussels, this is precisely what I saw happen. In a strategy re-shaping exercise over eighteen months, we turned the organisation on its head. All product design and innovation were propelled by what and how much value was brought to the customers and the team. No planning, project meeting, transaction or conversation was conducted without contextualising it to the end value impact it brought. As a result, everyone's work took on fresh and more substantial meaning. People became far more collaborative as it served their success better through co-operation etc..

The point at which the penny dropped was when the CEO and I toured around the business units across Europe, and we helped teams convert existing projects to become value-driven. It was compelling, palpable, clear, visibly generating customer, company, team, and personal success. There was no turning back, and then when the entire strategy program happened, there was great engagement and commitment. A culture was born which lives on to this day, well after the CEO had left. It is working with great success for the business and the individuals in it, their customers and the broader environment.

That same CEO now heads another organisation for seven years. He has grown the company three-fold, and when I asked him at lunch recently on a scale of one to ten what is the level of valuepreneurship in your organisation, i.e., to what extent are people working with, making decisions on, conversing and interacting through value, the answer was an emphatic eight (see p51).

And I know it was a level of two when he joined as he took my inputs in shaping it. Job done. He is a respected leader who doesn't just see himself as the leader but builds the culture of value leadership in his organisations.

Section 5

The Magnetism And Relationships Of A Valuepreneur

5.1

Unification And Dis-Unity

Working with people and organisations around the globe, it has become abundantly clear to me that one of the most significant problems which hold companies back and causes great pain and harm is dis-unity. In the deluded sense of self, every individual and function or department is working with a sense of self-preservation, self-importance, taking control and self-projection. This comes at a high cost to the organisation, to customers and above all to this so-called self.

Most often, it happens subconsciously, i.e., without people even being aware of it. It seems to be innate within us.

In dis-unity, we lose purpose, sense of value-impact which we are here to serve, shared goals and direction. It generates destructive politics, bureaucracy, poor decision-making and stifles creativity and innovation. It diminishes and degrades communication, cooperation, and collaboration.

Missed Deadlines For An IT Company, London

The London client of a global IT company recently complained to the project director about missed deadlines and delays in releasing a new software version.

The Director told the client:

- I'm sorry, but we've had issues in communication with our offshore team of programmers in India. The project manager in India said, 'There were issues and errors in the specifications sent by our colleagues in Spain.'

- The Spain team manager said that due to the extended festival period in India and key people in that team being on holiday, they couldn't properly communicate the design changes. They had to rely on less qualified staff, so errors occurred which the guys in London need to fix. 'But we are doing our best to solve it.'

It was a mess.

The client's reaction was, 'I don't care whether you are onshore, offshore, near-shore or frankly in the middle of the ocean. I need to release this version so our customer's systems don't crash...' which could cost them millions in poor customer service to their consumers, and that is all that matters.

Look at the level of dis-unity. A familiar story? Is it making you uncomfortable? Yes indeed, in one way or another, we have all experienced and regularly experience breakdowns in proper collaboration, blame each other, protect ourselves and impact the brand of our business.

5.2

Unification And The Cost Of Dis-Unity

So what is *unification*, and how can we achieve it? Think back to alignment – it is the same point. When we are aligned, we operate as one unified unit, and we are also aware that my colleagues' success will generate success for my company and, therefore, for me. In this case, we will consult each other, help each other and find solutions together rather than acting against each other. This is true collaboration. But we need to be unified over something in common to which we can both relate. Yes, indeed, you guessed it – that ultimate point of unification is the Value Onion of the end customer we exist in this role to serve, and it is the only reason we are paid.

Dis-unity has always been the scourge of humanity. In today's day and age, where we have instantly available information and everyone is connected to everyone, the power of dis-unity is amplified to destruction and disruption.

Brexit, UK

Look at what Brexit (the vote for Britain to exit the European Union) has done in the UK. Today, the country is divided between those who saw benefit in remaining within the European Union (and I stress the word Union) and those who wanted out. There is hatred, loss of productivity, dissipated energies and even violence. The *Leavers* narrowly won because many people in England were naively led to believe that foreigners had invaded their country. It's a misguided delusion. On top of this, unscrupulous politicians seeing an opportunity to grab power perpetuated this delusion and emotional fervour with the slogan *Take Back Control, Your Country Belongs To You.*

There is total dis-unity, and that notion of alignment has been entirely lost. The country has been in a mess and its respect in the world has definitely and visibly been depleted. This is an observational example of dis-unity rather than a political statement of whether Brexit is right or wrong – that is individual choice and I respect it.

The sad truth is that the EU is never about invasion but building a robust, united trading alliance globally. I fully subscribe to the fact it does considerable need improvement on this the *Leavers* had a point. The logical approach would have been to seek a modification of the EU and modernise and strengthen the alliance further for mutual gain of all members. So, you see, logic and rationality play a negligible part in the human psyche. Everything is always sourced in the emotion and therefore irrational.

So what is the answer? Find that point of alignment, which must be the genuine welfare, employment, health etc.., of all citizens of the UK. Why would anyone vote against that? But they did because sadly the loudest politicians consciously didn't make it about that but focused on *take back control.* If the welfare of the citizens of the UK was genuinely the driving centrepiece and at the heart of the politicians in that country, they would have had a better chance of achieving unity and, yes, remaining in power longer. But it isn't. Their motive is to be in power opportunistically at *any cost,* even if it hits the economy and disfavours the people. And as we have seen, this lack of integrity results in short term gain for the few but long-term pain for all. Integrity is the only lasting and sustainable method to success.

In the modern world, people are sick and tired of being manipulated and have genuine choices and the power to make those choices. Understand real and genuine Value Onions and build perfect Response Onions to match – this is integrity and the way of Valuepreneurs.

US Presidency

The same can be said of President Trump. On a scale of 1-100, 1 being low, how much of a valuepreneur is he? Was he a force for unity or disunity? Playing on people's emotions, making them hate others like Mexicans, withdrawing from important world accords like the environment and climate change, winning votes by dividing people and deluding them to think *I am for you so-called dis-favoured people etc.* The result? A divided nation. The power of instant information and polarising of emotions to form hardened clubs and collections of people who have been taken beyond logic into their more powerful emotions, has without doubt hurt the nation.

It's a macabre thought, but I'm glad all of this is happening as the upset and disharmony will soon reach a point of realisation by people that their interests and value are not well represented. People are essentially good and only want to be successful and happy. Add to this the new generations who are much more connected to values, be they societal or environmental. They will not tolerate the divisions through loss of integrity. I see in the younger people I work with around the globe who are genuinely concerned about welfare, the planet and honesty. The Phoenix must rise from the ashes, but there must be a fire, which is happening now, and this is why I say I'm happy about these events as they will give rise to a demand for integrity. It's why I say that the age of the valuepreneur is upon us. It is the only way for the future.

5.3

Unification Is Better Than Integration

The African Bank IT Project

I was asked to help a giant technology consulting company. The CEO of a large division told me they had acquired a strategic new client, a sizeable international bank in Africa. They inherited a team of 900 people from a third-party company doing the IT and support for the bank. These 900 people needed to be properly integrated into his company and added to an existing team with 1,200 people.

After three months of this change, the CEO told me that there is chaos, dis-harmony, massive conflicts. Productivity and service levels are in free fall; *our clients are suffering and unhappy with us.* It's because each team is trying to assert their self-importance, knowledge and methods, and there is total disagreement, and there have even been fights. I asked him what he would like, and he said integration, please. I said this word *integration* is in itself a problem and would cause further division.

Think about this. The minds of the 1,200 are saying, *I* need to integrate *you*, so the *I* and *you* are perpetuated. The 900 are asking, *Who are you to integrate me?* – so the *you* and *me* is still there.

He saw the problem and asked me how I wanted to approach it.

My answer was not *integration* but *unification.*

In *integration* we are separate trying to force ourselves together. In *unification*, we are one, so the sense of you and me dissolves. It may sound like semantics, but it is a vital distinction as the entire state of mind changes from the me and you to us, and ultimately it is the state of our minds that really influence what happens to us and around us.

Having agreed on the approach, we did a series of two-day workshops for 300 seniors in the combined team of 2,100 people. Barriers started to melt, and within four months, that team grew the business and began to forget they had come from different companies and had been grafted together. A year downstream, new account acquisition has been better than ever before. Business growth has well exceeded forecasts due to stronger and sincere delivery as one unit combined to serve Response Onions to the customer's Value Onions.

It's exciting that although these were unification workshops, we didn't mention the word even once. We didn't need to. Unification is not something you tell people to do or build; it is a result. It happens as a result of doing something.

So, what is that *something*?

Having taught them models like VORO, The Christmas Tree and SVOC very practically, they worked in small cross-functional teams on selected real projects applying the SVOC and Tree. As the common joining point was the famous Value Onion of customers, they became perfectly aligned. They went on to find creative, innovative solutions to serve the values collectively as a united team and constructively leveraged the expertise within the team to find these solutions.

The collaboration, communication and cooperation were electric to watch. The CEO and his director colleagues were astounded as they saw no disharmony or conflict.

It's simple: move the emphasis away from you and me to the only thing that binds us, shared value, and suddenly we are bound by a common purpose. We are united and magnificently performant.

There are many so-called management trainers and theoretically minded academics who try to force the issue by giving moral lectures like: communicate with each other; respect each other and so on. Sadly, they understand little of the source of the issue or human beings and think there will be enlightenment and awakening from their wonderful moral lectures and instructions. It's naïve at best. People must have a reason to align, and that reason is personal success which is always tied to the customer's success. Naïvely, they say, *Don't put self-interest first, but the company interest etc.*. Rubbish, why should they? Every human born of a mother on this planet has their own Value Onion, which defines their own success. There is nothing wrong with this at all, so long as we don't negatively impact anyone or anything else.

Only one of these two things can cause a disconnect:

- Our own values don't align to those of our customers – for example, a friend of mine who was working for a car manufacturer expanding their manufacture of high polluting diesel engine cars – he left. Fair enough, good decision. Or;

- We don't understand the true values of our customers and haven't therefore aligned our values to them – which is usually the case.

It is most often the latter. So, look hard to understand the values you are serving, align yours to it and to your company's values – like Jack and Claire (see below), or the 2,100 people in the above example and frankly all the many examples I am citing.

French Cardiology Devices

Remember the case of the Finance Director and Marketing Director in that medical device company in France coming near to blows over whether we should recruit an extra twenty-five maintenance engineers? Where was the unity, alignment, collaborative agreement? It was all *me* and *mine*. Each protective over their own skills, knowledge and so-called interest. I say *so-called* because they hadn't seen that ultimately their own success and interest was in reality tied to the success of the customer, the French private cardiology clinics and indeed the customer's customer, the cardiology patients. They didn't even see that value correctly, so how could they align to it? However, once we took the discussion from that point of value, suddenly the Finance Director saw the potential for €7.2m extra sales and €2.5m profits, which served his values of success. The Marketing Director saw market expansion and brand strengthening, which served his values. As a result, each would be personally more successful, achieve promotion and earn more.

We have it, and we just don't see it. Somewhere deep down, we don't have bad intentions, but overtly, the need for self-preservation takes us down the wrong behaviour paths and actions.

Now you have the understanding and analysis of the source of the issue and the practical tools to handle it. I can safely say to you, collaborate, listen, respect each other and drive your conversations, communication, meetings, projects, plans and strategies from an indisputable *Point Of Zero Conflict* and alignment. At that point you will be unified and therefore strengthened.

Let's examine this together.

5.4

The Point Of Zero Conflict
– Alignment At Its Best

Its Benefits In Agreement, Collaboration, Results, Negotiation And Even Marriage

Is there such a thing as a Point Of Zero Conflict? I hear you ask. Yes, absolutely, without a doubt. And if we begin every conversation, communication, project, plan, transaction or strategy from that point and cross-refer everything to that point, the conflict will come down to zero. At this point, no two people in any organisation or relationship can be misaligned; in disagreement or conflict, it isn't possible. Sounds theoretical? Even magical? Let's see.

What Is Conflict?

Let's start by firstly understanding what conflict really is and how it arises. Conflict comes from the human tendency to hold on to and push the *me* and *mine*. It's the pinnacle of dis-unity. Each person or collection of people clings to this – my way, my knowledge, my interest, my process. This *my* is a debilitating problem; we take ownership in the negative sense.

It's an expression of our ego that forces us into one of two motives – either an exertion of control and power or, alternatively, self-protection as we feel weak and seek safety in what is *mine*. To use the old cliché – it's our comfort zone.

Before we know it, the whole thing transforms into pride, and it feels like we will lose face by conceding. Resultantly, we harden our position further and remove any chance of recovery from it. Relationships break down; the one with the stronger voice wins, not necessarily because it was the right way. In this state, how will the person who lost out be committed with us, motivated, take responsibility and operate collaboratively? It's a mess. All of this may be happening overtly as described or subtly without much discussion or disagreement. The result is the same.

In such situations, we deludingly say to both *that you really must work properly together; please don't argue; respect each other; try to find a solution together.* A valiant attempt but misguided. Will this moral lecture make people suddenly drop the me and mine and start collaborating? Dream on.

What Is That Point At Which Conflict Is Zero?

That *Point Of Zero Conflict* at which we are aligned, collaborating, cooperating, communicating, and working together respectfully. Yes, you have the answer – the *Point Of Zero Conflict* is the Value Onion of the end customer. It's the end gain and benefit to whom we are serving.

We will take examples in a minute. But first, let's examine why is the customer's Value Onion the *Point Of Zero Conflict*? It's because if conflict comes from the *me* and *mine*, then the beauty of the customer's Value Onion is that it doesn't belong to *you*, and it doesn't belong to *me*. It is independent of you and me. Whether you and I exist or not, it exists beyond us and regardless of us. So at the *Point Of Zero Conflict*, which is the customer's Value

Onion, the *me* and *mine* has gone, but here is the beautiful part, it's the only connection between you and me. Once again? – the *Point Of Zero Conflict* is independent of you and me *yet* it is the ONLY thing that binds us. It's the only reason we are communicating with each other, working with each other, and if *it* didn't exist, our relationship wouldn't exist. It's the only reason we are paid, i.e., customers pay us to serve their value.

No apologies for repeatedly labouring this point folks. Look how glaringly simple it is and how we unnecessarily complicate it. Now, if the centrepiece, reference point, ultimate context and the goal for each of us is the *Point Of Zero Conflict*, i.e., the value-impact to whom we work to serve, then this must be our shared goal, and we are genuinely inseparable on this point. The result? – conflict is gone, collaboration assured, productivity raised, best outcomes are a certainty.

So, in reality, there is no conflict. It is man-made by the collision of perspectives, not the meeting of reality, the objective truth. If we approach situations with this understanding, the only and last stand for disagreement which can come in our way is to disagree on the Value Onion of the customer. There is no problem with this, and the disagreement can be easily nullified. Think about this - who knows the customer's Value Onion best? Of course, the customer, so there is no need to argue; simply go and ask the customer. There cannot be two views on this as it is one reality independent of us and our different opinions. So even the last stand of the difference between us has been eliminated.

Now that we have established our goal and purpose, all that remains is to find the best way to serve that value. And it's the same one for each of us. We have a much greater chance of being aligned as serving that ultimate value will make us both individually and collectively successful. Clear, powerful, effective, simple and real. *It* isn't complicated – we are!

How Many PowerPoints Do We Need In The SlideDeck?

Last week I heard two managers arguing strongly over a presentation to the client. Jack said, 'We need to create a robust PowerPoint slide deck to impress the client.' Claire said, 'We only need two slides but communicate the rest verbally.'

No one was prepared to give way. They were mis-aligned, in conflict.

It would either result in some pathetic halfway compromise or their boss may take the decision, making one of them unhappy or worse they would make a mess of it for the client. But as their collaboration and mutual expertise are vital for the success of this presentation to win the contract, if Jack wins, then Claire's morale and contribution will fall and vice-versa.

I asked, 'Who will be at the presentation?' They said the Finance Director, Business Unit head and Operations Director.

I then asked them what the Value Onions of each of these people are – they seemed to disagree on half of those.

Next step, I requested them to get on a call with each stakeholder separately and ask intelligent questions to understand their values.

I was listening in, and even feeding them with open questions to ask during the conversation. Jack and Claire discovered a lot more than they knew. Many points of value came out.

For example, the FD needed to see creative ways of spreading the cash flow in the project; the Business Unit head needed to launch the product well ahead of the competition; the Ops Director wanted the support and collaboration of his whole team by involving them. And they all needed to present to the board in three days. This was invaluable information, and when Jack and Claire worked on how to help the customer on each of these values, their personal preferences seemed to automatically and drastically diminish from the conversation. And their individual distinctive expertise took on greater importance and came together.

The focus turned to how to make a value-impact on each of the three directors.

Without realising it, they were out of conflict and in collaboration. Each of them knew that making these three stakeholders successful would serve their company's and, therefore their own personal values. As this was common to both, they were aligned. The me and mine didn't disappear - it transformed from taking defensive positions on the process, to aligning their expertise to serve that common value, bringing beneficial personal outcomes to both Claire and Jack. So, the me moved from the process to the outcome. This me is highly desirable as each is looking for personal success. And so they should, but the success comes from a common goal and shared outcomes for mutual, individual, non-conflicting achievement. And that is value-impact to whom we serve.

Alignment

Let's talk more about everyone in the organisation being aligned with each other. All leaders I see are chasing alignment as a priority, and they must. But despite excellent intentions, they miss what alignment really means and how to achieve it. Let's sort it out once and for all.

Indian Telecom Mis-Aligned

The India CEO of a global a telecom giant asked for my help. He told me his fourteen function heads, the executive management team, are not aligned. He said, 'We have incoherent strategies because of this misalignment, and we are missing significant opportunities in the market. Further, the thousands of people under this team are also not *aligned* and not collaborating.'

Before helping him, I wanted to see what was in his mind, what he thought alignment was; and I asked him what he would like.

He asked, 'Can you train them, coach them, do whatever is needed to get them *aligned*?'

'Aligned to what?'

'To each other', he replied. 'They should speak to each other, understand each other, respect each other.'

'Do you really think we can knock together fourteen strong individuals who can't see eye-to-eye and get them to suddenly see the light by me telling them to *collaborate*? Is this *alignment*; and will it achieve it?'

He said, 'You are right; that doesn't seem plausible; and no, it's not alignment. OK, get them to align with the strategies.'

'You just told me the strategies were incoherent, and they each have different ideas not only on the strategies to go for but also the very definition of *strategy.*'

Again, he said, 'You are right. OK how about to the products?'

I said, 'The recent merger seems to have created deeper divisions on deciding which products and services we should have in our portfolio, with everyone trying to defend their own position and interests.'

This conversation went on to processes, financial results etc..

He still couldn't find alignment.

Please understand I wasn't being obstructive, I know him well, and I was concerned for his company and his people's success. I was merely awakening his own realisation of what *alignment* is so he can properly commit to bringing about the change.

Finally, he said, 'OK, I give up. What should we align them to?'

You know my response by now. I said, 'We are all aligned to and by only one thing and nothing else in any business. It gives us a common purpose, common goal, and it is the reason those fourteen people and thousands under them are even in a working relationship together. And that, dear Mr CEO is the Value Onions of your customers, and further still, the Value Onions of your customer's customers.'

It was simple but revelatory and powerful, and he was entirely on board.

We went to a beautiful beach resort near Chennai for three days with all fifteen of them. I facilitated the workshop using my SVOC strategy framework, discussed in 2.11 and 2.12.

In essence, this involved starting from a complete understanding of our customer segments and their Value Onions. Then deciding on the matching Response Onions and all the activities (*Tactics*) needed to make that response deliver the maximum value-impact.

The result was terrific, and interestingly, I never even mentioned the word *alignment* in the workshops. I didn't need to; it was one of the great bi-products.

Alignment is not something to impose, tell or even do. It is the result of the approach I have briefly described (see *The Christmas Tree Model –With Cross Functional Alignment - see 2.2*). They didn't even realise they were in strong collaboration during the workshop, which is what this compelling thinking does.

On the next day at 4pm, I remember a fun activity had been arranged on the ocean, and at 3pm, one person said, 'Do we have to do it?' The others agreed that what we were doing was far more beneficial, and they didn't want to break that rhythm – activity cancelled.

When the benefit is evident, engagement is inevitable.

Not only did they come up with innovative and creative solutions – even products and services for the market having calculated the Value Onions – but they were united on which existing ones to keep and scrap. With the clear mutual interest established through total alignment to the Value Onions, no one held on defensively to their personal preferences.

To quote their head of Legal Services, who wrote to me two weeks later – '… *we went into this workshop as fourteen disparate, unaligned individuals. You de-constructed us, re-constructed us and already after two weeks, we are in dialogue, implementing the plans which came out of Chennai.'*

Please understand this is not about me. With humble gratitude, I am sharing with you the approach, thinking, and tools that I see working in practice and are definitely the way forward as valuepreneurs.

5.5

Never Compromise
– There Is Better Way

Compromise. It's a dirty word leaving nothing but dissatisfaction all around. Never compromise. You never need to. This is radical and probably shocking for you. Do I sound inflexible? Do I sound selfish? So far, yes, but it is precisely the opposite. Please understand the point when I say you never need to compromise, but you do need to get the job done and leave the table with all parties satisfied. The task and outcome are usually half-baked in a compromise, leaving all feeling they have missed out. I'm setting the scene - the answer is coming. The problem is that most negotiations end up in sad compromise. And in most situations between people, some form of negotiation is involved.

The origin or etymology of the word *compromise* – it's from the Latin word *compromittere* and made up of three parts:

- Com = together
- Pro = before, prior
- Mitre = to release, let go, throw

It's the last part which is the killer. Essentially, compromise asks both parties to throw something away together. Throw away what? Yes, unfortunately, your points of view, ideas, and values. And it applies to both parties, which is where the *com* element comes in. So, the very word is drenched in negativity and not minded to construct anything. It is sad, destructive, counter-productive. Far from satisfaction, it will generate unhappiness in the end. Please don't do it. There is something much more constructive.

The Cake

Think about this, there is a delicious cake, and we agree to cut it in half. You get one half, and I get the other. It's a compromise. Then afterwards, which part do you think more about? Yes, it's the part you didn't get. Am I right? It feels like you let it go, threw it away. Is this a happy and satisfying outcome? Does it result in trusted and strong relationships?

In marriages, all the so-called wise advisors naively tell you to compromise to make a successful relationship. I have seen many marriages where one spouse or both compromise to adjust with each other. It may solve a short-term problem and issue, but I have never seen such marriages flourish to a level where both people are individually and collectively deeply happy and satisfied. Marriages are a perfect model for showing the failure of compromise.   In the same way, in organisations, people are tied to each other and quite often forced to each other. We need to find a better way than compromise.

So, the answer is, understand and genuinely listen to the Value Onion you both co-exist to serve. It is the way of the valuepreneur. Establish a collective understanding of this value. If there is any doubt or even disagreement over this, then simply go and ask the owner of that Value Onion – remember it is independent of you both. This sets up our common purpose and goal, which is the essence of any relationship. Now keeping that value at the forefront of our task, you will find that one of you can bring x and the other y. They combine to give the right answer, so no one has to concede or feel they have lost anything as again the result will be good for both. Even if one person's approach is a better response to the value and the other person has to drop theirs, there is no loss to the second person as the result and outcome will be more beneficial to them than holding on to their own way or point.

In Jack and Claire's example above, they were in conflict, one pushing for a PowerPoint slide driven presentation and the other favouring fewer slides and more conversation. There was an impasse, and a so-called wise person would have said you should compromise. Why don't you do half the presentation with slides and half as a conversation? These are the kind of naive messages being peddled. It is precisely the same as splitting the cake into two halves, and then neither is happy, and we will have also missed the real point.

In Claire and Jack's case, this real point missed was the Value Onions of the three stakeholders – the FD, BU head and Ops director. These priorities would have remained unaddressed, and it's pretty likely the contract lost. As a result, Jack and Claire both would have lost out, as would the customer.

By genuinely and jointly listening to, caring for and understanding the Value Onions, which becomes the common purpose and goal for Jack and Claire, they discovered more powerful responses well above their initial personal preferences. They became mutually and collectively successful by bringing success to the customer and their company too.

As it happens, Jack's method was closer to the best answer, but now it didn't disturb Claire or make her feel she had lost out because she won equally from the outcome.

Focus on purpose and outcomes, and the method will clearly appear. Initially the conversation between the two circled around each pushing their own ideas – *my idea* no *my idea*. Now imagine if Jack says to Claire – to win this contract and both our objectives met, how about helping these three stakeholders to manage the board meeting much better, i.e., clear ROI etc.. Claire, seeing her own success by serving the value of the customers, will certainly agree that a more structured presentation, as proposed by Jack, will help in this case. In another situation, it may be her approach of a conversational presentation that has the highest value-impact. This is real win-win. Win on the results, irrespective of who's way.

Sounds simple? It is.

It's the same principle in marriage, although the customer, in this case, is the couple themselves. I heard a couple recently arguing heavily about the choice of school for their daughter. The father wanted a more academic school, and the mother's choice was the school with more sports and activities. By truly understanding the child, her talent and interests and therefore happiness which was the common goal and purpose to both, they chose a school specialising in music and drama – no compromise. Or a couple fighting, one saying why didn't you do it, the other saying it wasn't necessary. Had they focused on the outcome of that task, they would have had a better discussion, and neither would feel their way was compromised. The marriages I have seen succeed the most is where:

1. There was something of mutual and shared interest – it could be art, history, a sport, charitable activity or as in our case, classical music and performance. This automatically sets up the end Value Onions of someone

to serve, and then the couple work together, and the more they serve that value, the more satisfied and successful they are themselves.

2. Each wants to see the other unconditionally successful in whatever their work or interest in and does everything to enable that success.

3. It doesn't work where one is dedicated to the other, but the other is dedicated to themselves. At times, it will seem that one is getting more and the other times the other, but the overall graph is upward. I believe this unconditional wanting to see the other achieve, succeed, and be happy is true love. I've done this for you, and you didn't do that for me brings down to being cheap traders trying to squeeze as much out of the other for mutual gain.

What Does Winning Mean?

Deludedly, when we get our way, we think we have won. Maybe it's true, but only if your way happened to serve the end and mutual value and brought the win to all. There are too many *ifs* and *buts* here. Let's get straight to the point - winning means collectively, collaboratively and successfully impacting the end value, which is common to us both of us. And common value always exists; otherwise, our relationship wouldn't exist. On a cricket pitch, you can't bowl all the time. Sometimes you bowl, sometimes you field. If another bowler is chosen because their style will work better against a particular batsman, then you haven't lost – you will benefit from winning the game. In an orchestra, sometimes the violins have to give way to the cellos and vice-versa - no one loses you win by creating beautiful music. No compromise is needed - you are giving up nothing. You are combining in the best way.

Frankly, it's the same in organisations and in work generally. Jack was concerned for Claire's welfare in the better conversation above, and vice-versa they found mutual success.

Or in the example of the Finance Director and Marketing Director arguing over whether we should recruit another twenty-five maintenance engineers. Both dropped their positions when they took it from the *Point Of Zero Conflict,* i.e., the success of private cardiology clinics in France and their patient's welfare. They found the best answers on which both were united – no compromise required.

Think of the example of the client John, who wanted to have Excel restored as his working platform, and Rakesh, who insisted on his expert ideas and SQL. The answer was in the Value Onion of the client on which neither could disagree. SQL happened to be the correct answer in this case. But when the argument was on Excel v SQL, there was conflict, and when it moved to the *Point Of Zero Conflict,* it was clear which solution was the best. No-compromise was needed, and we achieved simple and indeed grateful acceptance of the right solution – in this case Rakesh's SQL (see 1.22).

5.6

Successful Negotiation Without Compromise – The Valuepreneurial Way

The word *negotiate* comes from the Latin *negotium* and begins with a negative term. *Neg = no* and suggests in business dealings that it is the negation of differences. The problem lies here as it starts with the assumption that there are differences. With this in mind, negotiation by default becomes a desperate and often aggressive act of trying to get more than the other. This destructively selfish attitude results in each party trying to score over the other, in-fact in its subtle reality, it is about hurting the other so I can gain the most. Can this ever end up in satisfaction? It may provide immediate apparent success and even pleasure but satisfaction? Sustained success? Stronger relationships and trust? Certainly not. At its very best, this approach in business dealing ends up in a compromise, and you know what I think about that!

Win-Win Is A Flawed Ideal

There is no need for this unnecessary pain, stress and ambiguous uncertainty. There is a better way.

Firstly, all those naïve books and training on negotiation are centred around those two famous three-letter words *Win-Win*. The logic behind it is honourable, but the sentiment is anything but. It's a flawed ideal, and if you examine the method, the approach is how can I win the most and try not to let the other feel bad.

This is the true and flawed sentiment of *win-win*. It's about how to exert influence over others to further your interest or get your method, approach, or idea to succeed. It's actually *win-lose* in disguise. It's shameful and must be stamped out, not because I'm adopting a high moral idealistic position and giving you a lecture on moral values but because there is a better way to achieve success and a genuine *win-win*.

I recently heard an enlightened statement on a TV program where one character asks the other, *Did anyone come out of that meeting satisfied?* The other says, *No.* The first one says, *That's a successful negotiation.* A sad reality but that's how most negotiations conclude, and the compromise is a fait-accompli.

The *win-win* – or rather *win-lose* – goes back to my earlier point about the cake. It's a compromise.

I will always miss the part I didn't get, and most often, one or both parties in a negotiation feels cheated or hard done by and their own value or position has been compromised. Nevertheless, they grudgingly accepted it because they were desperate to get something, maybe a sale, a contract. They accept their lot; their loss and their position being compromised.

In this state, how can you work, operate, collaborate with confidence and build stronger relationships, which is at the heart of any business, organisation, activity or life?

The Valuepreneurial Negotiation = Collaborative Agreement

It's not about desperation or winning above the other or strengthening your position to weaken theirs. It is the opposite, the antithesis of what we have just discussed. A valuepreneur understands the true purpose of a negotiation is to collaborate to serve value. So firstly, let's replace the word *negotiation*, the premise of which is negation, with *Collaborative Agreement*.

Now here is the question. *Instead of dividing the cake* – which is classic negotiation – *if I give you the whole cake in its glorious entirety, will you not invest in me?*

Simple, isn't it?

So what does the *entire cake* practically mean? Yes, it's your Value Onion. If I see your true and complete value instead of splitting the cake, then provide perfect responses to match and serve that value, will you not be happy to invest in me and pay me well? This is a *Value-Based Collaborative Agreement* and the true meaning of *Win-Win*.

For example, in the Excel/SQL case, in the second conversation with John, the client, Rakesh wasn't focused on himself *(Me sFear)* but on John *(You Sphere)*. He showed John *how* he would never again lose millions on transactions, support his team's currency decisions remotely when travelling and beat his targets – this is the whole cake in its glorious entirety. In this case, can John afford to let Rakesh go? He will definitely want to buy from Rakesh and, within reason, pay him the asking price.

This is what I mean: if you give the whole cake, won't the other person invest in you?

So, Rakesh and John both win because the focus was not *what can I squeeze out of this negotiation* but a genuine understanding of John's Value Onion. The result is excellent outcomes for both and, most importantly, a long relationship of respect, collaboration and trust.

Trump And North Korea

When President Trump went to negotiate in North Korea, he came back empty-handed and a laughing stock in the world, having failed to nail the deal with a dictator he had only weeks before called *Rocket Man;* and had threatened to obliterate.

Ironically, *Mr Champion Negotiator* and author of *The Art of The Deal* – which in essence is all about how to squeeze the other – failed miserably. He went unprepared on the North Korean dictator's Value Onion, whose PV (personal value) was all about legitimising himself as a world leader, which he more or less achieved, and BV (business value) was lifting of sanctions which partially happened. Mr Trump, in his arrogance, went with a show of power, *I am the most powerful leader of the free world, and I will @#!* you.* Shameful. Whichever way your political allegiances lie, would you call him a valuepreneur?

Getting back to our discussion about classic negotiations i.e., an entrepreneur's eye is on the bigger slice of the cake, but the valuepreneur's mind is obsessively on the value of the other. Who will win? With whom will you prefer to do business and argue less on price. So, who will be richer in any case? A classic negotiator or the valuepreneur?

I want to stress this point, and it is imperative to recognise that the valuepreneur making collaborative agreements will be more prosperous than the negotiating entrepreneur.

Again, I'll cite Apple under Steve Jobs. When did he ever have to negotiate hard and make deals? His obsession was value, and as a result, he named his price. Don't forget that a MacBook Air was selling at three times the price of competitors; this is your investment in him as he serves your value, assuming you are in that segment. Unsurprisingly, Apple became the wealthiest company globally and the first one to be worth one trillion dollars and, shortly afterwards, two trillion dollars.

Without him, the future is less bright, and it's running on his legacy but fast becoming just another competing corporation. Even the price differential is negligible now.

Terminology Clarification

The following terms I am using mean the same thing with some subtle differences in application:

- Common Purpose and Goal.
- Value Onions.
- Value-Impact.
- Point Of Zero Conflict.
- Collaborative Agreement Point.
- Point of Alignment.
- Point of Unification.

They are all different expressions of the same thing because they are driven by and a direct outcome of the Value Onions of the end customer. It really is as simple as that, and yes, it is magical!

5.7

Trust Capital And Valued Relationships – The New Currency

Building Trust Capital through excellent relationships is the new currency to propel us with impetus and longevity. These relationships could be with customers, suppliers, people in the organisation, other collaborators, government bodies, and the list goes on. As we increasingly automate, deploy technology, and artificial intelligence, relationships and human interaction are becoming significantly more valued. Their importance is further fuelled by the pandemic, global disharmony, questionable motives and fall in integrity.

What Is Trust Capital?

Why am I saying this is the new currency, which will take you much further in your work, endeavours, organisations and as an individual. How do you inculcate it? What are the methods, what are the techniques for building *Trust Capital*?

In the new age, there's a shift from buying products and services into buying the value-impact or the outcomes they represent to us.

How do they enhance our business, work, and lives? How do they improve things for us? That's really what we engage with and what we buy now.

Think like a customer – the product or service you are buying is readily available from many suppliers, then how important is who you are buying from. How much faith, confidence, and even trust do you have in them. And that person who engages with your value, understands it, obsesses with it, and then and only then develops and presents their products and services or positions them to you, is what we call a valuepreneur. And this is the trusted advisor who will have longevity in their business. They will make a lot more money in any case because there will be fewer negotiations. Why would a customer look at other suppliers when they are getting their problems solved?

So, it's not about selling products; it's about bringing solutions to the end value. Only 20-30% of the deal is to do with your product or services in today's day and age, and it's shifting fast. Seventy to eighty percent of it is to do with the relationship.

How Much Value Have You Understood?

Let's say you're selling to a business; do you understand what's happening behind the scenes? Who are the other stakeholders, what values are they're looking for? What are the business's priorities, and what are their customers demanding and, therefore, shaping their priorities? This engagement with customers and understanding their values is what I call a *Spirit of Enquiry*, which builds *Trust Capital*.

Let's demonstrate this with an example.

Agile Vs. Waterfall

I was conducting a program for a major IT company, and two of their senior executive directors, Elke and Sean, fell into disagreement.

Elke: Our client wants to develop the entire program using the Agile methodology. (Don't worry about these technical terms, that's not the point; and you'll still get the principle).

Sean: No, I think we should do this in the Waterfall method (which is another way).

Elke: Yes, but the client is still asking for Agile.

Sean: Fair enough, but you know Waterfall will be much better. Let's try and convince the client that we're going to do this in Waterfall.

Do you know why Sean wanted to do it in Waterfall? Because Waterfall works to fixed outcomes and fixed objectives. In Waterfall, you're able to fix and know the budget, have clarity of how much will be earned from the project, plan the manning and resources, and manage it with greater ease. In other words, *it's about me, my convenience, my processes and how I can make it easier for myself.*

The client, however, wanted to do this under Agile. They are a major medical devices company in electro-cardiology developing a new cardiology machine to launch ahead of competitors. For this, it is critical they engage their customers - physicians, cardiologists, doctors in giving feedback and be involved in the whole development process. Agile helps to serve this major value. With it they'll be able to design the product much better and launch, ahead of the competition and gain market share. So, it was pretty important. Further, their finance director was looking for a return on investment and a much better handle on cost - Agile gives you this better than Waterfall.

This huge customer value was the real issue.

Still, no one had developed that *Spirit of Enquiry* to engage at that level with the customer to genuinely understand *why* Agile was needed to serve that value. How can we become a trusted advisor?

Guess what happened? Unsurprisingly, they ended up losing the deal. They lost the contract. The client went to another competitor of theirs. And the client didn't work this out logically, saying, *Let me go to someone else because I wanted it in Agile, and these people are pushing Waterfall.* It wasn't as logical as that. It was far more emotional, and it was in the subconscious mind of the client. Remember the Icebergs in Section 3?

Trust is an emotional issue; it's not a logical issue. We're deluded into thinking that we sell logically. We propose to the client with –*Look at my product, isn't it great? I'll offer you a special deal, etc..* It doesn't work like that. It's far more subconscious, far subtler and emotional.

We missed a big part of the emotional and subconscious response of the client and the opportunity to build trust by engaging with them through their value and becoming trusted advisers. And these words, trusted advisor, are being loosely thrown around these days. I hear it a lot from my clients and the corporations with whom I am working. The intention is excellent, but the substance is missing, and people are not actually doing it. They'd like to, but they're missing the technique, and that's what we are building here for practical use.

So, this is the point. Do you want to build longevity in your business as a trusted adviser, or do you want to become a vendor and grab as much as much business in the short term as you can? Then you'll be fighting against competition. And this word *vendor* comes from a Latin word, *to vend; to sell.* So you'll become a desperate seller, and the moment you know that your customers call you a *vendor,* you're in big trouble.

You're not a trusted adviser, and they'll negotiate with you, and they'll position you against competitors. You might undercut your competitors and get a deal today, but if tomorrow someone else comes and undercuts you and they'll buy from them.

This is the antithesis of building relationships.

Business now is all about relationships. It's true even in the consumer environment, I'm not just talking about the business-to-business environment. In a consumer environment, where as a producer we are even further removed from the customer, they can perceive how genuinely we are interested in them and listening to their values. Whether buying, washing powder, or food - how much are we interested in understanding the nutritional content and advising consumers you on that value etc.. Building relationships by serving value is now a universal phenomenon.

Laptop Sale

Let's say you want to buy a laptop. As you enter the shop, the salesperson comes and asks, 'May I help you?'

And you say, 'I'm looking for a laptop.'

He says, 'Sure we have a good choice...' and takes you to the computer section and says, 'Here they are...' and from left to right they are increasing in price as the features improve like processing speed and storage. Then he points to one and says, 'This is our best-seller at the moment, and we have a promotion on it, and if you buy it this weekend we have a 10% discount, and it comes with a free bag.'

This tedious style is a pretty normal and familiar conversation, and I'm sure you recognise it. But where is the *Spirit of Discovery?* Your normal response is, 'Thanks, I'll have a look around...'. You will then look at laptops, select the two or three you like, and then go home and check the prices online and buy on Amazon or similar.

Is he behaving like a desperate vendor or as a trusted advisor?

Note: Although I am using a sales example, it applies to all of us each day in many different situations. If selling means bringing value, then we are all selling all the time.

A trusted adviser, i.e., a valuepreneurial salesperson's approach is different and rooted in the *Spirit of Discovery* of the Value Onion of the customer.

Once you have told him you are looking for a laptop, and he says, 'Come I'll show you our range.' As you are walking there, he says, 'I'd like to show you the right laptop for you, and it would help me to know about your usage. May I ask, what's your current laptop like?' This is an excellent question to start understanding value with the *Spirit of Discovery*. He's taking an interest.

'Well, it's okay, but it's quite large.'

'Ah, I see... how would a smaller one help you?'

'I'm travelling a lot and I need something lighter with a long battery life. And I need to be able to... etc..'

'I see, so you need to be far more productive on your travels. Anything else?

'Yeah, I make movies and enter competitions; so I need fast processing speed and more storage, and I need a bigger screen with superb clarity and definition...'

The valuepreneurial salesman points him to the right product and says, 'This one has high processing speed... a lot of storage capacity. And it will hotlink to a large screen... which you just keep at home or in your study... it has the highest image definition available. It's also has real-time screen refresh modes pro editing suites. So, you will be more productive when you're travelling, and you can make your movies very smoothly without speed and storage problems...'

Let me ask you folks - who will get that business, where will that customer go to, who will they recommend, and who will they advocate when they're speaking to their friends? Not only will they recommend your shop but you as well.

Look at it in reverse – as a customer – wouldn't you trust such a person and return to them the next time you need something?

You're not here to sell but to bring a solution. Sell nothing, bring solutions. Your product or service will certainly be bought. But to bring a solution, you need to understand the value to which your solution is responding. For this, you need to engage with their value, understand it, be obsessed by it.

I call this a *dare to care* mindset.

I'm talking about the ultimate of integrity. You are working with integrity when you genuinely understand value and build your products and services to bring value-impact. You've become a trusted advisor. This awareness resides in us all, and it is our nature, whether consciously or subconsciously – we just need a way to make it happen; that way is valuepreneurship. You will win the deal, the sale, and you will not just be differentiated but distinguished.

I invite you to become a trusted advisor and shift your team and entire organisation into this way of thinking and valuepreneurship.

5.8

Conversity
– Conversing For Collaboration

I am using an artistic licence with this made-up word to describe the universe and university of conversations. Ultimately business is about people, and people are about relationships. At the centre of every relationship is communication and the mechanism of communication is conversation. The way we converse will determine the quality of the relationship, and even make or break it. The principles, tools and techniques we will discuss below are as applicable to written communication as verbal.

Who are these conversations with? Going back to *Value Leadership* and our *Total People Environment* (Section 4), you converse with your customers or clients, other externals like suppliers, internal colleagues, members of your team, as well as your managers and seniors.

We comprehensively described these conversations in the Hotel Serve Ltd case (see 4.4) and in many other examples like the Excel SQL case, the medical devices company and twenty-five maintenance engineers etc.. Now let's put more structure to these collaborative conversations and equip you with the technique for making them productive for you all the time.

Before we look at the steps in making a conversation or interaction collaborative, I want to emphasise one crucial point.

I'm dissecting, analysing and describing each step below to give deeper insights and the reasoning behind it, rather than just a set of menu driven instructions. In one way or another, you are doing all of these things, but now we are ensuring you are doing it consistently and well. However, in application, they are straightforward and will feel totally natural.

**The Two Fundamental Principles
For Successful Conversations And Communication**

- Capturing the Interest – of whom you are conversing with.
- Being Interested in them.

It's two-way traffic. And you may correctly argue that the more you are being interested in people, the more you will capture their interest. Yes, indeed, the two go hand-in-hand.

5.9

The 7 Steps In Excellent Collaborative Conversations

The seven steps are:

- Step 1 - Prepare Your Mind To Be Confident, Clear And Right Focused.

- Step 2 - Connect With The Person - The First Contact.

- Step 3 - Context – The 'Why'.

- Step 4 - Spirit of Discovery or Spirit of Enquiry.

- Step 5 – Validate.

- Step 6 – Provide Solutions / Responses.

- Step 7 – Agree And Get A Commitment.

In the seven steps of excellent collaborative conversations below:

- Capturing interest is covered mainly in Steps 1, 2 and 3.

- Being Interested is principally covered in Steps 4 to 7 as well Questions and Listening.

5.10

Step 1 – Prepare Your Mind To Be Confident, Clear And Right Focused

Ensure nothing in your subconscious is distracting you.

Your confidence or lack of it, fears, apprehensions, hesitations show upfront as anticipation of and expectations from the conversation and its outcome make your emotional state more evident and revealed. You give the game away. Not that it's a game, but until people see their value being addressed, they could take advantage of it and see it as your weakness.

To prepare the mind, there are two things:

1. Before the meeting, think about the person's EV BV PV. Please write it down, shut your eyes for a few seconds and imagine you are that person with that Value Onion. Make sure it is genuinely their value and not what you would like their value to be to suit you. This will take you out of the *Me sFear* and put you into the *You Sphere*.

2. Having built the consciousness of their value in your mind, check your mind to ensure that nothing is distracting you, for example, any negative ideas about them, prejudices, concerns and fears.

This will disturb and distract, but as you have now moved from
the receiving to the giving mode, through value, fears will be replaced by
care, nervousness with confidence and expectation with delivery.
You know the result. In other words, dis-engage (look at Step 1
of *Handling Difficult People Situations And Tough Attirtudes* - see 3.26).

Try this on just three selected issues each week and please
be diligent about it. Please don't apply it to all situations as
it may get tiresome and shift the focus to the process rather than
the outcome. By actively applying it to three a week it will remain
manageable and over a few weeks it will organically turn into
reflex on all conversations you have. Within a month, you will
see that it will start to become automatic, and you will not even
be conscious that you have gone into the You Sphere. It will be
a reflex, and your conversations excellent. You are through.

One further point to prepare the mind – meditate to achieve
mind equilibrium, balance and freedom at all times. It will still
the mind. You will not be distracted by yourself, and you will be
more available to yourself. Your conversations and interactions
will be truly objective, productive and collaborative. There are
many great methods available, please pick one which suits
you and stick with it. In a future text I will be happy to share a
structured technique.

5.11

Step 2 – Connect With The Person – The First Contact

This is the first part of the conversation, the opening. Whether you are communicating with them for the first time or have known them for years, opening the conversation well is essential. Why? Because as the saying goes, first impressions are usually the last ones. In other words, they tend to remain and are indelible, and they influence the rest of the communication and, therefore, your relationship. So how do we get the first contact to be strong?

Firstly, link with the person with a compliment, an observation, a kind word. It could be, *Thanks for the report, and it's looking good...* or *Great to see you how was the holiday?* Nothing complicated.

You might think this is mundane and obvious, and most of the time, especially in a professional context, we forget it. However, it profoundly impacts communication and instantly positions us as collaborators in a constructive dialogue.

The French have an excellent term for this; it's called *construire un climat de confiance*, literally meaning *building a climate of confidence*. It implies that we are engaged constructively and respectfully to solve something together, irrespective of the subject.

Also, ensure that there is a smile in your attitude and warmth in your tone. Just be your natural self - stresses and strains of the topic or over-thinking the issue makes us unnatural. It sounds obvious, but you will be shocked how it escapes us, especially when your mind is distracted with emotions like fear, concerns, expectations. We will take full examples of this later.

The Key Captivating Phrase (KCP)

Secondly, your first important words should be what I call a KCP, a *Key Captivating Phrase*. Something which makes the other person or people sit up and become interested in listening to you and conversing with you. So, what constitutes this KCP? Let me first tell you a story on this.

The French Cardiologist

Recently I was coaching a very senior cardiologist in France to present with a more personal impact. He is a brilliant cardiologist and in the elite group in Europe called *Key Opinion Leaders*. The following week, he was presenting his new technique of interventions using stents to keep arteries unblocked and open in one of the biggest cardiology conferences in the world called PCR.

I arrived in Paris and asked him to do a mock presentation. There he was, standing behind a podium, looking into his laptop, spectacles halfway down his nose and the giant screen behind him projecting his slides. Three thousand people would have been in the audience, and the presentation began, *Good morning dear colleagues, my name is Dr___ I am the professor of cardiology at xxx university...* and so on.

Laboriously, technically and in an over-professionally monotonous tone, he described his work on the different types of stents, drug-eluting, non-drug-eluting, balloon type, etc.., the number of patients in the study, the research protocols and processes...

It went on and on, and I was asleep as would have been half of his audience and right at the end, buried deep into the presentation, was the conclusion.

I said, 'Professor, why did you keep the best part to the end?'

He said in a beautiful French accent, '...because I am a scientist, and the conclusion always comes at the end.'

'Doctor, I have studied science, and I appreciate that this is the accepted norm but making a scientific presentation is no joke.'

'You are absolutely right, it is no joke. How do you mean?'

'Because, in a joke, you keep the punch line at the end! That's why it is no joke. Start with it up at the front. No one was born a scientist or engineer, or artist. Everyone was born a human, and our first and most potent interactions are as humans and then anything else.'

He got it, and next week in PCR, to which he had invited me, the presentation was completely different. He stood in the middle of the stage with proximity to the audience, not behind a podium to distance himself. He opened with his personal style and comfortably and confidently said:

'Dear colleagues, imagine you come into your catheter lab (operating room) in the morning, and there is a patient on the table with a complicated lesion (blockage) near the aorta. What goes through your mind?

That:

- The intervention is so successful; you don't see the patient for at least six years and not six months because they need a re-intervention.
- The patient's safety and prognosis are significantly raised.
- You can handle two extra patients on your daily list.
- The cost of intervention comes down by 20%.
- This is what we are speaking about today.

This was the KCP. He had struck the Value Onion of his audience as a masterstroke. I heard a vocal buzz around the auditorium, everyone was perked up, and a couple of doctors sitting in front of me turned to each other, and one said, *What? How does he achieve that?* The audience's interest had been ignited with the *Key Capturing Phrase* (KCP). He then gave the details of the entire research, but at every point and slide, he was cross-referring back to the KCP and, therefore, the value-impacts.

The doctor had become a valuepreneur, delivered the presentation without nervousness, with confidence and a voice fully intonated and at his natural best. Why wouldn't he? After all, he had moved from *receiving* mode to *giving* mode. At the end of his exposé, amongst rapturous applause, he came off the stage and shook my hand. A few weeks later, he told me the take up of his method had been the best he had ever seen in his illustrious career.

When you are obsessively in value and its delivery, you are magnificent yet humble and, most importantly, impactful and effective.

I am speaking about a lot more than just the KCP here but getting back to the question of *what constitutes a KCP?* It's the Value Onion of who you are interacting with. It's the most powerful point in capturing their interest. We don't communicate to communicate. We communicate so there will be a more decisive outcome, a result, a decision, an agreement. By capturing the interest of the person or people I am conversing with, I will sure up those outcomes, bring value-impact and success to people through my skills and talents and bring success and deep satisfaction to myself.

Confidence is not something you tell yourself to have. The more you try and tell yourself to have it, the more you will perpetuate the lack of confidence as you will be over-conscious of it, uncomfortable and lower your confidence.

Confidence is a result - the source is something else. Work on the source and the symptom, result or outcome will be confidence.

The source? Shift from the *Me sFear* to the *You Sphere,* from *receiving* mode to *giving* mode. Impact their Value Onion – confidence is guaranteed, nervousness will be reduced, even eliminated.

5.12

Step 3 – Context – The 'Why'

If you don't know the destination, frankly, take any road, and the chances of getting anywhere meaningful are slim to zero. A journey without purpose can never be fulfilling and motivating. Success will delude you. However, with a clear and worthwhile purpose, people apply themselves to the maximum, innovate, create and be committed.

In conversations and all interactions, begin with the why, the end outcome, value impact or the benefit, only then go to the *what*, the topic and the actions. The conversation will then move with more purpose, and both are aligned through this why, which is also the *Point Of Zero Conflict* or the Value Onion of the end customer whose value we co-exist to serve.

When no context is given, one of two things will happen. Either they will do the task without commitment and engagement, or worse, they will assign their own why, and usually this is not a reasoned assignment but a less rational one from our prejudices, assumptions or worse still from our fears and other emotions.

Think back to the case where the client was asking for a workload optimisation report. No context was given. The *why* was missing, and he went straight to the *what – I need a workload optimisation report by tomorrow 3pm*. In this case, the project manager assigned his own *why*, as did the whole team, falsely concluding the client is checking up on us, he thinks we don't work hard enough, but this was far from the truth. This assumption was an irrational one made through fear and concern. They took the wrong action i.e., showing they were 120% occupied, yet the real *why* was the client was looking to award a new contract to the team who had some spare capacity. They lost out. In-fact they all lost out – including the client as these were the right people for the job.

Was this a collaborative conversation? No, but a good example of the importance of leading with the context and the *why* in all conversations. In most cases, this is the Value Onion of whom we are serving. Of course, when stating mundane, simple facts like, it's getting chilly these days, or the water is hot you don't need the why or context – I am speaking about important conversations.

Another virtue of starting with the context is respecting the person with whom you are communicating. When you bring someone into the why first, they feel valued and respected and, as a result, will be more engaged, enthused, positive and contribute more to the discussion and action.

The final point is that Steps 2 and 3 may be combined, depending on the situation. Where the Value Onion is fully known and well expressed in the KCP, then that is also the context. For example, in the case of our cardiologist, his four points of KCP are the complete Value Onion of his audience and their patients.

The difference between the two is the KCP is short, sharp and punchy, and the context is more detailed and complete. So, you may start with quick fire points in the KCP. This will capture their attention and then go on to expand on these points to frame the context and destination.

5.13

Step 4 – Spirit Of Discovery Or Spirit of Enquiry

A *Spirit of Enquiry* is a mindset and technique to fully understand the Value Onions of our customers. Remember, the word *customer* means anyone whose values we serve with our talent, knowledge and capabilities, so it applies equally to our managers, teams and colleagues, external customers, suppliers, etc..

As we have amply discussed (see 1.39), it is essential to understand the Value Onions of our customers, not just the Essential Value (EV) but the Business Value (BV) and ultimately Personal Value (PV). Only then can we genuinely build Response Onions to serve all three levels of value. By this we not only reassure our customers (on EV) but also win their confidence (on BV) and most significantly their trust (on PV). At this level, we become trusted and valued partners. All of this happens through collaborative conversations and interactions.

Returning To The Example Of The Laptop Salesman

In the valuepreneurial conversation, there is a genuine *Spirit of Discovery* of value. There is care, not only for the product the customer wants but why they want it, i.e., for the value-impact and outcome they will derive from it. The laptop now is a mere tool. He is really selling or addressing their *productivity* when travelling and enjoying making movies – focusing on the creative process rather than managing the technology.

For the customer then (see 1.39):

- EV is the laptop, eight hours battery life, small screen, xyz storage capacity.
- BV is work productivity - using his travelling time to get a lot of work done.
- PV is to make more movies and win awards.

Having understood the customer's Value Onion, the salesperson takes you to the perfect computer and also shows a high-speed connection with the TV to facilitate the movie editing. So, his Response Onion matches your Value Onion perfectly, but this can only happen if he has the mindset of and the heart for caring and bringing value as well as the technique and mechanics to navigate the conversation and ask the right questions.

I request that you never again in a conversation jump to offer solutions without a proper *Spirit of Discovery*, which I also call a *Spirit of Enquiry*.

All of this sounds logical and straightforward, and when I ask people what is *selling*? In today's day and age people rarely give me the wrong answer: showing your product and services to customers and getting them to buy as much as possible at the highest price.

Everyone says selling is about understanding customers' needs then showing them how your product can help, i.e., find the Value Onion and serve the Response Onion to match that value. All very well and honourable, but 90% of the time, if not more, what we actually do is precisely the opposite, and we end up not listening and then trying to sell as much as we can. The shift from the *Me sFear* to the *You Sphere* is the bottom line, the ultimate formula for growth, satisfaction and success.

Throughout this book, we have taken so many examples of where the *Spirit of Discovery* is critical in all conversations, whether the Excel SQL case or the twenty-five maintenance engineers, workload optimisation reports etc..

No More #002653

I heard of a conversation at one of my engineering company clients recently. Their distributor said to the salesperson, 'We are stopping orders of tool #002653 from next month as our customers want something different.'

A minor panic set in immediately, and he told his boss, who then called the distributor to say, 'We have been supplying this part for a long time. Our product is the best in the world, and we have just brought out a new model – please speak to your customers, and we can come to a better price arrangement.'

Which sphere are they in as desperation set in? I coached them to move to the *You Sphere* and have a better conversation through a *Spirit of Discovery*, and they discovered several values:

The value of the distributor was that he wasn't making enough margin on this tool, so he didn't encourage the customer to continue buying it. The value of the customer, the engineering head of an automotive production company, was that they had automated the part of the production process where this tool was used and needed a tool that could set the screw tightening to the exact strength automatically rather than manually. The current tool would cause costly bottlenecks in production. What a revelation, and we were trying to drop our price to sell him more of the manual tool. How will the customer ever have faith and trust in us? Look how remaining in the *Me sFear* and not having a *Spirit of Discovery* damages our own success, and we miss real opportunities.

Having discovered this value, they showed the customer and the distributor that if we could step up the design of an automated tool to the customer's exact specification and have it ready in two months, it would prevent the bottlenecks and save costs. The result was that the customer gained so much faith and trust in the engineering company they pushed back their automation by four weeks, partnered with them in the design and gave orders for a year's supply on the prototype. The customer, distributor and the company were all delighted.

How did they discover this value?

1. Conversed with the distributor to understand his Value Onion.

2. By reassuring the distributor of more sales and better margins, they convinced the distributor to arrange a three-way conversation directly with the end customer. This is something distributors always resist as they feel it's giving away control, but they agreed, and frankly, why wouldn't they if they can see it's in their own interest – it's the power of value and shifting to the *You Sphere*.

3. They remained open minded. A productive three-way conversation in the *Spirit of Discovery* between the customer, distributor and my client, the engineering company, brought excellent results for all. It wasn't about pushing their products or desperately trying to win business (*Me sFear*-ism) but genuinely a heart and mind to understand their Value Onion.

4. Proposed and agreed with ease, built perfect Response Onions, and presented the solution of accelerating the design of the automated tool etc..

5. Conversed to propose working in partnership with the customer and distributor in providing the best solution.

A *Spirit of Discovery* is the centrepiece of all collaborative conversations and, therefore, Conversity. It sets up our first enabling nature, understanding, and makes all actions right and rewarding and not just reactions which will at best end up as a fluke if it works.

Having understood the mindset, thinking, and examples of a *Spirit of Discovery* we will examine the tools and mechanics of making it happen after the seven steps below. This is the technique, science and art of asking the right questions at the right time in the right way.

5.14

Step 5 – Validate

At every step in the conversation, validate your understanding. It is a critical step that we will discuss under *Questions To Navigate The Conversation* (see 5.17).

You will see how necessary it is, how badly it is done and how easy it is to do.

5.15

Step 6 – Provide Solutions/Responses

Having understood the true value and only after you have understood it, bring matching responses, layer by layer of the Value Onion.

Further, as you are giving the responses, cross-refer them to the value points they are serving. It is straightforward and virtually impossible that they will not buy your product, service or idea.

In The Laptop Purchase Example

VALUE DISCOVERED	MATCHING RESPONSES
Ease of opening and using a laptop on aircraft.	Dell Inspiron model... Detachable touch screen in case there is no space for a keyboard.
Productivity and work continuation during travelling.	Long-life battery; power optimisation software; convenient, lightweight spare battery etc..
Making short films and winning awards.	High processing speeds; data capacity; easy connection to a large TV screen...

5.16

Step 7 – Agree And Get A Commitment

This simplest step of all is just one question, and again we will explore this below under *Questions to Navigate the Conversation.*

5.17

Questions To Navigate
The Conversation
And Build Trusted Relationships

Let's start with that famous wisdom. There are two types of
Questions – *Open* and *Closed*. I will split these into two further
categories – *Neutral* and *Oriented* (or Influenced).

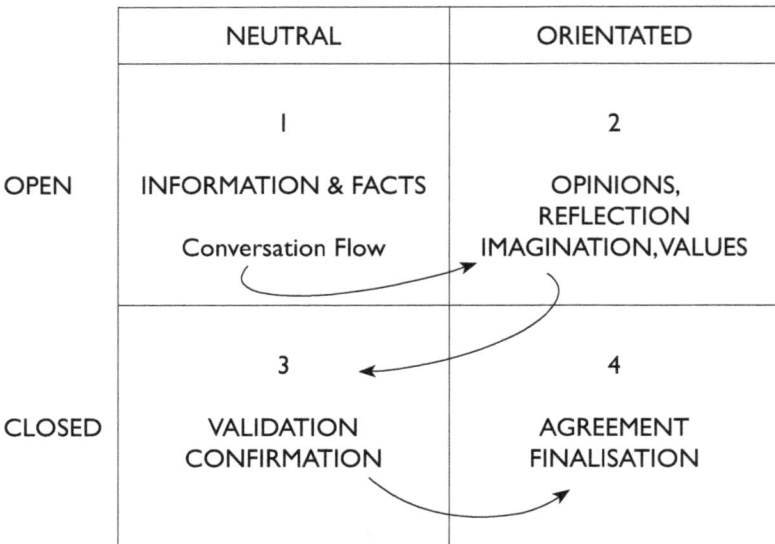

	NEUTRAL	ORIENTATED
OPEN	1 INFORMATION & FACTS Conversation Flow	2 OPINIONS, REFLECTION IMAGINATION, VALUES
CLOSED	3 VALIDATION CONFIRMATION	4 AGREEMENT FINALISATION

These are not just questions - together they give us the entire structure and flow of conversations.

Reminder – What Are Open Questions?

Open questions begin with *Who, What, Where, When, How, Why, Which*. They *can't* be answered with a *Yes* or *No*. They require elaboration. And elicit information. It's as simple as that. These seven friends are invaluable in the *Spirit of Discovery* and indeed any conversation, regardless of how mundane or important it is.

Step 1 - Open Neutral Questions

With these, we discover factual information. We call them *neutral* as they are neutral to you, the person asking the questions, i.e., there is no opinion expressed. They are simply the observed reality. Getting the facts is the crucial first step in any conversation. This is where understanding begins, and much too often, we tend to miss this – the result is we are working with nebulous conclusions and assumptions, usually driven by our prejudices. It leads to misconceptions, false interpretations and misunderstandings with whom we are communicating. How can there be a collaborative, trusted relationship? So first, understand reality in its raw form, unadulterated by opinions and emotionally configured interpretations.

Example Of Open Neutral Questions
Using The Laptop Seller Example

- What is your current laptop like? Which make is it?

- When did you buy it? How long have you had it?

- For what do you use it?

- How fast is the processor?

- Which was the last movie-making award you won? – Which one are you targeting?

Step 2 – Open Oriented Questions

With these, you are orientating them towards their value and success. Far from neutral, with these questions, we will discover the real Value Onion and priorities of the person with whom we are communicating.

Importantly, they will incite opinions, reflection, imagination – it's powerful indeed, and it is true discovery with a *Spirit of Enquiry*. People will enjoy answering these questions even more than *Open Neutral* questions as it concerns them, their improvement, value and success. They will be more engaged and open with you, reassured that you are genuinely interested in their value and, therefore, the potential answer to their success. It's all about making people comfortable to open up to you. The more you know their value, the better you can truly respond to their Value Onion.

Again, these questions begin with *Who, What, Where, When, How, Why, Which,* but they will orientate the other person towards improvement.

Examples Of Open Oriented Questions

- How would you describe your perfect laptop?

- Which features would help you most and how?

- What is essential for making better movies?

- What is critical for improving your productivity on your journeys?

- …

Reminder – What Are Closed Questions?

They end up in a simple *yes* or *no* response, hence *closed*. They have vital applications in the process of conversations and begin with a verb. The moment you put an action word or verb in front, it will end up as a *yes* or *no*. For example, *Shall we? Is it? May I? Will you? Isn't it? Do you? etc.*

Step 3 – Closed Neutral Questions

If I say, *Do you follow me?* you will say *yes* or *no*. But for me, either of these responses from you is fine. I am neutral between these two answers, hence it's a closed neutral question.

If you answer, *Yes – great...* we can proceed. If you say, *No – isn't it important for me to find out why? It's only with this understanding that I can bring an answer so that we can proceed.

Closed neutral questions then are used for *validation* or *confirmation*, which is critical in the flow of conversation, collaboration, correct actions and best outcomes.

Too often, people are scared to ask this kind of question in-case they get an unfavourable response. But that is the point – there is no unfavourable response.

Let's say the answer to your question *Do you follow me?* is a *No*. You may think a *Yes* is a favourable response, and *No* isn't. Not at all – if they don't follow you and you continue without addressing it, how unfavourable would that be? They would get further lost and confused, you would lose credibility and maybe even respect, but overall, the work and hence the outcome would not be achieved.

So closed neutral questions are vital.

Be absolutely comfortable and therefore neutral to get a *yes* or a *no*. If you get a *yes*, move forward. If you get a *no*, then it's back to step 1 with an open neutral question, *Ah, so what have I missed?*

Which part would you like me to re-explain? And so on.

We also use these closed neutral questions as reformulations to confirm or validate a point. It's a critical part of any communication.

In The Laptop Sales Example

- Have I understood this correctly - you need both small size and large storage capacity in the same device, am I right?

- The response will be either *yes* or *no* – we are neutral on the response and either is acceptable.

Although I have put this validation as Step 3, it should be done after each step. Understand facts in Step 1, then confirm your understanding – e.g. *You said x, then y, then z – am I right? Have I missed anything?* If they say *yes* – then it's back to open neutral questions – *What did I miss? etc.*

Understand their entire Value Onion in step 2 – then validate.

Build the proper responses and solutions to their value – then validate that your proposals meet their values.

Step 4 – Closed Oriented Questions

Again, these begin with a verb and end up in a *yes* or *no*, but far from neutral, you are orienting them towards an answer you want. For example – *Do you like my project? Shall we sign the deal? Isn't my product the best?*

This is a most dangerous question as you may be looking for a *yes* but get a *no* or vice versa. It must be asked but at the very end. What is the essential condition under which you can ask this question? Yes, when you know what the answer will be. *But how can I be sure of that?* I hear you say.

Well, if you have applied the sequence of Steps 1 to 3 exactly as I have described above and especially well-validated in Step 3 with closed neutral questions, you will end up with the answer you want.

Laptop Sales

- So, are you OK with this size? *Yes.*

- And the clarity of the screen on this laptop? *Yes, it's perfect.*

- Continue and you validate all points.

- Is there anything remaining? If you get a *yes*, then go back to open neutral – *what is that?* You may discover a new value to which you bring a new response, then validate again with a closed neutral question – is that OK? *Yes.*

- Great, anything else remaining? *No.* Are you sure? *Yes.*

- Shall we complete your purchase? *Yes.*

In other words, when you asked, *is there anything else remaining* and they say *no,* you can be sure to get a favourable response from your closed oriented question – *shall we complete your purchase?*

This sequential four-question process from Steps 1-4 is not just about asking the four types of questions; it is also the structure and flow of excellent, collaborative, cooperative, productive and successful conversations. They build respect and bring excellent outcomes for both parties.

This is the way of valuepreneurs.

5.18

Conversing Through Value
Brings Automatic Alignment

The Small Sofa Conflict (see 2.31)

Last year, I was in Pune, India and visited a client, Vijay, the CEO of an IT company that exclusively handles the IT of one of the most prominent retail organisations in the world. That day Vijay was in a rage and very upset. I asked him, what was wrong.

'Look at these guys! *(speaking about his directors).* They aren't serious and behaving unprofessionally, bringing up petty issues. Please do something with them, coach them, train them, whatever you need to do but shape them up.

I said, 'Relax, Vijay and tell me what happened?'

'Our mother company has given us the mandate to do business with other customers in the open market, which is a great opportunity. We have a strategy to build, but these guys are concerned with petty issues. Amit was in my office just before you came, and he complained that the sofa in his office isn't big enough. It really made me upset that a senior director can be so irresponsible and speak of petty things at a time like this.

I said, 'When we finish our meeting, call Amit in and ask him to show you which sofa he wants? Oh, a Roche Bobois? The dark green one with a yellow pattern?'

How much? $15k?

'Tell him no problem at all, and that you will get it ordered.'

Now Vijay is looking at me perplexed, thinking I've lost my senses too. Then, I continued.

'As Amit is leaving your office, ask him, by the way, which Value Onion layer of which customer segment is this sofa serving?'

It's a simple question to which if he can answer that going out on the open market, there is a tremendous opportunity with media companies. From an $80m market this year, we could win a 4% share, i.e., over $3m. Further, these clients are very impressed with designer sofas etc.

'Dear Amit have *two* sofas and a bigger office.'

But if he can't match the $15k to a viable return by serving Value Onions, then the answer is simple.

When we inculcate this thinking, Amit himself would happily accept the *no* and, he would never bring that expenditure to Vijay, knowing it's not an investment with returns.

The best returns on investment occur when we build Response Onions perfectly matched to genuinely discovered Value Onions.

Do you see how simple it is? In the many organisations where this valuepreneurial ethos is established, the results are astonishing. Also, the constructive mood, thinking, planning, conversations, and execution are palpable and inspirational.

5.19

Redesign Your World
– Construct A Legacy

Congratulations! You are a valuepreneur! Valuepreneurship is your Ninth-Gear.

I am moved and inspired by your commitment to join me on this journey to valuepreneurship through this book. It's now time to apply it to elevate your immediate world and collectively let's ameliorate the wider world.

Being obsessed with the value-impact of whom you serve, understanding that value, and serving it with perfect responses is the path to becoming a fearless valuepreneur – distinguished, respected, admired and advocated.

Let us work with integrity and dedication to engage with and bring a depth of impact to whomever we serve. It could be your customers, your people and teams, your bosses, colleagues, organisations and people external to the organisations and indeed society in totality.

One of the incredible outcomes will be the amplified achievement, wealth and satisfaction for you and of course for your stakeholders and investors.

But this is the assured result and not the driver. Making it the driver will force us back into the *Me sFear*, we will not serve full value impact and our own results will be compromised.

Please treat this book as your manual and guide. Re-read the techniques, understand them fully, apply them in your work. And as you taste the results, which I guarantee so long as you use the principles and apply the methods, you will gain the confidence to continue on the path of lifting yourself and others through valuepreneurship.

- Valuepreneurship is that path of absolute integrity and now your future. Congratulations!
- Engage your Ninth Gear. Redesign your world, construct your legacy.

I wish you incredible progress, achievement, abundance and fulfilment on this journey.

Let's combine to reshape the way we work, live and run organisations.

About The Author

Sanjeev Loomba led global corporations over twenty years. Since then, he has transformed hundreds of organisations and thousands of people as clients. His experientially honed methods have brought exceptional growth, results and performance to individuals and businesses, from blue chips to SMEs.

Having turned around organisations from different sectors, he puts people at the centre of every triumph, capitalising on their talents and achieving the best of self. In addition to the skills and techniques of strategy and leadership he fortifies them with the availability and potency of their minds and emotional capabilities. The combination of both these dimensions amplifies people for immense achievements.

His vision – The world is tiring of the loss of integrity, the future will belong to people obsessed by bringing real value and they also be much wealthier – it's not just academic, it's real!

His mastery of strategy, leadership, customer relationships, communication and even finance, bring a *holistic* and complete development of people towards valuepreneurship.

After his MBA he was director of different functions – finance, business economics, strategy and then CEO in different industries and countries.

Whilst their results hugely escalated, he considers this experience as his laboratory – the formulae from which he shares with you in this book. Sanjeev is a Winner of *UK National Training Awards* and is now a judge on *UK Business Awards*.

Follow and connect with Sanjeev Loomba on Linkedin

Sanjeev Loomba, Valuepreneurship

Contact EA at

Ritu@valuepreneurship.com

www.ingramcontent.com/pod-product-compliance
Lightning Source LLC
Chambersburg PA
CBHW022042210326
41458CB00080B/6603/J